14 + 15 + 18

DATE DUE

		WITHDRAWN	

DEMCO 38-297

Human Problems
of a State Mental Hospital

Human Problems
of a State Mental Hospital

IVAN BELKNAP, PH.D.
Associate Professor of Sociology
The University of Texas

The Blakiston Division
McGraw-Hill Book Company, Inc.
New York   Toronto   London   1956

HUMAN PROBLEMS OF A STATE MENTAL HOSPITAL

Library of Congress Catalog Card Number: 56-11041

*Gratefully dedicated to W. E. Gettys,
to R. L. Sutherland, and to the employees
and patients of Southern State Hospital*

FOREWORD

Five hundred and fifty years ago Western culture produced the first institutions calculated to provide relief to society from the inconvenient presence of madmen. Segregation and subjugation of the violent was the specified purpose of these institutions. The story of their growth, evolution, and modification in succeeding centuries is well documented. Common to all times and to all countries is the fact that they were never capacious enough to house properly all those sent to them for care and never sufficiently staffed to provide a level of care high enough to relieve public guilt. Therefore, from time to time, the compassion of an individual, the interest of the press, or the collective conscience of society found, in the hospitals for the mentally ill, a subject for concern and an outlet for heroic action and reform. The plight of the bereft provided the door to immortality for Philippe Pinel, Dorothea Dix, Clifford Beers, and many others. In recent years, the names of many more—psychiatrists, journalists, jurists, and legislators—have been added to the list.

Against continual deficits of staff and materiel, and against occasional instances of indifference, neglect, or outright abuse, progress has been made from time to time; but the uneasy feeling exists that reform and regression in mental hospital affairs are inseparable processes. The cycle has repeated itself too often to be fortuitous. The sequence of exposé, reform, progress, indifference, apathy, and decline has been repeated with

vii

variations in a dozen states of the Union in the past twenty years. Professionals are drawn from one state to another and back again as interest in mental health waxes and wanes. Meanwhile the basic needs remain unchanged. It is easy for state hospital superintendents to browse through the records of speeches of fifty or a hundred years ago and find quotations and recommendations appropriate to the problems which beset them today.

The fact that reforms somehow have never quite satisfied acknowledged standards of either quality or quantity of care has generally been explained as due to the fact that the patient load placed upon us grows faster than our available resources. Occasionally political interference is an obvious explanation for the failure of a hospital program. The "unfair" competition offered by the financial rewards of private practice or of industry is frequently offered as the reason why clinicians are not attracted to work in state hospitals. Available public funds are often exhausted by educational and highway projects. These explanations have the common virtue that they absolve individual citizens, professional groups, and the general public of responsibility for conditions as they are. They make the task which confronts us so formidable that no one expects us to accomplish it. In a way, these explanations help to make heroes of those who dare to do even a little in the face of unreasonable odds.

Meanwhile, terrazzo and foam rubber have replaced concrete and hog's hair. Unfamiliar plastics, night lights, call systems, and acoustical ceilings give reassurance to the staff, if not to the patients. We strain our resources, and at times logic as well, to prove that psychotherapy, the shock therapies, or the newer pharmacotherapies have improved our discharge rates by a few per cent. One hospital boasts of its high per capita expenditure; another of how much it can do with how little. One trains the staff which money cannot buy; another does research; a third builds buildings. Each has something on which to rest its pride, but collectively we have not come very far. One-third of our patients still get well in spite of all we do, one-third go home with the help of our attention and some adaptive gestures on the part of their associates at home, and the remaining third accumulates.

The historical function of the state hospital can distort its social structure in such a way as to constrict spontaneity. As Dr. Belknap's study shows, personnel may be driven, as a result of this situation, to the practice of deception, defensiveness, authoritarianism, and coercion. Since modern mental treatment requires the most efficient social organization possible in which to operate successfully, it is small wonder that those efforts at state hospital reform which fail to recognize the hospital's social organization lead only to frustration and fruitlessness. Of even graver significance is the fact that the organization of the mental hospital is a fixed culture form in our society, a form which sets severe limits on what most states can reasonably be expected to accomplish in mental hospital improvement. The inertia of cultural traditions does not yield to legislation but only to the slower and steadier pressure of public education. If the mental hospital is to be redefined as an integrated part of a long treatment-and-rehabilitation continuum, having its focus in the patient's own community, with hospitalization regarded as only an episode in this continuum, then present mental health education will have to be sharply revised to emphasize acceptance of the mentally ill person as a community responsibility rather than a state responsibility.

Objections to this presentation are easy to anticipate. The particular hospital herein dissected may not be the best state hospital available for analysis, or even one of the better ones.

But what state hospital in the United States would contend that its program is so much more effective than that of Southern State Hospital that it would better lend itself to such a study? I am afraid that the internal anatomy of Southern State Hospital compares only too closely to that of the many state hospitals it has been my fortune to know. Some are better, some are worse—but none could serve as a model for others to follow.

It may seem that the study of only one hospital does not warrant general conclusions. It should be borne in mind, however, that this study consumed three years of effort. Surely we have had a surfeit of reports of superficial inspections of many state hospitals, which do little to reveal the answers to our needs. The findings of Dr. Belknap's penetrating study will have to stand by themselves until other equally thorough studies have been made. The conclusions are valid, at least for this one case, and they beg for confirmation or refutation.

Finally, a word should be said about the fact that, as a sociologist, Ivan Belknap is an "outsider" who has dared to walk alone in precincts which psychiatrists hold sacred. For this, and for the refreshing insights which he brings with him, he has my gratitude. More than a few of my colleagues, I hope, join me in welcoming his attention to our problems, in considering his observations, and in contemplating their implications. It can become our great task to test Dr. Belknap's ideas in program form. Together we might just possibly design more efficient methods of applying our special skills to the help of the mentally ill than we have been able to contrive independently

ALFRED P. BAY, M.D.
Topeka, Kansas

|The intention of this case study is to describe a problem I believe to be more pressing than any other in the field of mental health. Before we can expect substantial progress in our treatment of mental illness in the United States, the peculiar problems posed by the social organization of the state mental hospital must be faced and solved.|

In this country the state hospital represents for more than eight out of ten patients the only agency treating serious mental illness. Yet the bulk of research in mental disease treatment, as reported in professional sources, has been concentrated on the patient as he is treated in private hospitals, in private practice, or in special clinical institutions. This research has been promising in its results, but much of it is not applicable in state mental hospitals. A basic reason for this lack of applicability is that in most of these hospitals it seems impossible to establish some of the elementary social conditions essential for the practice of modern psychiatric treatment.

The present case study of Southern State Hospital attempts at several points to compare this hospital with similar institutions elsewhere in the United States. This comparison shows, I believe, that nearly all these hospitals have become organized in such a way during their historical growth that they are probably themselves obstacles in the development of an effective program for treatment of the mentally ill.

The deep-seated causes of this unfavorable development in

the state hospital do not appear clearly until the hospital as a whole is subjected to analysis at a broad level. The broad analysis shows that what is done or not done in the hospital is determined by the way in which the institution has been conceived by the state and local governments and their citizens. This conception of the hospital has dictated a form of organization imposing severe limitations on the effectiveness of professionals and laymen who are attempting to work with the problem of mental health in the hospital context. But the form of organization, which is itself causing these limitations, has so far escaped any systematic analysis.

The research reported in this book can be regarded only as the first of many studies which should be made of the larger social setting and internal organization of state mental hospitals. My generalizations on this social setting and its effects are offered as tentative and subject to revision by future research.

The negative tone of this report has resulted from the fact that I have taken as a point of departure the persistence of certain major problems in state hospital social organization. Another selection of materials might have given a more cheerful or constructive picture of Southern State Hospital. But the time has come for us to stop making the best of a bad situation in our state mental hospitals. It seems to me that it is much more constructive in the long run to ask why this bad situation has developed and what can be done about it.

The research reported in this book is primarily an exploratory case study. It is not intended as a strictly scientific analysis, but rather as an attempt to outline and describe a system of social relationships about which many more rigorous studies need to be made. All facts secured and used in this study, however, have been thoroughly validated. Research methods are described in Appendix Two. Enough minor changes have been introduced into this report to prevent identification of Southern State Hospital or of any person in, or connected with, the hospital.

I should like to acknowledge the advice and counsel of Professor H. Warren Dunham, of Wayne University, in establishing a basic perspective for the study, as well as the general stimulation received from the research of Professor S. Kirson Weinberg, Roosevelt College, Chicago, and from that of Dr. Maurice Grimes, of San Francisco, Calif. Drs. A. B. Hollingshead and Frederick C. Redlich, of Yale University, contributed criticism. The research, personal encouragement, and suggestions of Dr. Maxwell Jones of the University of London were of great importance. I owe a debt for interpretation and support of the study to two dedicated psychiatrists, Drs. Hayden Donahue and George Jackson. Dr. Morton Kramer of the National Institute of Mental Health was generous with advice and unpublished material, and B. W. Ramsey was of great assistance in completing the research.

Financial assistance in publication of this study has been provided by The Division Fund, Chicago; the Hogg Foundation for Mental Hygiene, The University of Texas; the H. E. Butt Foundation, Corpus Christi, Tex.; and Leonard Coe Scruggs, of New York.

The completion of the research and the present report have been achieved largely through the efforts of the Texas Research League and in particular through the assistance of Alvin Burger and Aris A. Mallas, Jr., of the League staff.

None of the above individuals or organizations is responsible for the views and conclusions of the present study.

IVAN BELKNAP

CONTENTS

xvi   *Contents*

CHAPTER ONE

How the Study Began

Shortly after World War II a journalist with a hard eye for facts and a strong moral sense took a look at the state mental hospitals in South State. He did not like what he saw, and he blanketed the state with a series of blistering articles and editorials. This is the gist of what he had to say:

Twenty-six years ago the number of mental patients first began to outgrow facilities of the South State hospital system. Each year since has seen conditions grow worse. Buildings have become dangerous and unlivable; doctors have quit and others have not come in sufficient numbers; modern medical equipment has not been obtainable.

This winter hundreds of mentally ill people in South State mental hospitals are sleeping on open, windswept porches and on cold concrete floors. The hospitals have overflowed and there is not enough space to give each patient a bed, even if beds were available. Why? Because South State has 14,000 mental patients, and, by reasonable medical standards, room for only half that number.

Thousands of sick people who need nourishment are eating chilled, tasteless food this winter. The hospital dining rooms are too small, and the kitchens have neither enough food nor the proper facilities to prepare what they do have. Why? Because the hospitals must feed the patients on an average of 47 cents a day, and sometimes for as little as 21 cents. And there are no funds at all for enlarging the kitchens.

The rest of the sunless days the thousands of forlorn and hopeless creatures who were once useful citizens sit and stare at the empty walls of murky basements and cheerless corridors. Why? Because most of them have no recreation rooms, no handicraft shops, no special therapy clinics. The few facilities that are available can hardly be used because there are not enough attendants and nurses.

The average patient in South State state hospitals has one chance in 280 of seeing a doctor. There are too many patients for each physician. In at least one hospital the chance is one in 750.

There are nine principal methods which American doctors are using to treat mental illness. Doctors in South State mental hospitals say that not a single one of these nine methods can be used adequately because of personnel and equipment shortages.

One of the most revolting things about the newspaperman's findings was not that such things could exist in South State or any other part of a world that refers to itself as civilized. It was rather that such things had in fact existed in South State before on at least four occasions. And four times these same conditions had been exposed by previous investigators. Moreover, earnest action had been taken by the South State legislatures and governors to remedy the conditions. The effectiveness of all this previous study and action can be judged from the journalist's report.

But South State is not unique among its sister states. The history of state mental hospitals throughout the United States shows much the same pattern of criticism and reform as that in South State. Reform is followed by slow but steady deterioration until the next criticism and reform. The persistence of this cycle in the state mental hospitals should be of interest to any citizen for a simple and intimate reason.

Of all mental health agencies, the state hospital treats the most resident patients and those suffering usually from the most severe mental disorders. For most Americans it is the only psychiatric treatment available. The National Association for Mental Health estimates that there is now probability that one out of each twelve children born in a given year will require treatment in a mental hospital sometime during his lifetime.[1] Since the state hospital treats 86 per cent of all resident cases of mental disease, the probability of state hospital care is quite high for everyone suffering mental disease except for a minority of war veterans and the very wealthy.[2]

A ferment of lay and professional discussion of state hospitals in South State followed the journalist's exposures. Among other action, an independent central board for the management of the state hospitals was set up, and Dr. Beddow, an energetic and capable psychiatrist, with unusual administrative experience and ability, was brought in to head up the board.

Dr. Beddow had come to the view that fundamental improvement of some kind was needed in institutional psychiatry. His experience in public health research had suggested to him that when medicine had to deal with a problem of the massive proportions of mental illness it was necessary to develop new procedures to lengthen the arm of the individual physician. The effective public health techniques did this by perfecting procedures which were inexpensive and simple, and which could be accomplished in many cases by individuals who lacked advanced technical education. Dr. Beddow felt that one source of the problems in the state mental hospitals might well lie in the fact that these hospitals had accepted uncritically the notion that their form should be set up to permit mainly individual practice, and that this form might be standing in the way of newer and more effective procedures in dealing with mental illness.

As a first step in getting at this problem, Dr. Beddow discussed with me the possibility of making a systematic study of the administrative structure of a particular hospital in South

State. Such a study might reveal resources that could be employed in more effective group therapy, or which might lead to the development of better community relations and more sustained extramural services than the hospitals had been able to give. The older views of Dr. Abraham Myerson [3] and new research then under way at Boston Psychopathic Hospital,[4] and projected at Stockton, Calif.,[5] seemed to Dr. Beddow to be pointing in this direction and to offer good opportunities for comparison if similar projects could be set up in South State.

The perspective for research indicated by Dr. Beddow was of considerable interest to me. During the year previous to Dr. Beddow's arrival, I had been attempting in Southern State Hospital to employ the hospital records as a source of data in a research project. In the course of this attempt it became clear why such records were regarded by most psychiatrists as of little research value. The social histories of patients were unevenly reported and almost never verified after initial interviews. Diagnosis was often cursory, and in 15 per cent of the cases I analyzed did not occur at all. Even where the patient was submitted to staff diagnosis—and this occurred in a minority of cases—my data on the qualifications of the staff present showed that in 30 per cent of the staff sessions no member of this staff was fully qualified from a professional psychiatric point of view to make a psychiatric diagnosis. Certainly the diagnosticians had little adequate case history material. Continuing records of treatment or progress were almost never present in the master files, except for routine reports of administrative actions, such as transfers or furloughs. And there were no administrative procedures for periodic review and audit of such action as was reflected in these files.

Comparative literature on state hospital records elsewhere in the United States suggested that Southern State Hospital was not unique in most of these deficiencies.[6] And while underfinancing, with consequent inadequate and low-quality staffing, was obviously part of the explanation, I was not personally satisfied with this as a single explanation. Many of the errors and omissions I found were the result of inertia and carelessness on the part of employees who I knew from my own observation had sufficient time, training, and intelligence to do a much better job. It seemed to me that in addition to the obvious causal effect of inadequate staffing, there were other somewhat independent forces at work in the hospital environment which had the effect of lowering morale and initiative among employees at nearly all levels. Dr. Beddow, who held a similar view, was interested in the idea of an exploratory study to identify such forces if they existed, to assess their effects, and perhaps to propose improvements. The focus of the study was to be on the relationships among the hospital employees, and, as far as this proved feasible, the patients as well, as they went about their daily activity in the hospital. My students and I divided the study tentatively into three phases, as given below:

1. Study of the history of the hospital and comparative study of other hospitals. This was accompanied by a review of the literature in sociology and social anthropology on the social organization not only of mental hospitals but also of institutions in business and government with administrative structures similar to those of the hospitals.[7]

2. Field study of the selected hospital itself. This phase was subdivided into three field subphases:

   a. An exploratory period of observation projected for about a year in the hospital by the author and graduate students, during which journals were to be kept, rapport was to be established with the people of the hospital, and an attempt was to be made to outline the important patterns of social organization in the functioning of the hospital. This exploratory period was to end in the preparation of relatively formal "open-ended" interview schedules for more systematic study.

b. Concurrently with *a*, two graduate students were to take jobs in the hospital as attendants without official connection with the project. These students were to keep journals during their employment and, at the end of a period of 2 or 3 months, were to report on their experience as participant observers in the hospital social organization.

c. A final field phase, of 6 to 8 months, during which the author of the present report was to take the open-ended schedules into the hospital and administer them both to the informants previously used and to new informants, using random sampling to secure representative informants. This sampling was deliberately postponed until subphase *c.* New information was to be accumulated during this subphase, but the primary purpose of the subphase was to verify by question and observation the information secured in the preceding phases.

3. Final analysis and synthesis of the data of the exploratory study and comparison of the results with other studies of similar type. At this point, we felt that we should be able to reach at least some tentative conclusions on the major systems of human relations present in the hospital, their effect on one another, and the general functions of the hospital.

The study was scheduled to last 2 years, including the third analysis phase. In fact, it did not near completion for almost 3 years, partly because of unforeseen difficulties in securing field material, partly because of the special problems posed by the large rate of turnover in employees in the hospital, and partly because it was necessary to turn aside from the field work on several occasions to make parallel studies in the history of social work, nursing, psychology, and psychiatry as these specialties were employed in mental hospitals. It was necessary also to analyze some of the legal problems and political development represented by the South State hospitals and those of other states. And during the course of our study we found an unexpectedly large amount of periodical literature bearing on segments of the social organization of mental hospitals.[8] In addition, toward the end of the study, two highly significant books on mental hospitals had been published, both of them requiring a restudy of data and in some cases changes in our conclusions.[9]

Phase One of the study benefited from good previous research. At the start of the study we had crucial advice and assistance from H. W. Dunham, as well as helpful suggestions from the research of S. K. Weinberg and from the pioneer studies in state hospital interaction processes of Rowland.[10]

Dr. Dunham had conducted studies at mental hospitals in Ohio and Michigan over a period of several years. Some had been aimed at the problem of measuring effects of hospitalization on given categories of patients;[11] others had been directed toward determining the effects of social organization on patient therapy.[12]

Dr. Dunham pointed out that while there were few cases of outstanding generosity on record, nevertheless considerable amounts of money had been spent on attempts to improve state hospitals throughout the country. In spite of this, however, these hospitals continued to be plagued by chronic personnel problems of procurement and turnover, indicating a serious morale problem in which there was no apparent improvement. Moreover, there was little reliable evidence showing just what effect hospitalization had on any given kind of patient.[13] Some of Dunham's unpublished data suggested, in fact, that in certain diagnoses, patients who were not committed to a mental hospital had a more favorable prognosis than those who were. Finally, Dunham felt that the historical tendency of state hospitals to deteriorate rapidly after periodic improvements in personnel and facilities suggested some kind of deep-seated flaw in the administrative design or social organization of the mental hospital. On the basis of his own research, Dunham considered that this flaw could be identified only by close observation of single institutions over a long period of time and by the use of intensive case-study methods in the field procedures.[14]

The research material of both Dunham and Weinberg dictated much of the initial direction of attention, as well as procedures, used in the present study. Both investigators had found and demonstrated a good deal of social organization in their hospitals which seemed to have little relation to therapy or patient treatment. Both had found cases in which social organization in the hospital seemed to result in effects contrary to patient welfare or employee morale. In one study, in fact, Bateman and Dunham found that the forces within the hospital environment which tended to work against recovery for the patient were about twice as numerous as those tending to work for recovery, excepting only those patients who were physically ill or whose mental disorders had a definite organic basis.[15] Weinberg's research indicated the presence in the mental hospital of an extraordinarily rigid administrative structure which tended to block communication and mobility between categories of staff members and communication between patients and staff.[16]

In addition to the research of Rowland, Dunham, Bateman, and Weinberg, three other studies of mental hospitals determined some of the questions we sought to answer. E. M. Lemert and Maurice Grimes had both suggested that forces exterior to the state hospital have tended to make a rigid and authoritarian internal organization of the hospital a necessity, to render innovations in treatment or organization unlikely, to hamper or exclude efforts to widen the preventive and rehabilitative activity of the hospital for its patients, and to hinder both professional and nonprofessional community relationships on the part of hospital personnel. Among these forces were such things as ill-defined public opinion on the status of mental illness and the functions of mental hospitals, entrenched political practices in state government, defensive and traditional attitudes on the part of professions in the state hospitals, and hostility or indifference on the part of professionals outside the state hospitals.[17] The studies of Lemert and Grimes suggested that adjustments to these exterior forces enter at many points into the formal and informal relationships of both employees and patients in the state hospital. We attempted in our own study to note such points and their effects in our interviews.

Another research study of importance in guiding our inquiry was that of Paul S. Barrabee.[18] In addition to the research material on hospital social structure provided by Barrabee, his study was particularly significant because it dealt with the social organization of Boston Psychopathic Hospital. This hospital is connected with Harvard Medical School and it ranks first in the nation's state hospitals in the ratio of attendants to patients, second in the ratio of physicians to patients, and fifth in the expenditure per day for food for patients.[19] The problems of lack of research atmosphere, understaffing, generally inadequate budget, and inadequate professional manpower which are usually offered as the main explanations for the difficulties of the state hospitals were at a minimum in this particular institution. The study thus was able to provide comparative data to be used in determining the extent to which other factors than those of inadequate financing might be at work in the mental hospital.

Barrabee's study suggested, although somewhat indirectly, that even under the most favorable conditions, large portions of this hospital's social organization were dominated by tradition and inertia and by an uncreative preoccupation with administrative operations. There was also much indifference and outright ignorance. Barrabee's material implied also that orientation of this hospital around an idea of total therapy for the patients would require a redefinition not only of the roles of the "non-therapist" staff members but also of the "therapist" staff members, to eliminate the many activities and attitudes possessed by all of them which are either indifferent or actually opposed to patient therapy.

The research of A. H. Stanton and Morris S. Schwartz was also significant in suggesting leads for study and in providing additional specific and critically important evidence on the possible influence of hospital social organization on everyone within the hospital. Their studies were important to us in several ways. As in the case of Barrabee's research, and to an even greater degree, the research of Stanton and Schwartz was conducted in a hospital where financial support, professional quality and supply, and general atmosphere were all equal to the best in the United States. The data of the Stanton and Schwartz investigations show beyond much doubt that even in a private mental hospital, closely connected to one of the most advanced psychiatric training institutions in the country, and restricting its clientele generally to those patients able to pay an average of $850 per month for treatment, many of the serious problems of the state mental hospital were still present.[20]

Perhaps an even more significant aspect of the Stanton and Schwartz studies, however, was their illuminating proof, first, of the great complexity of interpersonal relationships that exist among patients, between ward personnel and patients, and among all those employed in the hospital; and second, of the deep effects of these interpersonal relationships on the adjustment of personnel and patients and on the course of therapy. This research, when added to that of previous investigators, made a final and convincing case for the view that the social organization of mental hospitals needs intensive examination to determine, first, what effects—good and bad—it does exercise on patients and personnel, and second, what may be done to eliminate the bad effects and capitalize on the good ones.

That this adds to the already serious problem of the etiology of mental disease the further problem of the analysis and reassessment of the whole structure of our main agency for treatment is unfortunate, but inescapable.

At the beginning of our study, it appeared to us that one of the main implications of the literature on mental hospitals was that a good deal had been taken for granted about how these hospitals should be organized. The resulting organization had not been submitted to much scientific study until recently, and our review of these recent studies suggested that at least some of the recurrent problems in these hospitals might be caused by the operation of a certain kind of social organization both inside the hospital and between the hospital and exterior agencies in the community. Much of the material, on state hospitals in particular, implied that if this special social organization were studied carefully, ways might be found, first, for improvement in the hospital's effects on patients and personnel and, second, for improvement in the hospital's relation to other agencies, to communities, and to families concerned with the mentally ill.[21]

In applying our research schedule to the study of the hospital we assumed that unobtrusive and systematic observations of the day-by-day work and interpersonal relations of attendants, nurses, social workers, psychologists, physicians, and patients would permit us to develop a reasonably accurate picture of both the formal and informal side of the hospital. Our intention was to produce an exploratory and descriptive, rather than strictly scientific, study of hospital organization, to compare our results with other organization studies, and perhaps to lay a basis for more rigorous comparative studies of alternative organizational designs in the treatment of mental illness if that represented by the traditional form of the state mental hospital proved to be faulty.

CHAPTER TWO

Mental Hospitals in the United States

The history of state mental hospitals in the United States shows a development which compares unfavorably with that of most other state health or eleemosynary agencies. Modest gains in treatment effectiveness as measured by definite cures in such diseases as paresis, manic-depressive psychosis, and involutional melancholia have been overbalanced by increased commitments of patients generally, and particularly of those suffering from cerebral arteriosclerosis and senile psychoses. Improvement in physical care of patients in the hospitals has occurred, but it has resulted not in reduction of patient population through cure, but in greater average duration of hospital life for some schizophrenics, the mentally deficient with psychosis, and patients with mental diseases of the senium. Although nearly 50 per cent of patients committed to state hospitals are eventually discharged from the books of these hospitals, it is not known whether they are actually cured of their diseases by the hospital—or whether, in many cases, they are actually cured at all.[1]

That the state hospital is not responsible for this unfavorable treatment showing is obvious to anyone familiar with the facts about mental disease. The state mental hospital is charged with responsibility for the care and treatment of people suffering from the gravest types of mental illness. At the present time, the causes of the major mental disorders are not scientifically known, and most therapies used in treatment are without satisfactory validation.

At the same time, however, in terms of other criteria, the general conditions of the state hospitals are not satisfactory. The findings of the above-quoted journalist in the South State hospitals have their equivalents in many other states and many other times in the United States. The indictment that can reasonably be leveled at the state hospital is not so much that it lacks treatment effectiveness, but rather, first, that it has persistently developed conditions which are cruel and inhuman both for patients and employees, and, second, that it tends regularly to degenerate into the kind of social organization that does not permit the application of the little that is actually known about the treatment of mental disease. This indictment seems inescapable after a review of the history of mental hospitals.[2]

To the person who consults standard sources on the history of state hospitals it is soon apparent that the evolution of state care has certainly not involved cumulative additions of improvements, one upon the other. The entire development looks far more like a process of incoherent patchwork, interspersed with alternating periods of improvement and decay.

The history of state hospitals in the United States abounds with examples in which the advances of one decade are lost in the next. The nineteenth-century reformer Dorothea Dix discovered, upon later investigation, that many of the hospitals established through her work exhibited scenes of suffering and neglect little better than those she had encountered and so bitterly condemned a few years before. From the outset, efforts to improve conditions in state hospitals for the mentally ill have been repeatedly hindered by public indifference, political manipulation, insufficient capital, and inadequate personnel. These influences have persisted with varying degrees of intensity at different times and places over the past 100 years. And progress in the care of the mentally ill has been irregular and uncertain.

It is true that a small number of welcome and abiding changes have been made. Material facilities and physical treatment have been improved in the past several years, though they are still far from adequate. Most state hospitals are forced to operate with obsolete facilities, insufficient and untrained personnel, and distressing deficiencies in bed space. Between 1903 and 1948, the number of resident patients in mental hospitals in the United States increased 366 per cent, yet expansions and improvements in hospital accommodations have always been far behind this increase.[3] Here again the uncertain and irregular character of state care is plainly evident.

The sporadic character of the development of state hospitals presents a rather curious paradox which is of decisive sociological significance. On the one hand, it indicates that at times in the past hundred years enough energy, know-how, and effort have been mustered to permit substantial changes in the direction of better care of the insane. Yet, on the other hand, there is evidence that forces have operated to nullify the accomplishments effected through previous efforts. Whatever the solution to the rather curious problems presented by the history of the state hospitals, it is certain that the issue does not revolve entirely around inadequate information concerning the direction in which ameliorative steps must be taken. The central difficulty seems to be *how and through what means and by whom* they are to be taken. This fact becomes increasingly apparent when it is recognized that many of the best principles of hospital organization and mental therapeutics now in use were clearly understood and practiced by intelligent administrators nearly 100 years ago. Moreover, much earlier, such men as Benjamin Rush and

William Tuke, pursuing the precepts formulated by Pinel, had fully elaborated several important procedures and methods to be employed in the humane and at times therapeutically effective treatment of insane persons; many of these methods are regarded as valid today.[4] The modern character of many of these earlier notions is clear: the treatment involved, among other things, the provision of interesting activities, such as reading, entertainment, congenial occupational tasks, and the stimulation of frequent group activities. The patient was to be accorded genuine kindness and friendly consideration, and the entire hospital was to be operated in a manner designed to create an atmosphere of calm and good will. The existence of these practices makes inevitable the conclusion that, at the turn of the nineteenth century, there was a definite body of information, still regarded by contemporary medicine as valid, concerning the way in which insane persons were to be treated.

Yet, despite the fact that Rush and Tuke were able to introduce their methods successfully in hospitals under their supervision, few others followed directly in their footsteps. Most mental hospitals remained in a highly unsatisfactory state, and, in general, there seemed to be little concern on the part of the public with diminishing the acuteness of the problem. This does not mean that a certain number of improvements were not being effected. In the first quarter of the nineteenth century, we find hospitals for the mentally disordered being established in eight different states.[5] Although these establishments represented the first positive steps toward a more adequate and efficient care of the insane in those states, they did not substantially alter the gravity of the broader range of difficulties involved in the problem. Large numbers, especially the dependent insane, remained almost entirely neglected. Thus, while small advances were being made by a few interested persons, the prevailing attitude was one of indifference. Only the grosser and more conspicuous defects were alleviated, and these only in certain localities.[6]

Even where improvements were being made, no systematic policy of planning was pursued. Most hospitals in the middle of the nineteenth century were established as individual units without any attempt to organize them all into one responsible, autonomous system. Consequently, there developed a situation of an even more complex character, in which there were not only frequent obscurities in hospital organization and management, but also a considerable degree of inefficiency and unnecessary expense. In response to the increasing complications and difficulties involved in the care of the insane, many states began to create special administrative hospital boards and to endow them with powers to make recommendations and inspections. However, in those states in which the board was limited in its duties to mere advisory powers, the situation was such that no action could be taken even where conspicuous deficiencies were exposed. The board could enumerate abuses and organize information on much-needed reforms but was usually powerless to have them put into practice. In fact, on numerous occasions the intricacies of bureaucratic procedure operated to stifle recommendations before they reached the point where effective remedial action could be initiated. There was no understanding of the broad problems involved, and hence no technique of reform.

Not only was the problem met with awkwardness and general public apathy, but also, even where improvements were made, they were adopted in the spirit of alleviating a necessary evil and in a manner that would entail the least expenditure of time and money. Such an attitude was consistent with prevailing practices in most state hospitals. The patient was treated not as a human being to be cured but as an undesirable charge to be tolerated. In point of fact, one of the justifications used for erecting mental hospitals was that of protecting the public from the dangers of the insane. Prevailing conceptions of persons responsible for patient supervision were naturally consistent with the principal custodial function which the hospital avowedly performed. Hospitalization was regarded as an end in itself and, accordingly, little concern or effort was directed toward introducing positive therapeutic measures.

The fact that the problem of mental illness was never faced squarely—namely, as an adverse mental condition susceptible of therapeutic treatment—is brought out strikingly in the initial direction of the early ameliorative steps. The first efforts involved little frank recognition of the magnitude of the problem but were largely concerned with alleviating only the grosser aspects in the most economical possible way. The opening in 1833 of Massachusetts' Worcester State Hospital marked the inception of an extensive asylum-building program throughout the United States. Yet, new doors hardly opened before facilities were jammed with inmates drawn from the almshouses and jails of small towns and cities. Efforts of the early asylum superintendents—the psychiatric leaders of their time—to avoid this swamping of a medical institution by a miscellaneous and often untreatable avalanche of indigent, deviant, and mentally deficient people were frustrated. And during this period, the character of the state hospital in the United States, with its growing static population and contradictions in its functions, became set. The public in general, having achieved a comfortable disposition of its local responsibilities by sending its mentally ill citizens to a large, centralized, and somewhat isolated institution, now found it easy to forget them, and settled into an indifference which had persisted well into the twentieth century.

CHAPTER THREE

Mental Hospitals in South State

The disposition to avoid rather than to try to solve the problem of the insane occurs just as frequently in the history of South State as it does elsewhere.

The system of South State mental hospitals began with the establishment of Southern State Lunatic Asylum at Millville in 1860. For 24 years, this was the only state institution available for care and treatment of the mentally ill in South State.[1] An appropriation of $50,000 was approved by the Legislature in August, 1854, for the purpose of erecting a hospital for the care of the insane; however, it was not until March, 1861, that the formal opening of Southern Hospital took place. As originally organized, the hospital was directed by a board of managers, consisting of five members, appointed by the governor for a term of 2 years. The board was directly answerable to the governor but was dependent upon the Legislature for its appropriations. In 1915, a legislative change increased the board to six members and provided that during the 2-year term of office of each governor only two members could be appointed. The specific object of the latter change was to remove the board, as far as possible, from the political control or influence of any one administration.

The ultimate responsibility of the governor for the state hospitals served supposedly as a method by which the hospitals could be kept under close and continuous surveillance. Theoretically, this was of decisive importance in the era before outside agencies, such as the Public Health Service and professional associations, were utilized to appraise the needs and efficiency of the hospital system. Unfortunately, and true to the general character of prevailing attitudes toward care of the insane, most governors rarely concerned themselves seriously with the state hospitals. However, during the tenure of the liberal and public-spirited Governor Lipscomb, there occurred one of the few instances in which the governor took an active and even aggressive interest in the problem. An avid reader on the subject of mental disorder, Governor Lipscomb was acutely concerned with the development of positive improvements in the care of the insane. On numerous occasions he made personal and unannounced visits to the hospitals in Millville and elsewhere. He conducted thus a one-man survey of the hospitals and himself served as a check against many of the internal abuses to which the state hospitals were then prone, as well as an advocate for the genuine needs of the hospitals.

Yet, despite the efforts of Governor Lipscomb and of those few others who were similarly disposed, the almost inevitable pattern of negligence, mismanagement, and improper care persisted in one form or another. That no state administrator was inclined to work continuously under such conditions is reflected in the fact that, at Southern Hospital, changes occurred so frequently in the superintendency that no one person occupied the position more than 5 years until the incumbent of 1896. These circumstances, combined with a host of other imperfections—such as inadequate financial provision, unsatisfactory admission requirements, and the housing of patients in jails and almshouses rather than in state institutions —provoked a series of investigations which has continued to this day.

The first of these investigations was undertaken by Dr.

Arthur N. Trout, who, after making a close examination of the deplorable conditions of the insane in jails and almshouses, presented his findings before the South State Association of County Judges and Commissioners at Watertown in 1916. Among the most urgent and important features of his report was the recommendation that all eleemosynary institutions be brought under a central board of control, which would have, among other duties, the responsibility of initiating arrangements for removing mental patients from jails and almshouses. Action was taken on this recommendation, and in 1919 a central authority was established in the form of a board composed of three members with overlapping terms of 6 years each. Members of the board were appointed by the governor and confirmed by the Senate. The creation of this board represented the first in a number of welcome but limited improvements that were to come later. However, the fact that the new board could not substantially alter the situation is indicated by disclosures of subsequent investigations.

The next survey was initiated in 1924 by the National Committee for Mental Hygiene and was carried out under the direction of G. M. Kline and E. V. Eyman for a commission appointed by the South State Legislature. The findings of the investigation showed the necessity for introducing a number of reforms. Although not all the reforms suggested by the committee were put into effect, at least three significant changes can be ascribed to its efforts. The first was legislation to change the names of state institutions for the insane, the mentally deficient, and epileptics to "State Hospitals." Accordingly, Southern State Lunatic Asylum at Millville became the Southern State Hospital. Of course, it cannot be legitimately assumed that name changing is in itself a positive reform; on the contrary, it is significant only in so far as it represents a substantial transformation in the attitudes and thinking habits concerning the manner in which the phenomena of mental disorders are to be treated. In this case its meaning is significant only in the fact that the term *hospital* implies susceptibility of mental disorder to therapeutic treatment. We are still far from the transformation of attitudes.

A second change which may be ascribed to the efforts of the committee took the form of a legislative provision for the establishment of two psychopathic hospitals, one of which was opened at Mineral Springs in 1931. Unfortunately, the other hospital, projected for Bennington City at the other end of the state, was never built.[2]

The third recommendation by the committee was directly concerned with the problem of temporary commitment. Hitherto there was no legal provision by which it was possible to offer temporary commitment for observation and treatment of mentally disordered persons not charged with criminal offenses. In 1935, a statute providing for such commitment became effective.

The next major investigation was made in 1931, at which time the Legislature authorized a committee to conduct an extensive survey of all South State government departments, agencies, and institutions. The project was undertaken by the Joint Legislative Committee on Organization and Economy, with the special assistance of a professional firm of specialists in public administration research, Bruns Associates. The chief objective of this investigation was to ascertain the means by which government expenditures could be substantially curtailed through more efficient organization and operation of the various state agencies. This, of course, meant that evaluations of the state hospitals as one of these agencies would be made from a fiscal and administrative point of view. Therapeutic evaluations of the hospitals were somewhat secondary in this study.

Among the serious defects disclosed by the Bruns investigation was the conspicuous absence of clear-cut lines of authority in the internal organization of the mental hospitals. The report found that there was lack of effective organization for the administration of services of the different institutions, as evidenced by the large number of individuals and heads of small groups that reported separately to the superintendents of the institutions.

In Southern Hospital, as in others throughout the state, the Bruns study found an absence of efficiently organized administrative structure, as manifest in the ambiguous distinctions in the functional requirements between the various departments. To a certain extent, this situation was attributable to the fact that a number of important organizational functions had grown up by local tradition and administrative rule of thumb rather than by law or regulation. The report ascribed these defects in part to the lack of appreciation of the true function of a coherently organized administrative system, and to a failure by the Legislature to supply new positions with capable departmental heads.[3]

Among the several recommendations of the report, the most important stressed the urgency of securing more competent medical personnel whose routine of duties and responsibilities would be unified under the supervision of a capable clinical director. This improvement would not only require the creation and incorporation of a clinical directorship in the hospital system but would also entail revision of the administrative structure in the direction of a more precise delegation of functions and authorities.

Although these recommendations were made available to responsible state officials, most of them either were not put into effect or were deferred until a later date. Because of this fact many of the recommendations embodied in the Bruns report reappear in a subsequent survey of South State hospitals conducted by the Mental Hospital Survey Committee of the U.S. Public Health Service in 1938. One of the most important recommendations directed at the administrative level was the proposed establishment of the office of clinical director. The report also indicated that a number of inefficiencies could be reduced by securing better personnel through increased pay, introduction of an attendant-training program, and increasing the number of physicians to the average ratio of 1 to every 150 patients. (The 1952 average ratio was 1 to 350.) Again in 1943 many of these same deficiencies were exposed by the U.S. Public Health Service. *A Survey of the State Mental Institutions of South State*, by the Public Health Service, recommended in this year:

. . . more numerous and better trained medical, nursing, and adjunct personnel, better accommodations for certain groups of patients, better relations between the institutions and public, and a more energetic attack on all deficiencies.[4]

Although this survey received considerable publicity through the efforts of mental hygienists throughout the state, a 1947 publication in the Mental Health Society journal by Dr. James Tewell, a psychiatrist, indicated that there was still much to be desired. In comparing the recommended changes of the 1943 survey with the actual accomplishments, Dr. Tewell mentioned that although there had been some increases in salaries and a limited in-service training program had been instituted, there still was no arrangement for systematic and regular inspection, no increase in social service, and no budgetary provision for research.

By 1949, it became apparent that definite remedial measures would have to be undertaken if the state care of the insane was to be more than a steadily enlarging custodial function.

During World War II the lack of adequate personnel and the critical shortage of building materials resulted in the deterioration of the physical plants of the various state hospitals. Since these conditions were not corrected after the war, and since patient loads had increased substantially, the situation had become so grave that the matter was brought forcibly to the attention of the public through various periodicals and journals, notably by the journalist whose findings head Chapter One. These difficulties, combined with the fact that the State Board of Control was already overtaxed with mainly fiscal duties, resulted in the legislative establishment of the South State Hospital Board. Although this change constituted a marked improvement over the preceding administrative structure, and although it apparently eliminated many of the difficulties of administration and direction of the several state hospitals, there still remained a variety of internal defects in each of the different hospitals throughout the state, as well as a distinct lack of legal and administrative clarity in the relation of the board to its hospitals.

Shortly after the organization of the new state board, another survey was undertaken by Fancher and Beam, with the specific aim of evaluating the extent to which the fifteen state institutions under the board's jurisdiction were organized on a sound fiscal and administrative basis. The results of this survey disclosed that the management structure in the various institutions was, with one or two minor exceptions, poorly organized and inefficiently operated. The evidence upon which this interpretation was based included, among other things, the poor conditions of the buildings and equipment, poorly managed and controlled food services, defective and probably unprofitable and uncoordinated industrial and merchandising operations, and irregular and uncertain internal control. Although many hospitals had been able to maintain low operating costs, it was indicated that this "economy" was rather illusory and misleading, and actually constituted mainly a record of liquidated equipment that was not properly preserved or replaced. Hence, low costs were maintained only at the expense of allowing buildings and other equipment to deteriorate through negligence and mismanagement.

Granting the general accuracy of the Fancher and Beam diagnosis, the implications are quite consistent with the typical character of the state hospitals as revealed by the disclosures of other surveys. Although the investigation was mainly concerned with the economic, business, and financial resources and expenses of the South State hospitals, the research indicated also that the state institutions were therapeutically unsound and suffered from several organizational defects which obviously curtailed the medical effectiveness of the hospitals. It would be unreasonable to expect that effective and adequate care and treatment of patients could coexist with organizational and managerial inefficiency.

In certain respects, it could be argued that the state hospitals were forced into a situation of managerial uncertainty as a result of the burdens imposed upon them by sharply restricted financial resources. To a limited extent, this is true; however, in the Fancher and Beam report it was indicated that not all the imperfections in the state hospitals could be ascribed to limitations of financial resources. Many could be accounted for on the basis of defects of clarity concerning proper management procedures and organizational functions, along with a rather conspicuous absence of administrative talent in some of the key jobs within the institutional structure.

This interpretation is clearly supported by the findings of the hospital survey that took place almost simultaneously with the Fancher and Beam investigation.

This survey was undertaken by the U.S. Public Health

Service at the request of Governor Ewing Trumbull for the purpose of evaluating existing facilities and arriving at a reasonably accurate estimate of future needs. During 1949, Dr. Ralph Gammon and Miss Marian E. Coughlin visited all the state institutions, completing a report with findings similar to those of previous investigations.[5]

This most recent research resulted in thirty-four general recommendations concerning needed improvements in four general areas. The first set of recommendations concerned the necessity for augmenting psychiatric influence in the central office and introducing measures designed to clarify channels of communication and authority. Second, there was an obvious need for overcoming the deficiencies in personnel quotas, salaries, employee living conditions, and in-service training. Third, it was indicated that there was an apparent need for making a rather extensive capital outlay for the purpose of instituting a building-expansion program that would be carried out as a long-term project. Finally, it was recommended that definite steps should be taken toward increasing therapeutic function of the hospital by enlarging the medical staff, undertaking research projects, giving special training courses for professional workers, and utilizing the services of outside workers.

The nature of these recommendations is sufficiently clear to indicate that most of the same problems found in earlier decades in the hospitals continue to persist in one form or another. Typically, they have revolved around three distinct, but generally related, difficulties, viz., problems of (1) building space, (2) administration, (3) personnel.

To some extent these deficiencies can be accounted for on the basis of the way in which mental disorder has been traditionally conceived. That is, in the past the marked tendency has been to assume that hospitalization itself was sufficient and adequate as a means for solving the problem of mental illness. This is, of course, a variant form of the widespread custodial conception which arose simultaneously with the erection of the first state hospitals all over the United States. Since custody was conceived as an end in itself, it necessarily followed that primary emphasis was placed on the mechanics of institutionalization. Consequently, many of the more urgent problems of organization, administration, and methods of effective therapy were relegated to a position of relatively little importance. Only in a very few state hospitals in the United States has there been a systematic integration of functions and duties around the idea of therapy. The South State hospitals do not belong to this distinct minority. From the very outset, efforts to provide for the insane in South State have been handicapped by a variety of recurrent problem situations. Inadequate building space, insufficient and untrained personnel, and poor administration, as we have pointed out, are among the most prominent.

Everything about the South State mental hospitals, as in the case of the mental hospitals of most other states, has been marked with stigma and avoidance. From a sociological perspective it is quite clear that the sociocultural status of agencies for the care of the mentally ill is decidedly low. This conclusion is supported strongly by the evidence reviewed above. That state care of the insane has developed only because of a prevailing sentiment that insanity is an evil to be tolerated is clearly indicated by the fact that improvements are introduced, if at all, only after exposure of a series of abuses and defects. Even where such imperfections have been consistently exposed, they have been only temporarily removed. Removal is not accompanied by thoughtful future controls. Moreover, as the above reports indicate, there has been almost complete absence of any long-range medical or administrative planning in making provision for care of the insane. On the basis of the available evidence, it is apparent that South State has pursued an extemporizing policy according to which the needs and inadequacies of the mental hospitals have been treated as if they were merely temporary disturbances in an otherwise ordered system. It is clear that from either a medical or an administrative perspective such an orderly system has never existed, and that no systematic efforts have ever been consistently focused upon the psychiatric needs of the patient as the point from which to erect a reasonably efficient system of care and treatment. The general conclusion to be drawn from the foregoing facts is that treatment of the insane in the South State hospitals, as in other states, has developed only in a very irregular fashion, and progress has been largely a matter of patchwork on an otherwise inherently unstable and probably unsound institutional framework. It is clear from the historical record that South State has not treated the problem in terms of its long-range aspects and thereby anticipated the occurrence of future imperfections and needs, but has intervened only after conditions of insufficiency have become so severe that they must at last be faced.

As has been pointed out above, it is remarkable how unanimously the many recommendations made by the different surveys are uniformly concerned with the same set of problems. Again and again these investigations have revealed the pressing need for more organization with local communities, more personnel, more bed space, more efficient control of resources, and more psychiatric influence in the key points in the hospital. It is a fact of primary significance that such a variety of different investigations by physicians, laymen, and business research agencies has uniformly arrived at the same diagnosis of the problems of the agencies for the care of the insane.

Although it cannot be denied that this diagnosis is essentially correct, it is debatable whether the remedy lies in the recommendations which have been made on the basis of this diagnosis. All the recommendations emphasize the need for increasing the size of the medical staff, the number of the adjunct personnel, and the amount and quality of the various facilities within the hospital itself. Many of the problems of the state hospitals are indeed those of inadequate resources, both in personnel and in physical equipment. But it is still an open question whether these resources can be brought up to an efficient standard as the state hospitals have been traditionally organized and operated. Certainly, in view of the past history of these institutions, the time seems to have arrived to ask whether, in fact, institutions of this size, centralization, and even of this kind are actually adequate to meet the problem of mental illness or the state's responsibility for the mentally ill.

THE FINAL FORM OF THE SOUTH STATE HOSPITALS

The confusion in the social definition of the South State hospitals is clear enough from the review of their history. But within this confusion there is a rough pattern of accommodation among the many social needs and interests associated with the operation of the hospitals. It is a pattern pleasing to few people, but as a pattern it does provide an ordering of the hospitals' activities, minimizing conflicts which would otherwise occur.

In Southern State Hospital, this pattern or ordering of the hospital's organization was the result of compromise between

a number of hard facts. The first fact was that the people of
the state through the Legislature had set up the hospitals in
South State on a legal basis providing for custody of rather
broad classes of indigent people, rather than for mental patients requiring treatment. The second fact was that mental
disease in the state of our present knowledge is usually a long-
term disease of indefinite duration and uncertain cure, and one
requiring some control of patients in their own interest and
that of others. Psychiatric science, even up to the present time,
must be regarded as in its infancy as far as etiology of mental
disorders is concerned.[6] Those setting up and maintaining the
hospitals had to find ways to meet the characteristic problems
of mental disease with less explicit professional guidance than
exists in such fields as general medicine.

LEGAL FOUNDATIONS

From the very first, mental hospitals in the United States
have found it difficult to define their medical operations in a
way which would prevent such operations from being
swamped by the commitment of many patients who might
conceivably have been cared for in other kinds of institutions
or even by noninstitutional arrangements. Both in South State
and elsewhere in the country, mentally deficient individuals
and destitute older people have been committed to the hospitals in great numbers. The first group represents a problem of
the local community, primarily a problem in special education
and social adjustment and perhaps only secondarily in psychiatric therapy. The second group very often is primarily a
problem also of the local community in chronic physical illness and in old-age security. Both groups arrive in the mental
hospital because of the failure elsewhere in the state government or local communities to develop adequate measures of

education and care. And both of these patient groups exert pressure in the hospital tending to force it away from its primary mission of treating mental illness, and in the direction of care which can be only custodial.

In the years following the 1840s, in South State and elsewhere the tendency of most state legislatures was more and more evidently in the direction of defining the state hospital as a sort of residual agency where people could be sent when they exhibited fairly serious mental deviation or environmental maladjustment and could not be placed very well in existing welfare, custodial, or medical agencies in the home community.

In reviewing the legal structure of the state hospitals in South State, we found that this general tendency toward the dumping of miscellaneous groups of problematic people into the mental hospitals was well developed in statutes and decisions by 1900. Moreover, this process of legal definition had proceeded along these lines without much reference to parallel programs dealing with similar groups of people which were being set up by the health, welfare, veterans, and other special programs of the Federal government and by some local communities. By 1940 many of these programs overlapped or required coordination. But the legal growth and informal traditions surrounding the state hospitals made it increasingly difficult to do anything about the overlapping or to effect the substantial efficiencies that might come about through coordination.

Perhaps the most important point about the South State law governing the state hospitals is the basic view set forth in the South State constitution that the main purpose of hospitalization is to protect persons and property from the consequences of irrational acts. While other reasons may be recognized for temporary commitments to the South State hospitals, the only reason for which permanent or "indefinite" commitment is justified constitutionally is that the patient is in need of "restraint." Nothing in this basic law specifies that the purpose of hospitalization is to cure the patient through treatment in the hospital and ultimately to discharge him to his home community. Moreover, the constitutional provision seems to carry the implication that the mental hospital is to be regarded as an agency of poor law, or general-assistance law, as can be seen from this phrasing of the provision:

It shall be the duty of the Legislature to provide for the custody and maintenance of indigent lunatics, at the expense of the State, under such regulations and restrictions as the Legislature may prescribe.[7]

Up to the completion of this study, in spite of many kinds of pressure there seemed to be very little chance of securing a change in this fundamental law, with its clear implication of charity, protective or police, and custodial functions for the state hospitals. Of the five amplifying and interpretative statutes later added to this provision, only two defined mental illness as involving treatment, or defined the persons committed as patients. One of these statutes specified the admissibility of "any person needing immediate care and treatment"; the other allows voluntary entry to a state hospital by a "patient" if he was "desirous of submitting himself to treatment." The other statutes merely added provisions for observation and emergency commitment of persons to the hospital.

In South State, the legal definition of the state hospitals as agencies with only incidental functions as treatment institutions left it almost impossible for them to develop as actual medical agencies. The prevailing—and most important—process in the hospitals became that of making space and providing some kind of attention for growing numbers of people, many of whom, as in the case of some older people, indigents with episodic mental states, alcoholics, and the mentally retarded adults, came in, not because they were psychiatric problems as such, but because there was no other place to send them.

In realistic terms, the South State hospitals were actually being defined by state policy in a manner which made them in many respects the equivalent of the older county and city poor farms and homes. Nobody actually stated the policy in these terms; and in fact it would have been vigorously repudiated if stated in words. The investigative history and internal organization of the South State hospitals, however, provides evidence that leaves little doubt that the state actually created in substance what amounted to a centralized and hardly more humane form of the older county and city poor farms.

The significance of this development becomes manifest when the present scientific status and needs of psychiatry are seen in relation to the political development of a custodial institution. Since the population of the state asylums in South State was expected to represent many kinds of physical medical problems, and since in a vaguely defined way mental illness was regarded as a medical problem, these hospitals were from their inception placed under physicians as superintendents. It is doubtful whether the allocation of total responsibility for the management of the state hospitals to the medical profession—and its acceptance by the profession—was actually a step forward for anyone concerned.

During the first part of the history of the South State hospitals, from 1860 to 1890, the institutional care of the mentally ill was undergoing a reaction away from what Deutsch has described as the period of early optimism regarding the curability of the insane.[8] Many of the physicians in charge of the South State hospitals believed sincerely, and with ample scientific evidence, that for the majority of their serious mental cases very little could be done in the way of explicit psychiatric treatment. During this period, they worked out a medical system which functioned fairly well in maintaining physical health and which did afford opportunity for some psychiatric treatment on a highly selective basis. But this system was accommodated to the sociopolitical situation of the state hospital, rather than to developments in American psychiatry as a professional medical research and practice area.[9]

The accommodation of a certain kind of medical organization with the state hospitals in South State contained the seeds of many problems which we found flourishing in Southern State Hospital. The older medical organization was adjusted to centralized custodial care and to a particular type of staff and line organization which operated to maintain this custodial care. Personnel throughout the organization who remained for any length of time had come to some kind of terms with the line and staff organization.

This older system of medical organization had both merits and defects. It was realistic about what could be done in the hospital as the agency was legally defined and financed. It had set up and enforced reasonable standards of health and cleanliness on the wards. Physical treatment techniques and surgical standards were higher than should have been expected in view of the hospital's financing.

But this older medical organization was committed in its form and accommodation with the state government to a general idea which is inconsistent with dominant theories in modern psychiatry. This idea was that mental disease can in fact be treated with main emphasis on a single intramural treatment phase—the hospital itself. This idea, which ignores the fact that prevention and rehabilitation are professionally regarded as both potentially at least as significant as intramural treatment, is not medical in origin at all. Rather it is clearly an accommodation forced on medicine in the sociopolitical development of South State. It is this accommodation which seems to create the problems to be considered in the following chapters.

CHAPTER FOUR

The Organization of Southern State Hospital

Southern State Hospital is located in Millville, population 215,000, the third city in size in South State, on land now inside the Millville city limits. The hospital has an attractive campus of 95 acres, and the entire hospital installation controls about 200 acres of land where hospital agricultural and other industries are carried on. On the hospital's 200 acres there are 69 buildings. The 1950 official rated capacity of the hospital was for 2,000 beds. The actual number of patients was 2,960, an excess of 960 patients over the rated capacity.[1] The hospital employs a yearly average of approximately 424 medical and 186 nonmedical employees, such as maintenance men, engineers, and skilled tradesmen.[2] In 1952 there were 33 treatment wards in the hospital, which serves fourteen counties in eastern South State, one of four mental hospital districts maintained by the state.

Construction of Southern State Hospital started in 1857. The hospital was named the State Lunatic Asylum and was formally opened in 1861, with fifteen patients, under the superintendency of Dr. M. P. McConnel. All of the twenty-four superintendents in the hospital's history have been physicians.

In 1950, Southern State Hospital was a big business from any point of view. The institution included almost every kind of medical function, and complex functions of administration, accounting, housekeeping, food management, purchasing, and storage. The hospital produced or processed and handled groceries, meats, dairy products, ice, clothing, and dry goods. The physical plant included utilities and equipment power plant. Crews and facilities were maintained for plumbing, sheet metal, electrical, general carpentry, steam fitting, and other plant maintenance work. The hospital had a bakery, creamery, sewing room, laundry, shoe shop, mattress factory, and barber and beauty shops. In the agriculture department there were farms, gardens, and a park. A very large cooking, food, and kitchen service was required for the institution. Food was provided and served to all patients and most of the staff members. Quarters were supplied and maintained for professional and subprofessional staff members and for about 20 per cent of the other employees.

In its large size, partly self-contained structure, and complexity of functions, Southern State Hospital is typical of the majority of state mental hospitals in the United States.

GENERAL ORGANIZATION OF THE HOSPITAL

During the ninety-odd years of Southern State Hospital's history prior to our investigation only one organization chart based on modern administrative principles had been worked out for the institution. This chart was largely the work of an outside business survey team rather than of administrators within the hospital, and it was based less on careful job analysis than was desirable. What the chart actually did was to mark out functional areas in the hospital where business experience indicated jobs should be better defined than the survey investigators found them to be. The survey had not dealt to any great extent with medical job analysis, since this was considered a professional matter to be carried out by medical personnel in the hospital in relation to national standard-

Fig. 1*A*. Organization Chart, Management

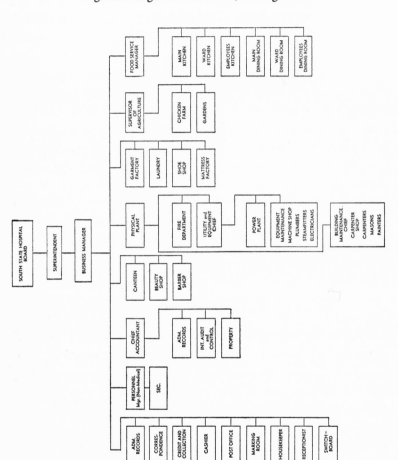

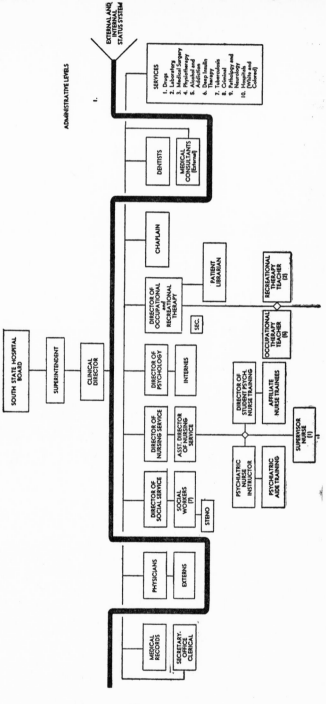

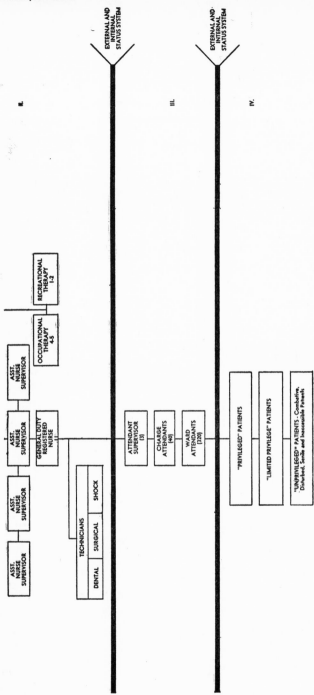

setting and evaluation agencies, such as the U.S. Public Health Service, the American Psychiatric Association, and the American Medical Association. Such medical job analysis was supplied in the form of systematic analyses of positions and functions and evaluations by the professional studies referred to in Chapter Three.

By putting these two sources of information together and interviewing a sample of employees throughout the hospital, we were able to establish a preliminary organization chart of the hospital's social organization. The most serious gaps in this preliminary chart were those dealing with the nursing functions, including registered nurses down through the attendants, and the ward organization.

It was apparent from the very first that we were dealing with a highly sensitive area in these latter functions. It was not until we had become thoroughly acquainted with physicians, nurses, and attendants and had established some degree of confidence among them concerning our scientific aims and personal discretion that we were given enough information to chart the main nursing functions and relate them with at least formal accuracy to the lines of authority and functional levels of the hospital. The general chart of Southern State Hospital which we finally established is shown in Figures 1*A* and 1*B*.

In a common-sense way, people concerned with the hospital consider the system in Figure 1*A* as the "business" part of the hospital; the system in Figure 1*B* as the "clinical" or "medical" system. While in practice there are many interrelations between these systems, there was clearly a tendency among most employees to think of themselves as belonging primarily either to one or the other.

In over-all characteristics, the business system differed markedly from the clinical system, not only in its general functions, but in such matters as job stability, lines of promotion, and amount of leisure-time association of different grades of employees with one another. Turnover rates for employees on the medical side of the hospital were much higher than those on the business side, on an annual basis. Sixty per cent of the employees on the business side of the hospital had been employed in Southern State Hospital for 10 years or more. On the clinical or medical side, this was true of only 22 per cent of the employees. On the business side, 86 per cent of all employees with supervisory functions had risen to their present positions by promotions either from lower positions on the business side or from the category of attendants on the clinical side. Such lines of promotion do not of course exist by definition on the clinical side, except in the case of the career lines from attendant to charge and to attendant supervisor and, in a limited number of cases, to recreational and occupational therapist.

Leisure-time association between employees of differing rank on the business side of the hospital was continuous and almost completely democratic, except for the clannishness of some of the skilled tradesmen. This was true not only of the roughly 35 per cent of employees who lived in the Southern State Hospital grounds or closely adjacent to the hospital in Millville, but also of the 65 per cent of the employees who lived in outlying parts of Millville or in the small surrounding cities 25 to 40 miles away from Millville. On the clinical side we found fewer than 2 per cent of cases in which there was any continuous leisure-time association between differing ranks. The attendants spent much off-the-job time with one another and with employees on the business side, but any association with professionals and subprofessionals on the clinical side was so rare as to be almost nonexistent.

The characteristic grading and barrier relationships on the clinical side of the hospital are perhaps one of the most critical features of the hospital organization. They are a natural consequence of both the custodial functions and the professional organization of the hospital, and they determine some of the most important things that the hospital can and cannot do.

The three double lines between each of the main clinical administrative systems in Figure 1*B* marks off both prestige and functional differences between categories of personnel on the clinical side. We found these differences to be most pronounced, both inside and outside the hospital, and the double lines, therefore, designate both internal and external status levels.

In its over-all structure, the clinical system closely resembled a military command system; so closely, in fact, that a previous superintendent of 20 years ago used military terminology in communicating with his staff, and punishment and privilege systems corresponding almost exactly to those of American infantry organization. As he translated the system into military terminology, the line between levels II and III was equivalent to the line between commissioned and enlisted personnel.

Between the attendants (level III) and the professional and office groups (levels I and II) social differences are great in rural-urban origin, education and previous occupation, and age. The average educational level in the professional and office group amounted to 15 years, or the equivalent of 3 years of college. The educational years of a 20 per cent random sample [3] of the attendants were 9, or the equivalent of 1 year in high school. Eighty per cent of the level II personnel came from cities of 10,000 and above; 40 per cent of the sample of attendants came from farms, another 30 per cent from towns and cities below 10,000. The level II personnel came from college or high school (70 per cent) or office clerical jobs (30 per cent); the level III personnel came to the hospital from farms (40 per cent), jobs as common laborers (20 per cent), or semiskilled construction laborers (15 per cent), as orderlies in general hospitals or attendants in other state hospitals (10 per cent).[4] Seventy-four per cent of the level II employees were under forty years of age; 80 per cent of the level III employees were over forty years of age.

While the social differences between level II and level I were not so pronounced as those between level II and level III, they were fully recognized by people inside and outside the hospital. Level I, being made up entirely of physicians and dentists, all of whom possess professional degrees, outranks most of the second-level professionals and office staff both inside and outside the hospital.

Our interviews and observations in the hospital indicate that levels I, II, and III are separated from each other by wide differences in social class background, with a particularly wide gulf between level III and the two upper levels. These social differences are sufficient to prevent any intimate communication between the professionals and the attendants, except in very rare cases. The attendant and professional literally do not talk the same language. As a result there is much avoidance between the groups, and a large amount of hostility, particularly on the part of the attendants. The ideas of the upper and lower groups on the subject of mental disease are quite different.

The effects of the divisions between the categories of hospital personnel are quite important, and will be discussed further in following chapters.

DISCREPANCY AND CONFLICT BETWEEN THE FORMAL
AND INFORMAL ORGANIZATION

It should be kept in mind that the organization chart of
the hospital is an abstraction. In many respects it represents an
ideal organization of authority and functions in the system,
rather than a description of actual operations. This situation
is true to some extent of all organization charts in both private
and public concerns, but Southern State Hospital departs
more widely than is customary from its chart in actual operations. The explanation for this departure lies in the history
and social functions of the hospital, which we have reviewed
briefly in preceding chapters—a history which has placed the
institution in a position wherein it is primarily and permanently responsible for custody of the mentally ill without
having clear and efficient techniques for dealing with most
mental disorders.

One of the unique features of mental disease as compared
with the acute infectious diseases is that medical success in
treatment often covers a year or more of time, and medical
failure in treatment is not generally followed by death, or by
termination of the disease through getting well, but rather by
a long period of custody. One way of viewing the mental
hospital is, thus, as an adjustment to the objective fact that a
large number of persons suffering from mental disease recover
slowly, or are not able to recover at all.[5] Each year of operation now confronts the institution with from 1,000 to 1,200
incoming new and readmitted patients, about 70 of whom
remain for an average of between 9 and 10 years in the
hospital.

As a result, Southern State Hospital has grown in size, both
from new admissions and from an increasing static load, and
this growth has been accompanied by inevitable complexities

in functioning. Duties once well within the capacities of an able superintendent have had to be delegated to secondary executives, who in turn have been forced to delegate some of their functions to tertiary executives. The medical functions in the system have been particularly problematic in this process, since in many respects medical competencies in the field of psychiatry are not amenable to parceling out into the hands of relatively untrained technicians.[6]

The process of growth and delegation had been going on for 90 years at the time of the study. Until 1931 very little of the process was the result of careful formal planning in terms of long-range analysis. For 85 years of its history Southern State Hospital had no accurate chart of its formal organization. As needs became evident and means available, new positions were created. The storekeeper became the Business Manager, the Superintendent added an Assistant Superintendent, who sometimes also functioned as a Clinical Director, and sometimes also as a personnel officer. A clerk was taken from filing duties and converted to a part-time receptionist. Except for occasional notation in the budget and on payrolls, little formal action went along with these changes, and new superintendents and employees learned what was going on by observation and informal instruction.[7]

The result of this expansion was that the actual working organization of the hospital really consisted in fact of two somewhat autonomous parallel systems. These systems were, and probably always will be, officially unrecognized as such, but our interview and observation data leave no doubt of their existence and of the reality of their functioning. These informal systems are shown in Figure 2.

In terms of the realistic purposes of Southern State Hospital, which will appear below to be mainly custodial and only secondarily medical, this informal organization is a reasonably

Fig. 2. Informal Organization Systems, Southern State Hospital

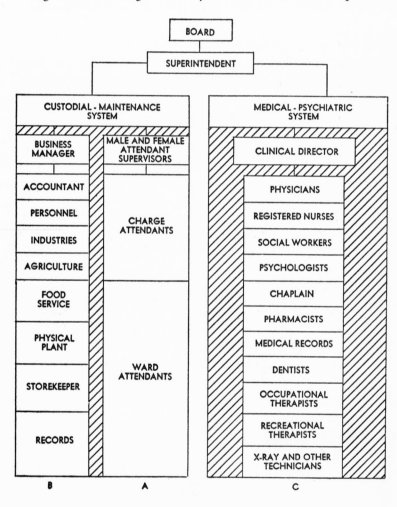

efficient one. The radical departure from the line and staff organization given in Figures 1*A* and 1*B* is evident. And it should be stressed that the informal organization as a whole is not particularly concerned with therapy of most patients, except perhaps on a routine physical maintenance basis similar to that in military organization.

Figures 1*A* and 1*B* represent a theory of what the state hospital should do; Figure 2 represents an attempt to describe what the hospital has done and is doing. The order of importance of the three systems in Figure 2 is suggested in their letters. System A must function continuously in relation to system B, or the hospital will collapse as an organized agency, through failure to meet its legally defined responsibility. It is the function of system A to receive and care for mental patients on a 24-hour basis in the wards, to establish routines for their deportment, health, dress, eating, and sleeping, to maintain maximum security for the patient and those around him. It is the function of system B to maintain a physical and social environment which makes the functions of system A possible. This includes provision and maintenance of physical facilities, such as buildings, water, light, heat, food, and housekeeping supplies, and the large apparatus of administrative and fiscal measures required for a big plant. Involved in this function is a definite responsibility to the Superintendent to prepare budgets and generally to organize his fiscal and administrative relations to his state board and to the state Legislature.

The status of system C is not so clear as that of the other systems. Officially it functions in a symbolic way to represent the traditional formal interest of the mental hospital in psychiatric therapy. It also functions in an intermittent way to give a certain amount of psychiatric attention to highly selected groups of patients. Judged in terms of what the system did in the daily round of hospital activities, system C served the function of providing professionally certified medical and auxiliary personnel to furnish physical treatment and a loose supervisory control of the other two systems. The personnel in system C were administratively necessary to the hospital's formal operation, since in South State the mental patient is formally defined as a person who represents a medical problem. His commitment, treatment, and discharge under the law have to be legally accomplished, and the state has legal responsibilities for his health. Thus the qualifications of personnel representing system C include the M.D. degree or the graduate degrees or some formal professional training in the case of the psychologists and social workers, and graduation from a recognized nursing school and some additional training for the registered nurse staff.

This statement departs widely from the usual view of the functions of state hospitals, which usually begin by assigning paramount importance to system C and its formal function of psychiatric therapy. The other systems are then interpreted as if they had little to do with the essential purposes of the hospital, or as if they were temporary obstacles in the way of a more "therapeutic" institution. This interpretation may be satisfactory to the outside expert or the casual critic, but in practice it would be fatal in the Superintendent of Southern State Hospital or the members of his medical and business staff.

Because of the dependence of hospital functioning on system A, the informal position of the two male and two female attendant supervisors has been throughout the history of the hospital much closer to the Superintendent in actual operation of the hospital than were most of the more highly paid professional services in system C, or the responsible fiscal and administrative positions in system B. These supervisors were all old employees in the system, who understood the realities of the hospital's daily functions and were able to keep the Superintendent reasonably well informed about the problems which might require his action. The Personnel Manager, also an old employee, who had worked his way up in the system, usually had an equivalent status. He was able, in addition, to report on and interpret the situation in system B. The Business Manager acted both as the chief authority over system B and as a consultant to the Superintendent on all equipment maintenance and fiscal matters and on most of the problems of space and budget involved in medical programs. The Assistant Superintendent had some responsibility (acting as a personnel officer) for overseeing professional services in system C; he also kept in touch with the chief problems of the other two systems.

Shortly after our study was begun the hospital was reorganized by the new state hospital board to bring its organization closer to that shown in Figures 1*A* and 1*B*. The new position of Director of Nursing Service (now filled by a registered nurse with high administrative experience qualifications) was instituted to replace the informal positions of male and female supervisors. The position of Assistant Superintendent was abolished, and the position of Clinical Director set up to replace it. Behind these changes, however, the organization of Figure 2 continued throughout our study to operate in a fashion which departed widely from the official organization of the hospital.

The new formal line and staff organization of the hospital (Figures 1*A* and 1*B*) represented partly a response to the criticisms of the Bruns and the Fancher and Beam investigations. When we began our study, this organization chart was described to us as a reasonably accurate picture of how the system should operate and of its intended future design. But we did not find that the line and staff definitions at work in the system followed or tended to follow the design.

Mainly the discrepancy between design and execution came from the fact that the chart recommended by Fancher and Beam put the cart before the horse. It ignored the evolution of the complex system of relationships by which the hospital actually managed its affairs, and the existing informal top-level staff relationships between the Business Manager, the Personnel Manager, the Assistant Superintendent, the male and female supervisors, and the Superintendent. These were the positions which belonged administratively at the top of the hospital organization, since they represented and heavily influenced the three main systems through which the hospital worked. These working relationships were not seen or described but instead were covered over by verbal procedures.

To take one example, the attendants in Fancher and Beam's theory were "medical" personnel, with medical functions. Therefore they belonged under the Supervisor of Medical Services rather than under the semi-independent male and female supervisors of Figure 2. This relationship is in line with current psychiatric theory but completely discordant with the facts about attendants in this and other mental hospitals. Our observations in Southern State Hospital show that at least 90 per cent of the activities of the ward attendants are supervisory, rather than medical, as the hospital is organized. Calling the attendants nurses or aides does not make them such, and it does not free them to devote their time to nursing service. Means to make them treatment persons in fact, rather than in theory, should have been worked out before the change was made.

At the end of about a year of our observation, the informal organization of the attendant staff was reestablishing itself through a system of direct and indirect channels. The attendant supervisors bypassed the director of nursing service by going directly to the superintendent when a policy was causing trouble in the attendant system, or when they wished to initiate action. Other detour channels were through the ward physician to the superintendent, through the social service workers, and through the personnel manager. This bypassing was causing much friction between the director of nursing service and doctors and the attendants.

It is always dangerous to try to summarize a complex social organization like that of Southern State Hospital, but the attempt is necessary to provide a starting point for the discussion of the chief positions in the system and their problems which is to follow.

Figure 2 is a rough representation of the concrete historical development of our particular state hospital. As a system it is not so much a medical-treatment institution as it is a modernized, more humane custodial asylum, showing clear signs of its descent from eighteenth-century madhouses for the segregation of the mentally ill from society. Like other social organizations it represents a concept, or an idea with a structure which maintains and carries out this idea. Basically, the latent idea back of this system is that the mentally ill are mostly not responsive to any treatment, that mental disease does not yield to public health measures of a preventive or rehabilitative sort, and that in the handling of the problem an agency that provides minimum decent custodial care is about the only realistic adjustment.

This idea, expressed in Figure 2, forms the central part of the operating structure of the hospital, not because it is correct—though it is by no means entirely false, either—but because by and large it reflects current opinion of a majority of people in the society in which the institution is operating.

Figure 1*B* represents a newer idea, held by an influential minority of leaders in the fields of psychiatry and medicine, that much, if not most, mental illness is treatable and responsive to a medical approach, most of which can be carried out by the hospital. This idea is trying to express itself in system C, but not very successfully. There are two main reasons for this lack of success. The first is the sheer weight of the custodial-maintenance structure of systems A and B. The second reason is that while much lip service is rendered to the ideas of these medical-psychiatric leaders by the public, there is at present no aroused public opinion in back of these ideas expressed in definite state action.

The bias of most professional investigators who have studied our hospital is naturally toward the organization of system C. Our results in the present study have led us to the view that there is something valid in all three systems in Figure 2 but that a number of drastic changes in the organization of the state's hospital and welfare services will be required before these valid elements can be expected to produce results.

In the day-to-day functioning of Southern State Hospital these two rather opposed ideas on the nature of a mental hospital are expressed by the operation of nearly all the positions having to do with the reception, diagnosis, treatment, and discharge of patients. The pattern indicated by Figures 1*A* and 1*B* is usually that given first by people interviewed as formally governing what they are trying to do. But as they carry out their duties, it generally becomes evident that much of this activity is consciously or unconsciously directed toward carrying out the pattern prescribed by Figure 2. Some of the details and effects of this situation will be given in succeeding chapters describing the concrete work problems which have developed in the psychiatric or treatment system of Southern State Hospital.

CHAPTER FIVE

The Hospital at Work: The Patients and the Organization of Treatment

There are four ways to become a patient in Southern State Hospital. One is by voluntary commitment, in which the patient himself comes to the hospital and asks to be admitted for treatment.[1] A second type of commitment is the involuntary, or 90-day, commitment. Under this procedure, a person may be committed to a state institution for a period not to exceed 90 days without benefit of trial by jury. This may be done by the testimony of two examining physicians, followed by notice served on the patient, a hearing without jury trial, and a court order of commitment by the county court.[2] At the end of 90 days, the patient under this commitment is automatically discharged from the hospital, unless upon recommendation of the physician further hospitalization is required. At the end of a 60-day period, the supervising physician submits his opinion of the patient as being dischargeable; improved and in need of no further hospitalization; or as unimproved and in need of further hospitalization. In the case of this last finding, arrangements are made for court commitment, and the patient is then officially committed to the hospital for an indefinite term by action of a six-man county jury from the county in which the patient is located.[3]

A third type of commitment is the indefinite commitment. Actually this is also the type which terminates the 90-day commitment for those patients who are not discharged from the hospital at the end of the 90-day period. The county judge, receiving information in writing to the effect that a person in his county, not charged with a criminal offense, is a person of unsound mind and in need of restraint, issues a warrant for the "arrest" of this person. The judge sets the time and place of the hearing in the warrant and takes steps to obtain a six-man jury for the trial. At the hearing, if the jury finds the defendant to be of unsound mind and needing restraint, he is then transported by county officers, or relatives or friends, under court bond, to the state hospital.

A fourth type of commitment is the 5-day emergency commitment, in which a person may be involuntarily held by the superintendent of a mental institution upon certification of two physicians that he is violently and dangerously insane.[4]

ENTRY OF THE MENTAL HOSPITAL PATIENT

Patients committed under the indefinite commitment or 90-day commitment rules form the bulk of admissions. There is no contact to speak of between the hospital and the patient's family before he arrives. At Southern State Hospital the patients are treated in much the same way regardless of their mental condition on arrival. When the patient comes to the hospital, he is immediately taken to the reception room where he is given an examination by the physician serving as officer of the day on receiving service. A member of the social service department is usually present, as are the male or female supervising attendant and a ward attendant.

Whether a patient goes to one admission ward or another depends upon sex and color and upon the current status of bed space in the wards. There are admission wards for the white males and females, and for the Negro males and females. The patient is escorted to one of these by an attendant. Formally these admission wards are set up as points from which the incoming patients can be reassigned to other wards; they are thought of as part of the hospital's receiving service. From the wards in the receiving section, the patient then goes to a more permanent ward. Senile patients, for example, usually go directly to a ward composed mainly of other senile patients. Patients with legal or criminal complications in their cases may go to a ward in which there are others of the same type.

In Southern State Hospital there is no separate receiving unit or admission unit. The patient is brought into the foyer of the main building by his relatives, friends, or by an officer of the county court. He is expected in the hospital, in the sense that the county judge has formally requested the Superintendent to receive him, and the Superintendent has agreed, usually by correspondence, but sometimes by telephone.

The receptionist and information clerk usually sets the receiving service in operation, directing the patient and his escort to wait, if necessary, while the physician on receiving duty, the male or female supervising attendant, and the social service worker are notified, and the hospital secretary secures or begins preparation of the patient's ward chart and file folder. Also the secretary routinely notifies the appropriate community social service exchanges that the patient has been hospitalized. The patient is taken as quickly as possible by the supervisor or attendant to the receiving or admission room and prepared for examination. Temperature, height, and weight are checked routinely, and the patient's valuables are received and noted for storage and safekeeping. While the physician is completing the initial examination, the social service worker completes as much of the patient's case history as he can secure from the relatives, officers, or on occasion from the patient himself. Hospital procedure requires this history to be completed within 10 days.

In Southern State Hospital, as in other hospitals of this type, the social service worker plays a critical part in the admission procedure. She has the responsibility of securing complete and accurate data on the patient's entire social background, including the reported symptomatology, history of illness, names of responsible or near relatives, or friends. She must complete this information for the general hospital records, and also a special summary for the physician to whose ward the patient is to be sent initially. In addition, she must attempt some interpretation of the state hospital's facilities and program to the patient's relatives and lay a sound basis for future correspondence with these relatives or other interested and responsible persons. She must initiate procedure for the relatives, if possible, to pay a charge assessed by the state on the families of patients able to pay for hospitalization.[5]

On admission, the social service worker is also responsible for notifying special agencies, such as Selective Service, if the patient is a male between the ages of eighteen and thirty; the Veterans Administration regional hospital if the patient is a veteran; and a special deportation officer if the patient is a potential alien. In addition, she secures adequate social history data on the patient and sends form letters to members of the family, social agencies, doctors, hospitals, police departments, and schools. Finally, she is expected to work in cooperation with doctor, attendant, patient, and community agencies during the treatment and discharge process.

From the point of admission, the patient is under the continuous 24-hour supervision of the ward attendants until he achieves a position in the hospital society in which he has ground privileges or work which permits him to go unsupervised about the hospital for brief periods of time. If he does not achieve such a position, he will remain under this supervision until he dies or is discharged, and even if he has some privileges these are subject to cancellation by the attendants if his behavior does not continue according to the standard established on his ward as desirable for patients.

During his life on the ward, the patient will receive routine supervision, attention to his daily wants, and his physical health needs. Clothing and such minor luxuries as tobacco will be provided if needed. In a small number of cases patients will also receive such psychiatric attention as the ward physician finds it possible to give, and will have some opportunity to participate in group recreation or occupational therapy programs carried on in the hospital. He will have some contact with the social service worker and perhaps with his relatives, but in the case of the patient who is not discharged, these contacts will dwindle as his residence in the hospital lengthens past the first year. If he falls into a minority of 15 to 20 per cent of the incoming patients he will have some psychological testing,[6] and a joint diagnosis by the medical staff of his case. In about 49 per cent of the cases, he will eventually be furloughed or discharged from the hospital after a year.[7]

If he remains in the hospital, the patient follows a fairly predictable process of transfer, moving down through certain stages into what may be termed wards of final destination, or into positions on other wards occupied by patients who are expected to live out the remainder of their lives in the hospital. In either of these cases, he forms part of the increasing static population of the hospital. Patients of this static type, who number about 1,700 in Southern State Hospital, fall usually into one of four main formal diagnoses: schizophrenia; psychosis with cerebral arteriosclerosis; senile psychoses; and a group of psychotic disorders "associated with" mental deficiency. In the day-to-day operation of the hospital one group of static patients is thought of as the "hopeless" cases, the other, "institutional cures" (those who are well enough as long as they stay in the hospital). Much of the ward house-keeping, some maintenance work in the hospital, as well as some agricultural and food-processing work is carried on by the institutional cures, with a few of the convalescent cases who are preparing to leave the hospital.

The patients who leave the hospital by discharge usually do so within a year. These patients may be discharged as improved, unimproved, or cured, "furloughed" in the first two cases to the custody of relatives. When furloughed, they may be carried officially on the books of the institution as patients, but traditionally Southern State Hospital defines its responsibility for the discharged patient as ending with his release from the hospital. There is no administrative apparatus for follow-up on the hospital experience or to check up in any continuous way on the patient's adjustment, rehabilitation, or general welfare once he has left the hospital.[8] Both officially and in practice, those discharged from the hospital have no further connection with the institution. A small amount of administrative connection is maintained with patients furloughed to the custody of relatives, but this connection is mainly through correspondence.

FORMAL ORGANIZATION OF THE TREATMENT SYSTEM

It is of course clear in a general way what Southern State Hospital is supposed to do with reference to the flow of patients into and out of the system. The medical staff of physicians, interns, consultants, dentists, psychologists, nurses, social workers, and medical technicians is responsible for physical and psychiatric diagnosis, for the maintenance of physical health of the patients, for the determination of what treatment is to be given the patients, and for the decisions as to which patients are to be retained in the hospital or discharged. It is because of these medical functions that the hospital is set up under medical rather than lay directorship. In theory, all aspects of the hospital are considered to be under the control and executive direction of the Superintendent. The Superintendent as a physician exercises this executive control over both the medical-psychiatric and the "business" side of the hospital's organization in such a fashion that the hospital functions to receive, treat, and discharge mentally diseased citizens of the state according to modern principles of psychiatry.

The ideal structure of treatment for an individual patient which this statement presupposes is represented in the following diagram (Figure 3).

Essentially this diagram represents a translation of the individual medical treatment of a psychiatric case into an institutional form. It is analogous to the organization of medical service in general medical practice, with some minor modifications to allow for the peculiarities of psychiatric disorders. In theory, the Superintendent is responsible for the patient. This responsibility, however, is delegated through a Clinical Director and thence to an individual ward physician, a member of the regular medical staff of the hospital. Formally, responsibility remains at this point in the system. All important administrative and medical action connected with any patient must be carried out in the name of his physician or the Superintendent as chief of physicians. In carrying out this responsibility the ward physician has available the consultation services provided by the Clinical Director as head of the medical staff of the hospital. Meeting as a staff, both formally and informally, the other doctors of the hospital, including the Clinical Director, can assist any ward physician in problems of diagnosis and treatment.

In addition to the consultation service available to him, the

Fig. 3. The Ideal Structure of Patient Treatment

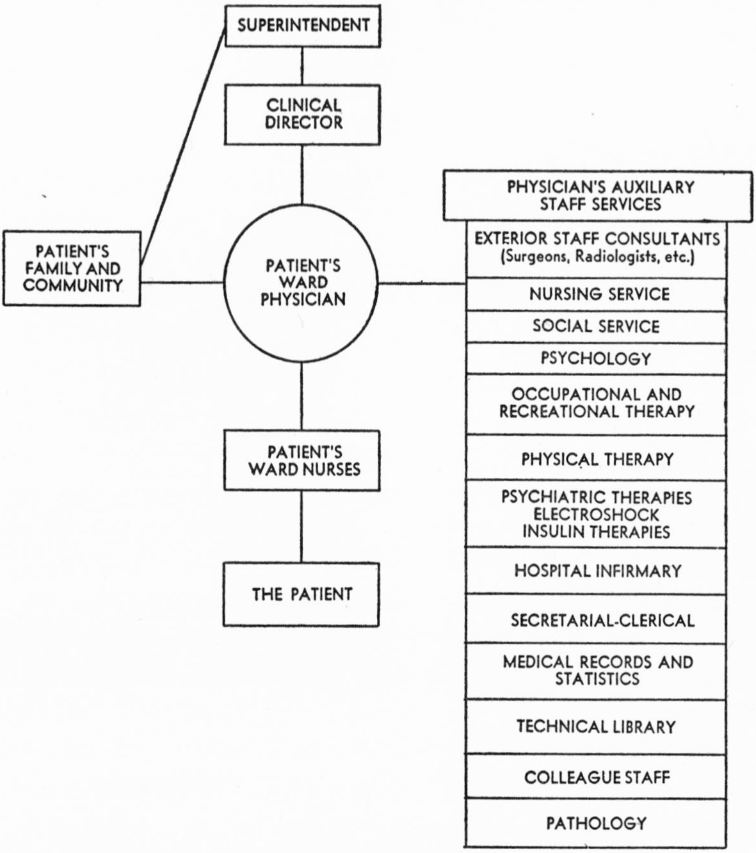

ward physician has a group of auxiliary services provided by the hospital. These are rendered by social service workers, clinical psychologists, occupational and recreational therapy personnel, physical therapy services, including surgery, registered nurse service, and secretarial and clerical personnel to aid in correspondence, case-history taking, and record keeping.

With the consultative and auxiliary services, the ward physician acts from his knowledge of the patient's condition to prescribe appropriate treatment procedures to the patient's ward nurses or attendants. The attendants are the contact point between the medical administrative system and the patient, and they are the only personnel in the system who have direct and continuous relationships with the patients on a 24-hour basis.

The functions of the attendant are to carry out prescribed treatment for the physician in charge and to maintain the patient under continuous observation, reporting to the physician any symptoms, physical or mental, which require action or bear in any way on treatment. The attendant has the further responsibility of seeing that the patient is protected from himself and harmless to others, properly dressed, clean and presentable in appearance, and that he is fed. With these duties, which are primarily of a nursing character, the attendant also has others more related to those of an orderly in a general hospital. These have to do with ward housekeeping: seeing that the ward is sanitary, swept, mopped, and tidy, and that necessary treatment and maintenance equipment is present on the ward.[9] In our observations we found that most of these duties are performed by patients, but they are nevertheless the official responsibility of the attendant and constitute part of his responsibility to the physician in charge. The attendant is also responsible for maintaining order on the ward.

INFORMAL ORGANIZATION OF THE TREATMENT SYSTEM

The preceding description of the ideal structure of treatment for an individual patient does not correspond, except at certain points, to the facts of the hospital's actual operation. The actual, rather than the ideal, structure of patient care is a matter of group assignment rather than individual treatment.

On his entry into the hospital, the patient is given a status in the hospital's informal classification system which assigns him automatically to the bottom of four status levels in the hospital. In this fourth status level, he may be classified as a member of a further set of subdivisions, depending on his initial diagnosis by the medical officer of the day and further observation of his behavior and speech by ward attendants and other patients. In nontechnical language, the patient will be classified roughly within this fourth level as (1) privileged and cooperative, (2) neutral and partly privileged, (3) un-privileged, dangerous, disturbed, or listless. This system of actual patient treatment is shown in outline in Figure 4.

Fig. 4. The Actual Structure of Patient Treatment

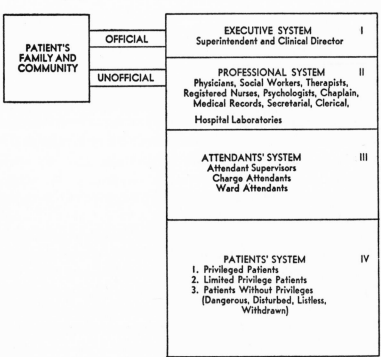

Depending on his initial classification and later conduct on the ward, the average new patient will become part of the fourth-level patients' social system in one of the three categories of the system. He may begin receiving definite therapies, such as electroshock or insulin treatment, almost at once. Moderate or complete restraints may be employed if he is highly disturbed. In the majority of cases, however, the new patient spends a good deal of his time in being informally instructed in ward rules by his observation, by other patients, and occasionally by attendants, in adjusting himself to these rules, in occasional diversional therapy programs conducted by the hospital, and finally in sitting or milling about with other patients on the ward as he goes through his individual process of adjustment to the hospital.

The main contact of the patient with the hospital's administrative superstructure is through the six to eight ward attendants who typically make up the group in charge of his ward. These attendants are part of the hospital's next higher status level (level III). The attendants govern both the patient's position in the patients' social system and his relations to the physician. They do this not in terms of the individual patient's psychiatric condition or needs but rather in terms of the requirements of their own social system. This fact means that the patient's first job is that of adjusting to the requirements set by the relations of the patients' system to the attendants' system. Adjustment is a critical problem for the average patient, since his contact with the other personnel in the system besides the attendant and other patients amounts only to a small fraction of time through the year. Even this small amount is usually mediated through the attendant, who often interprets the patient to the ward physician, the social service worker, or the occupational and recreational therapists.

Personnel in system II, shown in Figure 4, are functionally

insulated from the patients' social system by the attendants' social system. Their theoretical function is that of acting as auxiliaries to the treatment prescribed from system I. For several reasons which will appear below, however, the main work performed by the people in this system is related only partly to their theoretical function and to their professional titles. In large part, the second-level personnel are continually occupied in the supervisory and clerical duties required by the hospital's administrative structure. The social service workers, psychologists, and registered nurses have many occasional contacts with patients, but these contacts are determined more by the administrative requirements of social system II than by the patient's needs. Moreover, they occur in a highly irregular fashion, without much sustained relationship to any individual program of treatment.[10]

The double line between system II and system I corresponds in certain ways, as we have suggested, to the line between noncommissioned and commissioned officers in military organizations. As was pointed out, the Superintendent's formal medical authority is delegated downward through the Clinical Director to the individual ward physicians. The formal authority as such does not go below this line. The distribution of this authority assumes the patient-treatment structure of Figure 3, with most of the personnel in system II acting as auxiliaries to the physician, and with the ward attendants functioning as the physician's direct agents in the management and treatment of patients.

This authority structure is apparently rather typical of American state mental hospitals, and, as was indicated previously, shows clearly that mental disorders are considered at least on the surface to be medical problems. The American society is well supplied with physicians, compared with other countries, and it is therefore logical that, in the United States, as mental hospitals developed, treatment would be organized around a core of physicians in a medically oriented hospital, with treatment responsibility being restricted as far as possible to holders of the M.D. degree.[11]

In the actual rather than theoretical operation of the hospital, however, system I is insulated in the same fashion as system II from contact with the patient. This insulation occurs in several ways which will be described in detail in the following sections. Basically, however, the physician's contact with the patient is diminished, first, by the sheer weight of his average load of patient responsibility, which fluctuates between 300 and 500 per physician and occasionally rises above a thousand; secondly, by the administrative and clerical work required by this load; third, by the unavoidable necessity for the physician to delegate some of his patient responsibility to the ward attendants and second-level personnel, and the lack of both time and effective administrative machinery to supervise this delegated responsibility. Finally, it must be kept in mind that much of his contact with the patient is not of a psychiatric order but has to do with the physical problems of the patient.

In our treatment of the functions of the hospital, we pointed out that the medical function ranked third in the concrete responsibilities of the institution. The first responsibility is custodial; the second, one of institutional maintenance; and the third, those medical functions which may be discharged after the first two requirements are met. When the day-to-day role of the hospital physician is studied over a sufficient period of time, it becomes evident that as much as 60 per cent of his activity is usually devoted to work of an administrative nature resulting from the first two responsibilities of the hospital. This amounts to a near swamping of the medical-treatment function by administrative functions.

In practice, as it deals with its patients, the hospital operates in terms of four somewhat separate groups arranged as a hierarchy, with physicians at the top, social workers, psychologists, registered nurses, and office workers in the second level, ward attendants and supervisors in the third, and patients in the fourth. These levels not only reflect the formal authority of the internal hospital system but also conform rather closely to the relative status of the groups in the world outside the hospital. A characteristic of this total system is that the levels with the most authority, training, and prestige are the farthest removed from the patient population of the hospital in terms of daily individual contact, and administrative work is the most heavily concentrated on those positions, in the system which also carry the greatest medical and psychiatric responsibility for treating the patient.

CHAPTER SIX

The Executive System and Its Problems
(Level I)

A good-sized book could be written on the job functions
and interrelationships of each of the staff and line positions in
Southern State Hospital. Something of this sort must in fact
be done by investigators before institutions of this class are
thoroughly understood. In the present study, however, we
have selected only the major characteristics of these jobs and
their most important personal problems for treatment.

The necessity of selection in the study required us to con-
centrate most of our attention on certain positions historically
important in the functioning of the hospital. These positions
are those of the Superintendent, the Clinical Director, the staff
physicians, the social workers, and the nursing service and
attendants. These positions, with the dentists, the registered
nurses, and the personnel assigned to the laboratory, surgery,
and various diversional therapies, represent the professional
and semiprofessional persons upon whom the minimum functioning of the hospital has depended since 1880. There are
other positions, some of great potential importance to the
hospital, like those of the psychologists and the occupational
and recreational directorate. But at the time of our study the
position of the psychologist was very new and inadequately
organized in the system. The psychologist was treated as a
prescription or consultative person rather than as a member of
the staff with a routine relationship to all the patients; his tests
were required only in 15 to 20 per cent of the cases of unusual

interest, difficulty, or legal involvement, and adequate arrangements were lacking to make it possible for him to do satisfactory psychological research. Moreover, the position was poorly paid on a comparative basis and unsatisfactory as a research position, and it seemed unlikely that it would be filled very long. The position of occupational and recreational therapy director was authorized but not filled until about the time our study was completed. At this time it was becoming apparent to us that this new director would have great difficulty in adding the new functions of her department to the duties of physicians, social workers, charge attendants, and ward attendants, who were already overloaded with their own requirements. In a realistic sense, these two potentially important positions and certain others have to be regarded as somewhat external to the main lines of functioning of the hospital as it is presently financed and organized.

THE SUPERINTENDENT

Formal and Informal Functions and
Chief Problems of the Position

The job of the Superintendent of Southern State Hospital is to see that the hospital is maintained as a going concern. He acts as the chief executive and medical officer for the State Hospital Board. Specifically, the Superintendent is under the executive authority of the Medical Director of the state board.

Within the general framework of responsibility and accountability to the directorship of the state board, the Superintendent carries perhaps the heaviest administrative and medical burden in the state hospital system. At the present time the state board has developed five classifications of superintendents, beginning with Superintendents I, II, and III, who are required to have had long administrative experience, and in the case of the latter two, advanced educational training in institutional management as well. Superintendents IV and V are required to have, in addition to experience in institutional management, an M.D. degree from a Class A medical school, a completed residency training in a specialized field, with a certification in their specialty—ideally psychiatry and neurology—by the American Medical Specialty Board, and must be licensed to practice medicine in the state.

In Southern State Hospital the superintendency is held by the highest class of Superintendent in terms of the classification system. The formal requirements of the Superintendent's job can be divided into five general areas:

1. He reports to and receives directives from the board.

2. He serves as chief medical and administrative officer in the hospital.

3. He directs the hospital's planning program, in consultation with the state board, including plans for meeting all standards for patient, personnel, equipment, plant, and other needs; plans organizational functions and interprets them; and directs biennial budget requests.

4. He establishes and coordinates all policies and activities of the hospital program; ensures that patients are admitted, treated, and discharged in accordance with legal and medical standards; assumes responsibility for the safety of patients and personnel, for training programs for personnel; integrates the medical and nonmedical programs of the hospital; functions as the responsible personnel executive; ensures maintenance of proper institutional records and reporting of population, personnel, and property; develops and maintains cooperative relations with professional organizations, community agencies, and other hospitals; interprets hospitals to community and press; and carries out volunteer programs.

5. He performs duties in professional specialized fields: he

serves as chief medical officer, gives general direction to treatment programs, acts as consultant among staff physicians, initiates staff medical action, diagnoses individual cases, consults in unusual and difficult cases, and studies and develops new techniques to specific hospital needs. In addition, he may perform the general duties of a physician in his specialty in the hospital.

To anyone familiar with the operation of an institution of the size of Southern State Hospital, this set of responsibilities is formidable. It is no less formidable when it is translated into action as the Superintendent assumes the day-to-day tasks of the position.

The Job of the Superintendent in Operation

In our treatment of the functions of the hospital we pointed out that the hospital as it operates in actuality rather than in theory consists of three somewhat separate systems. These systems are, in order of functional importance, the custodial, the maintenance, and the treatment or medical-psychiatric system. Our research indicates that all job positions in the system necessarily reflect this same order of importance in their daily operation. This is particularly true of the position of the Superintendent.

As Southern State Hospital has grown to an institution with more than 600 employees and a yearly average of around 4,800 patients, superintendents have increasingly tended to rely for executive administration and control of the business side of the hospital on the individual who holds the position of Business Manager. This reliance has developed first out of the sheer impossibility of personally supervising the personnel, accounting, purchasing, and general maintenance of the business side of the hospital; second, from the growing intricacy of the medical-psychiatric organization of the hospital as it developed in response to increasing intake and static load of patients, accompanied by relatively low discharge and high readmission rates. A third cause stems from these other two: as patient load increases, the amount of correspondence and hospital public relations work with county judges, patients' relatives and friends, and various community agencies increases, and much of this can be handled only by the Superintendent.

But the delegation of the business and maintenance supervision to the Business Manager of the hospital has not meant that the Superintendent is actually able to devote himself to a position as chief of the medical-psychiatric services in a direct way. The major functions of the Superintendent must still be classified in order of importance as those of an executive concerned primarily with custody of patients, secondly with the maintenance problems of an existing organization, and only thirdly with problems of patient psychiatric treatment.

In looking at the executive problems of the Superintendent of Southern State Hospital, we can consider the clinical organization chart given in a preceding chapter (Figure 1B) as the formal mechanism through which he must achieve his ends.

In the preceding chapter we outlined briefly the medical-administrative organization of the hospital, as shown in this chart, and indicated some of the general differences between the three levels of personnel employed in the system. For the Superintendent of the hospital these levels represent an extremely intricate system of groups and individuals who must be instructed, evaluated, and continually supervised in the performance of their assigned jobs.

Within each of the major levels of the system there was at least one complex social group, made up of people who habitually interacted with each other in their work or other activity, who shared a common body of sentiments and ideas about their work and general position in the hospital, and who had a common set of attitudes toward other people in and out of the hospital.

Level I usually had one major group—the staff physicians and the regular consultants in surgery, orthopedics, and other frequently required specialties. The dentists were accepted, but were rather marginal to this group. Within the group of ten doctors there were two cliques during one year and three during the following year. During the working day much of the interaction between the doctors went on between the clique members, rather than between cliques. One clique was made up of rather energetic younger physicians; the other of the older, somewhat less active men. During past administrations there had been considerable conflict between the doctors' cliques, and at one time one of the cliques had systematically opposed almost every directive sent out by a superintendent. During our study, however, there were no serious instances of such conflict, and on the whole the cliques seemed to be serving about the purpose they did among other groups of employees in the hospital—of providing a friendly, relaxed, and technically helpful group among colleagues.

In level II there were at least four major groups centering around the professional people in social service, psychology, occupational therapy, and nursing. In addition, there was a fifth group made up of clerical and secretarial personnel.

In level III we found about three major prestige layers among the men and women attendants, based largely on differences in seniority and personal ability and reputation. The male and female supervisors and selected charge attendants made up the top layer, the senior charge attendants a layer below this, the newer charge attendants and other new attendants the lowest layer. There were two cliques in the top layer, divided largely on the basis of residence or nonresidence in the attendants' quarters in the hospital grounds. There were four cliques in the second layer, based on interests rather than residence. In the third group, because of very high turnover, there was little organization into cliques.

Below level III there seemed to be three layers of patients. The top group of level IV are the "privileged patients," made up largely of working patients on the ward or in the hospital and a few convalescent patients. There were at least thirty groups of patients in this layer, since they were separately organized on most of the wards. Next below this first level of patients was another less well-organized group of patients who were improving and who were beginning to learn and follow patterns of conduct which might eventually place them in the first group. The third group of patients were the incurable, "hopeless" patients. In approximate numerical terms there were about 1,200 patients in the first two patient groups and about 1,700 in the last.

This situation is sufficiently complex, but there are some added complications. In both level III and level II, some of the groups maintain continued relationships with some of the high-level positions in the business system. This is particularly true of the charge attendants and supervisors in level III and of the clerical-secretarial group in level II.[1] In our hospital and in the others where research had been done, we found reason to believe that the informal relationships between the attendants, the clerical personnel, and certain employees in the business system were among the most important in the hospital. The employees involved in this system were invariably the oldest in point of service in the hospital. Most of them had worked up through the ranks to the positions they held. Their uninterrupted tenure and experience made them reliable informants on what could and could not be done in the hospital. As compared to the physicians and other professional personnel at the top levels, these employees were unusually stable in their jobs, and they tended to carry along much of the informal knowledge of how the hospital operates. This fact made them critically important in hospital operation and in the instruction and handling of new personnel constantly coming into the system. Certain individuals in this group were constantly used as an informal advisory staff by the Superintendent, Clinical Director, the physicians, and the Director of Nursing Service. For the Superintendent, they had a functional importance far greater than their position in the formal line and staff organization chart would suggest.[2] Physicians and other professionals had an annual turnover rate of almost 70 per cent; the core of older employees had a rate of only about 1 per cent.

The informal system of communication to the Superintendent derives partly from the cultural gap between the personnel in level I and level II and those in level III. Both consciously and unconsciously the people in the top two levels identify themselves as upper-grade professional and white-collar employees. Most of them look down on the members of level III as people of lower class status than themselves. The members of level III respond to this attitude, of which they are well aware, with avoidance of any nonprofessional contact with the upper level, with the frequent statements that the upper-level people are snobbish and "stuck-up," and with a general attitude that they are doing all the real work in the system with the upper groups acting as parasites. We found only one or two special cases where there was any intimate personal association between the professional personnel in the two top levels and the attendant personnel in the bottom level.

This cleavage between the two upper levels and level III

is a persistent source of difficulty in the Superintendent's administration of the hospital. It sets up a barrier to the flow of directives downward into the system and to the upward flow of execution and communication. We found, for example, that the purposes of the psychiatric aide–training program for the attendants were poorly understood by the attendants who were the prospective trainees, and that this failure of understanding on the part of the attendants was puzzling to the executive and other professionals in the hospital. The cleavage operated to damage the psychological testing program designed to select good attendants. It prevented proper execution of the occupational and recreational therapy programs. In general treatment, the organization of the ideal operating "team" of physician, social worker, and attendant must operate across the barrier. It does not operate in fact because the barrier blocks communication.[3] The Superintendent must thus make constant use of the informal line of communication to keep his hospital functioning at all. If his relations with the upper members of level III are not reasonably good he can often get neither information nor action across the cleavage. Administratively, he must thus bypass his own formal chain of command in level II.

A second general complication of the task of the Superintendent is the management of the psychiatric and medical relationships within and between the groups in levels I and II. These relationships are exceedingly intricate. They must not only be kept in line with the custodial and maintenance requirements of the hospital, but they must also be made to operate as nearly as possible in conformity to the norms of the professional associations exterior to the hospital which they represent. Put more simply, this condition means that the Superintendent must find ways to permit the physicians, social workers, registered nurses, psychologists, and recreational and occupational therapists to operate in their professional capacities within the context of the hospital's custodial and maintenance organization.[4]

If the Superintendent is not able to find ways to reconcile the functions of his medical staff with the requirements of the primary custodial organization, conflicts and friction develop promptly in each system. In studying the operation of the Superintendent's office over a 14-month period, we found that about 20 per cent of his time was spent in getting information or hearing complaints on such developments and in trying to take some action to remedy the situation.[5] Typical problems were those in which one of the older attendants would complain because a laboratory technician used abusive language to him when he was delayed in getting a patient to the laboratory on schedule for a blood test. The complaint would be accompanied by a threat to quit if the incident were repeated. In this case, the technician, who was simply attempting to carry out his job efficiently, had to be admonished tactfully. On the same day a social worker appeared in tears to hand in her resignation because one of the physicians had told her to keep her psychiatric opinions to herself. On further inquiry it developed that the physician was actually acting in support of a ward attendant, who had complained to the physician that this particular social worker was disturbing several patients on his ward by "encouraging" them about being discharged. Again, this incident is an illustration of a legitimate attempt by a social worker to perform her job. She was, however, interfering in the attendant's informal organization of his ward. The superintendent had to nurse this situation along as best he could. Both the social worker and the physician were indispensable members of his staff. As friction continued in this situation, the superintendent finally transferred the attendant in question to another ward. Ill feeling between the physician and social worker persisted, however, until the social worker resigned.

The Superintendent receives a constant flow of problems of this sort every day. He may delegate some of them to the Clinical Director, who thus acts as an Assistant Superintendent, but the delegation, at least formally, can go no further down the administrative hierarchy. As the hospital is at present organized, frictions within and between the custodial and maintenance and medical systems have to be solved by the chief executive or by his immediate representative, since he is the only official in the hospital with final authority in all systems.

Up to this point we have been discussing the problems of the Superintendent in the hospital without reference to the historical context in which the job position has developed. But the problems and functions of this position cannot be fully understood without some knowledge of this history.

One of the most notable features of Southern State Hospital's development is the unplanned and almost random nature of its growth. This unplanned development has been further complicated by the growth of an informal structure of jobs bearing titles which have nothing to do with their functions, as in the case where a gardener and a part-time stenographer are carried as "attendants" on the payroll, and where a group of attendant supervisors actually discharge many of the functions of assistant superintendents.

From the hospital's beginning the superintendents have been confronted, as medical men, with a dilemma. If they conformed to the structure of the hospital as they found it, they could carry out a reasonably good, routine custodial administration. If, however, they attempted to establish modern psychiatric treatment of patients, the procedures necessary called

for changes in the traditional routines. This change amounted
to a change in the habits of most of the older employees and
immediately upset the routine custodial structure, thus preventing the Superintendent from acting efficiently as an executive.[6] But the professional training of any physician has been
for at least the past hundred years in the direction of seeking
and finding improvement in the condition of his patients.
Thus, the superintendents of Southern State Hospital have
found themselves confronted with a choice between being
good doctors and poor administrators, or good administrators
and poor doctors.

This dilemma probably accounts for much of the turnover
in the position of the Superintendent. During the total period
of the hospital's operation, from 1860 to 1952, the average
(arithmetic mean) tenure of superintendents has been 4 years.
The median tenure was 2.6 years. The superintendents with
the longest tenure were those who apparently accepted the
second horn of the dilemma and became efficient administrators.[7]

It is apparent that the difficulties of the Superintendent in
Southern State Hospital derive from the inability of the people
of the state and their legislatures to reach a clear decision as
to what can and cannot be done for the mental patients. This
difficulty is understandable in view of the status of modern
psychiatry, but more can be done about the problem than
has been done.

The appointment of physicians as superintendent and staff,
a few registered nurses, and a psychologist or two to the staff
of a mental hospital is not the means to guarantee that the
mentally ill patients will receive treatment. This means is actually no more effective than changing the name of the hospital
from "Lunatic Asylum" to "State Hospital."

Studies should have been made in the case of Southern State

Hospital to determine realistically what functions could and could not be performed by medical personnel in the hospital organization. Those medical functions which could be performed institutionally should have been separated from others which could not, and appropriate institutional arrangements made to handle these separate problems. Because of the planless growth of the hospital, no such studies were made. Two of the most serious and apparently insoluble clusters of difficulties in the Superintendent's position develop from failure to separate such functions.

The first cluster of difficulties is made up of those we have been discussing: they derive from the problem of managing the conflicting and poorly defined web of administrative practices which make up the social organization of the hospital, with its mixture of custodial, maintenance, and therapeutic functions. The tension built up around the attempt to reconcile these opposed ideas has made state hospital superintendencies one of the hardest medical administrative positions to fill in the United States.[8]

The second cluster of difficulties derives from the first. The administrative flaws in the hospital are such as to make it an unattractive place in which to work. To this are added the effects of underfinancing of salaries, poor quarters, and inferior food quality. There is a marked lack of opportunity for creative and effective work at any level in the system, from the physicians through the ward attendants.[9] The lack of such opportunity is particularly bad in the case of professional personnel.

Thus, in addition to the administrative problems deriving from the first cluster of difficulties, the Superintendent must also meet those coming from the second cluster. The chief consequence of this second cluster, from the Superintendent's point of view, is an appalling turnover rate in personnel of all classes. For the first two administrative levels in the system, the rate of turnover, as we calculated it for 2 years, was 67 per cent yearly. For level III, the turnover rate was 80 per cent.[10]

In concrete terms, this situation means that the Superintendent has to be constantly preoccupied with holding, recruiting, and training personnel for all levels of the system, and it means that the senior group of employees must be assigned at least informally to a constant on-the-job training program, much of which is usually nullified by resignations.

The chronic personnel problem of the Superintendent is reflected in the statistics of personnel strength and supply for the hospital.

In 1945 the American Psychiatric Association minimum standards specified that at least one physician be assigned to every 200 continued-treatment patients, and that at least one physician be assigned to every 50 convalescent patients.[11] Yet, at Southern State Hospital neither of these specifications has been fulfilled, and neither are any of the other personnel ratios. APA standards have been graded and adjusted to the different types of patients found in the hospital; although the breakdown given by APA is difficult to apply with any accuracy at our hospital, there are roughly three categories of patients that may be identified for purposes of illustrating the current discrepancy between existing personnel ratios and those recommended by APA.

These three classes of patients are (1) the continuous-treatment patients, for whom there is little hope of adequate social recovery; (2) the convalescent and newly admitted cases, who are potentially dischargeable provided sufficient attention is given them; (3) marginal cases, who may or may not recover sufficiently to be discharged or furloughed. In the first group there are approximately 1,700 patients; in the second, 800; and in the third, 400. Since only 14 doctors were authorized by the Legislature as staff physicians, in none of the above groups is it possible to comply with the standards set by APA. According to the recommended standards, 9 doctors would be required for the first group (the continuous-treatment patients), approximately 20 physicians for the second, and 10 for the third. In effect, the medical staff is less than half the size it should be in order to comply with APA minimum standards. Yet even here the outlook is more favorably presented than is actually the case in the hospital. The above calculations are based upon the authorized medical personnel, not upon the actual number of doctors employed throughout the year in the hospital. The medical staff is almost invariably fewer than the number authorized, and at the end of the first year of this study, the total number of staff physicians, not including the superintendent and clinical director, amounted to only 10 persons. And one of these already has made arrangements to resign in the near future.

A similar situation exists in the case of the nurses and attendants. While the number of the latter approaches APA standards more closely than the former, there is still much to be desired in both groups. As is apparent in Table 1 below, the discrepancy between the recommended and the actual ratio among the nurses at Southern State Hospital is tremendous. The existing ratio is approximately 1 to 250, while the minimum recommended by APA, even for continued-treatment cases, is 1 to 40. Although the number of qualified nursing personnel is inadequate, at least this group has the advantage of being properly trained for their work, while among the attendants well-trained workers are virtually nonexistent. The APA recommends a ratio of one trained attendant for every six or seven patients. At the present time Southern State

TABLE 1. SELECTED PERSONNEL GROUPS OF SOUTHERN STATE HOSPITAL:
RATIO OF PATIENTS TO PERSONNEL—FISCAL YEARS 1935–1951

Year	ATTENDANTS		STAFF PHYSICIANS		REGISTERED NURSES		TOTAL EMPLOYEES	
	Number	Patients per attendant	Number	Patients per physician	Number	Patients per nurse	Number	Patients per employee
1951	360	9	14	233	13	251	633	5
1950	282	12	10	332	6	553	606	5
1949	236	12	6	487	5	585	469	6
1948	229	13	7	423	2	1,479	459	6
1947	181	16	9	331	2	1,490	354	8
1946	158	18	8	360	2	1,439	330	9
1945	139	20	8	344	2	1,377	320	9
1944	140	19	6	450	4	675	316	9
1943	158	17	7	391	5	548	343	8
1942	163	17	8	349	6	465	350	8
1941	156	18	7	398	6	464	345	8
1940	156	17	7	388	6	453	347	8
1939	173	15	6	420	5	482	314	8
1937	147	16	6	389	6	389	305	8
1936	140	17	6	219	6	219	293	8
1935	265	9	5	454	5	454	292	8

Hospital is able to sustain a working force of attendants at a ratio almost approaching this, the current ratio being 1 to 9, but chronic turnover among the attendants makes this something of an overstatement; the attendants furthermore are not "trained."

It is almost needless to indicate that the level of efficiency of any organization is in part dependent upon the quality and training of its personnel. The figures in Table 1 show that, quite apart from other severe limitations, the superintendent is plagued by a relatively untrained group of employees, not only among the lower classes of employees but also among the medical staff as well. While we found little reason to assume that the members of the superintendent's medical staff are personally incompetent, the fact remains that none of them, except the clinical director, has had formal certification in psychiatry.[12] It is almost certain that no organization can be effectively operated without a thoroughly understood system of rules governing the work relations between its various groups of employees, and it is likewise certain that even a well-planned administrative system cannot be successfully managed by an executive without sufficient numbers of stable and trained personnel. In the past, as well as in the present, Southern State Hospital has suffered constantly from inadequacies in both respects. The consequences of these deficiencies have merely served to accentuate the already existing management difficulties of the superintendent.

THE CLINICAL DIRECTOR

Formal Functions

The formal position of Clinical Director is somewhat analogous to that of the Business Manager. He serves as the Superintendent's deputy for the medical-psychiatric system of the hospital, as the Business Manager acts as deputy for the business system. In terms of line and staff organization, the Clinical Director reports directly to the Superintendent and is answerable only to him. On occasion, he may assume the duties of the Superintendent, and he acts in many ways as an Assistant Superintendent.

The present classification system of the hospital provides two types of clinical directors. Both are required to possess the M.D. degree from a Class A medical school and to be licensed to practice medicine in the state. The higher of the two classifications (Clinical Director II) must have completed residency training in a specialized field and preferably should be certified in that specialty by the American Specialties Board. The lower (Clinical Director I) must have completed 3 years of accredited residency training in a specialized field. Holders of the higher positions are expected to have had about 5 years of previous hospital experience; the lower, about 4.

During our investigation the hospital was experimenting with this position, which had been newly created in the state hospital system. The Clinical Director's job was set up to meet two of the chronic executive problems of the hospital. Because of the increasing size of the hospital and the resulting load of nonmedical functions on the Superintendent's position, it had become customary for one of the senior physicians to exercise informally the duties of Assistant Superintendent. Such a position had been officially set up for Southern State Hospital by 1950 but was abolished in 1951 by the Legislature. In both its official and unofficial forms, the position of Assistant Superintendent combined three sets of duties, not necessarily closely related, which made him (1) assistant executive officer for the Superintendent on all matters of hospital administration; (2) chief of medical-psychiatric services, or chief of the group of physicians and other technical or professional people in residence or practicing in the hospital; (3) director of research and training.

Traditionally the Assistant Superintendent in Southern State Hospital, as appears to be the case in other hospitals throughout the system, has moved upward into the position of Superintendent. There are some exceptions to this rule, as far as we can determine from the records. These exceptions go into private practice, the armed forces, or the Veterans Administration. The Clinical Director's position appears likely to follow the same pattern as that of the Assistant Superintendent. Both positions thus may be regarded as, in part, training areas for the superintendency.

The two problems which the position of Clinical Director was designed to meet were, first, those which would face any executive in charge of a large institution or company: personnel administration, policy formation and execution, performance supervision, studying and taking action on operating problems; second, a group of more narrowly medical problems: the problem of coordinating professional medical-psychiatric services, research, and training in the hospital and exercising executive control over the interrelation of these services and the medical function of the hospital. The first group of problems can be described as an administrative overflow from the Superintendent's position, without any particular bearing on the professional medical functions of the hospital, stemming mainly from the increasing size and specialization of the hospital. The second group comprised specifically those problems of a medical-administrative officer concerned with supervision of the entire therapeutic system of the hospital and responsible to the Superintendent for the efficiency of this system. Essentially the second set of duties involved responsibility for the complete individual care of each patient, for his diagnosis and assignment to the appropriate ward, and for the conduct of all the medical-psychiatric functions in levels I and II, including those of physicians and the social service, secretarial-clerical, medical library, occupational and recreational therapy, psychology, and nursing services. Partly through nursing service and partly through the physicians, to whom he distributed patient loads and ward assignments, the Clinical Director was also responsible for the functions of the personnel in level III, including all attendants.

The formal job classification developed for the Clinical Director's functions assigns his work to four broad areas:

1. He plans the hospital medical and administrative program with the Superintendent, supplementing the latter at all points.

2. He is responsible for the administration of the hospital medical program. Here he integrates the interdepartmental operation of medical, nursing, and auxiliary services, evaluates the efficiency of the hospital medical programs, and works with the Superintendent in preparation of the biennial budget in the medical-administrative and related areas of the hospital's functioning.

3. He is directly responsible for the treatment of patients, overseeing diagnosis, treatment, care of patients, furlough and discharge of patients when appropriate. He directs medical research in all aspects of psychiatric treatment in the hospital, and he may on occasion perform the duties of a physician-specialist.

4. He supervises and controls personnel activities in the hospital. It is his responsibility to see that new personnel are adequately instructed in the requirements of their jobs, and that they are given the information necessary to carry out these jobs in the hospital. He directs much of the in-service training of various personnel and may on occasion assume direction of such parts of the academic training programs as

that of registered-nurse training. Finally, he is the responsible personnel officer for all professional personnel, hiring, evaluating, transferring, promoting, and discharging such personnel.

The Job of the Clinical Director in Operation

Informal Functions. Our study of the Clinical Director's job in day-to-day operation led us to feel that it includes three major functions. Efficient discharge of these functions would require at least three different executives. One of these three functions is that of assistant executive officer to the Superintendent on all matters of administration, both in the medical-psychiatric and the business systems of the hospital. The latter must always be coordinated with medical-psychiatric service. The second function is that of chief of all medical services in the organization and supervision of psychiatric and medical treatment, and the organization of technical exterior consultative services to the hospital—surgery, radiology, and other specialties. The third is that of chief of training and research in the hospital. This last function includes orientation and guidance of personnel, supervision of personnel policy, organization, and supervision of training programs for personnel, including the affiliate progams, such as psychiatric registered-nurse training, the organization of continuing refresher training for professional personnel, and the maintenance of a research program.[13]

Each of these three functions seems to require the full-time attention of a competent specialist in an institution of the size of Southern State Hospital. As we found the position of Clinical Director in actual operation, the three individuals who held the position successively during the study had to decide for themselves, or be informed by the Superintendent, which of the three functions would be emphasized. There was no real possibility of balancing the functions, since any one of them is a full-time job.[14]

It would be easy to label the problem of the Clinical Director as one of the problems of the general understaffing that does exist in Southern State Hospital. While it is indeed one of such problems, this is by no means the sole explanation. The addition of further personnel at this point in the system of the hospital will not solve any problem until a thorough redefinition of staff and line relationships above, in, and below the position is made. Some of this redefinition—such as, for example, a reduction in the responsibilities of the Superintendent —could conceivably alter the requirements of the Clinical Director's job. Improvement in the turnover rate of all personnel in the system would also alter the requirements of the position, as would a real improvement in the discharge rate for patients.

As matters stand at present, however, the clinical directors we have been able to observe have selected either the assistant executive duties or the medical-psychiatric duties. When the first selection is made, much of the administrative pressure on the Superintendent's position is relieved and general administrative relationships throughout the hospital seem more satisfactory. But this choice siphons executive control away from the medical-psychiatric functions. Those medical programs which require liaison between departments deteriorate, and, as communication becomes poor between departments, there is a marked tendency for each of the second-level departments like social service, occupational therapy, nursing service, psychology, secretarial-clerical, and medical records to withdraw into themselves, and even to develop slight hostilities. Interest in in-service education and training dwindles, and the physicians tend to become somewhat isolated from each other in their conduct of the wards.

Some of the deterioration of the medical program can be reversed if the Superintendent is himself able to take over the supervision. Both superintendents we observed did in fact attempt to do so. But the administrative load of the Superintendent's job in the hospital does not allow time for full control of the medical program, and too energetic an attempt to exert such control is dysfunctional either for the superintendent's other administrative responsibilities, or for the department heads responsible for medical functions. On either one side or the other the Superintendent is apt to be exerting control without full knowledge of the facts.

If the Clinical Director selects the strictly medical-psychiatric functions, a reverse imbalance to that discussed above seems to set in. In some ways this selection is less desirable than the selection of the functions of assistant executive officer. The reason for this is that when the Clinical Director ceases to take part of the administrative duties off the Superintendent's job, the latter is immediately overwhelmed with his administrative duties. The Clinical Director then becomes the medical-psychiatric head of the hospital *de facto* but not *de jure*. Since hospital tradition does not assign him authority to go with this position, he is not always in a position to exert control over the medical-psychiatric system of the hospital. Medical personnel and their adjuncts tend to go around him to the Superintendent with their problems. The Superintendent is too busy to accept his responsibility and sends them to the Clinical Director or tells them to solve the problem at their own level. Ultimately, this leads to a situation in which neither executive is consulted. The medical-psychiatric system of the hospital then tends to have actual executive control and organization only around those programs in which the Clinical Director is actively and personally interested.

During the 2 years of our observation, the lower levels of

the hospital administrative system were subjected to an oscillation of executive control, with changes in the functions of the two top executives. Inspection of the records of the hospital suggests that this situation is actually a result of the medical progress of the system. In the years preceding 1943, the administrators of the Board of Control and the superintendents of the hospital were inclined to accept the notion that the curative functions of the mental hospital, practically speaking, were secondary to the main function of decent care and custody of the unfortunate mentally ill. This was a thoroughly realistic attitude in view of the funds available to the hospital for personnel and equipment, and it was accompanied by administrative procedures which were on the whole kindly and considerate for the patients, but not medically oriented.

By 1943, however, the improvement in the prestige and power of psychiatry in the United States was creating a new social context for the state hospitals, and the effect of this improvement was visible in Southern State Hospital. From 1943 to the present time the curative mission of the hospital, as compared to its custodial mission, has been more and more in evidence. This should not be overstated. It can easily be shown that the hospital is still primarily a custodial agency, but comparison of the records of the hospital and the statements of informants for the period 1910 to 1920 with those of 1943 to 1953 leaves no doubt that the medical-psychiatric system of the hospital is now much more prominent and pervasive than it was in the early period. Very noticeably, since the superintendency in 1940 to 1943 of Dr. Edwin Murray, who served as president of the South State Medical Neuropsychiatric Association during his tenure, the medical and psychiatric influences both in and outside the Southern State Hospital have increased. This has been paralleled by developments in the central State Hospital Board, which is now under medical executive dominance.

Prior to the development of medical-psychiatric dominance in the state and in our particular hospital, the psychiatric, training, and research functions of the Clinical Director were discharged largely by individual physicians. As these functions became more important, the Clinical Director's job was established to carry them out. But as this was done, the functions of the assistant superintendent, which were of increasing importance as the hospital increased in size, were left without proper definition or assignment. The present oscillation in roles of the two top executives in the medical-psychiatric system is the result.

While the problems of the Superintendent and the Clinical Director are rather clearly of the order of growing pains, and perhaps transitional, they are not any less serious for this reason. Certainly they were evident during 14 months of our study. Until these problems are solved, many other problems in the system will not be solved. Some of these can be reviewed briefly.

Since the top control in the hospital is not clearly defined, the channels by which orders are sent down and information is reported upward are either nonexistent or not clear. One superintendent complained that when he ordered treatment or procedure of any sort, he was never certain of the form in which this order would arrive at the bottom of the system. Moreover, he could find no means to evaluate the effect of the order, either on the patients or on the personnel involved. Each level in the system is adjusted to a weak or oscillating top and intermediate executive structure to such an extent that the habit of solving problems according to a self-sufficient system is ingrained, and the habit of accurately reporting upward is nearly lost. Orders carried out and information transmitted upward are apt to be such as will interfere as little as possible with the self-sufficient system established in each level.

This process has been carried to the point where negative and positive decisions as to treatment are sometimes actually in the hands of ward attendants rather than of professional personnel. Negatively, the older attendants are in a position to decide which of the ward physician's orders they shall elect to carry out. Doctors who feel that they are getting results with certain types of advanced therapy on some wards are actually regarded with irritation and tolerant pity by many attendants, who make no effort whatever to carry out the physician's orders. Positively, the attendant can and does shape his report to the doctor on the conduct of given patients so that these patients are under the attendant's control.

The absence of efficient channels of executive control in the hospital means that poor work constantly escapes censure, and good work is seldom known or rewarded. This is particularly true of the work of attendants, charge attendants, and attendant supervisors in level III and is in general true of all departments which do not communicate directly with the Superintendent or Clinical Director. A further effect of this situation is the development of a chronic suspicion of the intermediate level II employees on the part of level III employees—a suspicion not altogether without foundation—that credit and rewards for good performance on the wards by the attendants will be absorbed by level II department members or heads. The effect of the strong social barrier which we have mentioned previously between levels II and III is to aggravate this suspicion, as well as other poor social relationships which exist because of the general status of executive control.

The failure to evaluate correctly good and poor work in the hospital has effects which are not confined to level III. In the second level, all the department heads in one way or another have had occasion to feel unappreciated. By way of brief illustration, diligent special work in preparing certain patients for discharge in Social Service was not used or acknowledged by the executive who had ordered it. Special efforts by the psychologist to set up a research program with certain groups of patients were nullified by failure of the executive to control the treatment of the experimental groups, and by the indifference of level III to the problem. The psychologist's efforts and difficulties were unacknowledged and unremedied. One of the special therapy services in the hospital was built up with great personal effort and care by one of the doctors and one of the social workers. The service was practically unknown to the chief executive, and little acknowledgment—but considerable criticism—of the service was made. Good planning and organizational work by the occupational and recreational therapy service was not known and appreciated. The effects of these and numerous other similar occurrences in the hospital on morale and initiative are obvious. Since this hospital has been confronted with this situation for most of its recent history, there is a developing tradition that efforts are not appreciated. Older employees pass this tradition along to newer ones, both directly and through a general cynical attitude. The new employee, with energy and fresh ideas, is now likely to be put under a damper at once by being labeled an "eager beaver" and is quickly informed as to what will happen to his plans. Unfortunately, this information is usually quite true. Disillusionment on this score is certainly one of the explanations for the tremendous labor turnover throughout the hospital. But no matter what his intentions are, the executive has no procedures to remedy most of this problem.

The problems faced by the Clinical Director as a person

trying to carry out a job are those of an executive responsible for the management of an intricate administrative machine. They are also those of a special professional administrator responsible for the translation of the techniques of modern psychiatry and medicine into an institutional setting. The administrative mechanism with which the Clinical Director must work is poorly defined in most respects and characterized by such turnover rates that executive energy which should go into policy and work supervision must be expended on constant procurement, orientation, and training of personnel. This difficulty can be combined with another equally grave one: modern psychiatry, with all its progress, has not made great strides in developing techniques which can be used in an institutional setting. Thus the job of translating psychiatric techniques into the hospital organization is not a simple matter of the application of known and tested medical procedures. It is a matter of constant experimentation, much of it of a trial-and-error type. Even with a stable personnel situation and with competent medical and adjunct personnel, the task would be difficult enough; as the hospital is at present organized, it is almost hopeless.[15]

This situation has its effect on the men holding the top positions in the system. Our observation of the Clinical Director's job suggests that in almost every respect it represents a combination of responsibility without power. The position carries the duties of providing psychiatric treatment, providing for the best medical service to patients, selecting and training the best staff, maintaining in-service education, organizing and furthering research. Yet on any realistic basis, the machinery for carrying out all these duties is almost nonexistent.

This kind of problem in a job is one which guarantees a continued mobility of men through the position. The Clinical Director, like the former Assistant Superintendent, is usually, almost by definition, one of the best physicians on the staff. The formal requirements of the position are such that over any long period of time he will be one of the few staff physicians to hold certification in the specialty of neurology and psychiatry. Of all the personnel below the Superintendent, he is, because of his training and experience, in the best personal and professional competitive position, and he is the most likely to be frustrated and irritated by the working conditions of the job.[16] It seems clear to us that in the future the position of Clinical Director will be increasingly difficult to fill on any permanent basis in view of its present working structure, the tendency for the directors to drift upward into the superintendency, and the competition of private practice and competing public and private agencies for psychiatric personnel of equivalent training.

SUMMARY: THE EXECUTIVE SYSTEM

The positions of Superintendent and Clinical Director share many problems. The functions of both of the jobs in the present organization of the hospital are probably too numerous and too unrelated to be discharged by single individuals, but the situation cannot be remedied by simply increasing the staff at this point. The present operation of the Clinical Director's position is causing serious problems to the Superintendent and to hospital employees below the position. These problems include administrative confusion, diffusion of executive action downward to levels where it does not belong, poor relations between equivalent departments, poor communication above and below each administrative level. One result is the dominance, in the treatment of the hospital patients, of the least well-trained hospital group—the attendants. Another is poor morale and poor job performance among most hospital employees. All these conditions are probably near the center of the causes for the unusual job turnover figures for the hospital. Because of the high level of professional and personal ability required for the Superintendent's and Clinical Director's positions and the unfavorable working conditions of the jobs, a high turnover rate in the positions seems to be inevitable.

CHAPTER SEVEN

The Physicians, Departments, and Services (Level II)

The resident physicians in the hospital are the chief responsible agents in carrying out the treatment program of the hospital. It is to them that the Superintendent and Clinical Director must actually delegate the hospital's job of physical and mental treatment and care. In theory at least the physician assumes personally the medical responsibility for diagnosis and care of the patient, with the additional responsibility for supervision and maintenance of security entailed in the care of the psychiatric patient.

The resident physician in the hospital is thus a part of the departmental system of the hospital, but he is also somewhat superior to the other members of the system, even those with the highest professional qualifications.[1] This follows from the fact that in the design of treatment, this hospital, like other mental hospitals, rests essentially on the doctor as the person responsible for final decisions on classification, treatment, and discharge of patients.

Since the doctor is the central figure in the operation of the departmental system, we concentrated our attention in studying this system on the problems of the physician as he attempts to employ the services of the major second-level departments in carrying out his job of treating patients on the wards. The chief problems of the physicians and key departments will be taken up specifically after a brief consideration of the medical-psychiatric services represented in the departmental system and of the general situation of understaffing and overcrowding in which the doctor must work. It should be kept in mind that our treatment deals only with the physician's major connections centering around ward treatment of patients. He has many other connections which must be left to other studies.[2]

ORGANIZATION OF THE DEPARTMENTS AND SERVICES

The plan of the medical-psychiatric system below the executive level of the hospital which was being developed at the time of our study included about twenty departments or services, as shown in Figure 1*B*.

This chart is not entirely accurate except as a description of progress toward which the actual organization of services in the hospital was supposed to be moving during 1951. The positions of Chaplain and Director of Occupational and Recreational Therapy were authorized but not filled. The pathology division was just being set up. The surgical division was also functioning, through the consulting surgeon, as the organizing point for several exterior consultative services, such as surgery and orthopedics, with the surgeon engaged in preparation of a plan for the organization of consultative services to the hospital.

- The nursing division was new in the hospital in the form proposed in 1951. It represented a new form of intermediate line authority between the Clinical Director and the ward attendant group, in the person of a Director of Nursing Service, who was a registered nurse. In addition, the Director of Nursing Service had under her control two new training positions, both to be occupied by registered nurses. One of these was that of director of affiliate nurse training for psychiatric-nursing education,[3] the other a director of psychiatric aide–

nursing training.[4] Two other supervisory registered nurses were budgeted under the Director of Nursing Service, together with eleven specialist and general-duty nurses.

The division of psychology was also new in the sense that for the first time it was headed by a full-time director, holding a Ph.D. degree in psychology, and had an additional psychologist's position allotted to it. Prior to this time, psychological testing and other professional psychological functions had been performed for the hospital largely by part-time—and sometimes unpaid—services from Millville Liberal Arts College.

In operation, the departments of the hospital were occupied with the duties of receiving, classifying, treating, maintaining, and discharging patients. The essential parts of this process are carried out by the physicians, the social workers, the secretarial-clerical staff, the attendants, the medical records service, with the occasional necessary service of the medical division, including the surgeon and consultants and registered nurses.

Perhaps the most characteristic difficulty shared by all the medical department heads, as in the case of the executive level, is the encroachment of the custodial-maintenance problems into the performance of the medical-psychiatric functions for which they are paid. This encroachment may be positive— through requiring medical-psychiatric personnel to spend most of their time doing administrative work; or it may be negative—through preventing these professional personnel from carrying out professional programs. In the case of most of the professional personnel, both the positive and negative effects were evident.

If we break down the functions of the hospital in a common-sense way and look at the day-to-day processes of work carried out by the departmental level and the lower levels in performing these functions, we can see that the hospital is trying to carry out nine operations:

1. Receiving all persons classified by medical and court opinion as either actually or potentially mentally ill, requiring treatment or observation, or both. This group may include criminals, alcoholics, the psychotic or neurotic feebleminded, the epileptic, and tuberculous patients showing mental symptoms.

2. Maintaining records on all persons committed.

3. Examining these persons and securing as much information from or about them as possible.

4. Diagnosing and classifying those committed.

5. Determining where those committed are to be assigned in the hospital, and how they are to be treated.

6. Maintaining the desired treatment under conditions giving the maximum security for the patient, for those dealing with him, and for the general public.

7. Determining when the patient is ready for discharge or requires further treatment.

8. Securing the patient's discharge.

9. Arranging for the patient's permanent care if he is undischargeable.

Our examination of the relation of the departments of the hospital to these nine functions shows that the professional personnel are restricted to a minimum level of performance on all of them. This minimum level represents a least common denominator determined by the organization and staffing of the positions (which was always substantially below national minimum standards) and also by the quality, quantity, and turnover of working personnel on the wards.

This situation represents a dilution of professional services which is not confined to Southern State Hospital but is actually present to some extent in all publicly supported hospitals for the treatment of the mentally ill in the United States, with the possible exception of the Veterans Administration facilities.[5]

The most conspicuous failure of Southern State Hospital seems to occur in the performance of functions 1, 2, 3, 7, and 8. The primary reason for this failure lies in a complete understaffing of the social service department, which is substandard in number and quality of personnel by a very great percentage.[6] Without trained social workers, it is impossible to set up any of the nationally recognized admission procedures to handle incoming patients properly, secure and maintain adequate records from a psychiatric point of view, determine when the patient is ready for discharge, and secure and supervise this discharge. If there are insufficient social workers to perform these functions, the hospital is guaranteed a steadily increasing static load of patients, some of whom might once have been dischargeable with vigorous efforts on the part of trained social workers. Also, none of the modern programs of home care, foster-home placement, or vocational rehabilitation of patients is possible without a competent social work staff.

Without something approaching an adequate number of social workers, none of the other members of the professional psychiatric staff, including physicians, psychologists, occupational therapists, chaplain, and nurses, can function properly on intake, treatment, and discharge of patients. The reason for this, as we have pointed out above, is that mental illness, unlike most of the other diseases, requires for treatment and rehabilitation considerable knowledge of the patient's social background and considerable contact with the people who form this background. The success of treatment in a case of mental disorder is often less dependent on the efficiency of hospital facilities than it is on the cooperation of the patient's family and accurate knowledge of his social relations.

A second reason for the failure of the hospital to perform the functions indicated above is the overcrowding of the institution by patients. We have indicated some of the facts about this overcrowding in a previous chapter. To the layman, overcrowding in the psychiatric hospital may appear merely aesthetically undesirable. But to the professional it is a deadly threat to all the modern types of hospital therapy. Psychiatric classification and treatment cannot be effective where patients of differing types must be mixed together; and this is likewise true of psychiatric research. Thus, even if the social workers are supplied the hospital, their work will not be effective unless an improvement in the space available for treatment is made at the same time.

The overcrowding of Southern State Hospital is actually part of a vicious circle. The overcrowding occurs slowly over the years, adding imperceptibly to the custodial load of the hospital. Some of the cases coming into the hospital are untreatable and must remain in the hospital until death. Many are treatable and/or dischargeable—a number varying between 40 and 60 per cent through the years. About 25 per cent have to be readmitted to the hospital. The disorders of old age are increasing with every decade in their percentage of hospital admissions, and while the older people live only 4 to 6 years after they enter the hospital, they still live longer than they did 20 years ago, and proportionately more of them are coming in each year. The longevity of certain types of incurable schizophrenic patients has improved with the increasingly better physical care given by the hospital. Longevity has increased for the mentally deficient. As the custodial group in the hospital grows, it requires a greater expenditure of administrative and medical energy. This, in turn, restricts the amount of such energy available for the hopeful cases. As a result, the hopeful cases, failing to receive the proper attention, eventually become part of the custodial load and begin to interfere in their turn with the treatment of new cases. As the static group in the hospital increases, the overloading of ward facilities interferes with assignment of patients to the proper type of hospital environment for their illness. This in turn blocks occupational and recreational therapy or other types of therapy which require some minimum of group homogeneity. Arbitrary transfers of patients have to be made without regard to sustaining or therapeutic social relationships the patient may have begun to develop in a particular ward. Treatment and research programs being carried out by professional personnel are often terminated by transfers which have to be made to relieve excessive overcrowding in some wards. Also, many of the treatment programs with particular patient groups cannot be initiated in the first instance because of overcrowding.

Thus, the vicious circle in the hospital is completed. Understaffing at key points, accompanied by overcrowding, prevents therapy and discharge. With the failure of active therapy and discharge, the understaffing and overcrowding grow worse. This is the general context in which the resident physician who works in the hospital must carry out his duties.

THE CHIEF PROBLEMS OF THE PHYSICIANS

The staff physician in Southern State Hospital, operating as he does in an understaffed and overcrowded institution, has many problems. We have selected only the most serious of those we found for consideration. The first of these problems is that of the qualification of the physician himself for the practice of psychiatric treatment; the second, the administrative overload of nonmedical duties under which the doctors are compelled to operate; third, the ill-defined staff and line relationships with his superiors and with his professional auxiliaries.

Qualifications of the Doctors

All but two of the average of ten physicians serving on the wards of Southern State Hospital were graduates of Class A medical schools, licensed to practice in South State.[7] None of the ward physicians, however, was certified in the specialty of neurology and psychiatry. Six of the physicians were preparing themselves in this specialty, but all of them were at least a year away from certification. The clinical director and superintendent, who do not practice on the wards, were the only diplomates in neurology and psychiatry.

At the present time, only about 3 per cent of the doctors practicing in all the South State mental hospitals hold certification in psychiatry, and only one of these is acting as a ward physician. The remainder, as in Southern State Hospital, hold administrative posts.[8] Of the doctors planning to complete certification in psychiatry, all but one informed us that they planned to leave for various positions in military service, the Veterans Administration, private practice, or higher administrative posts above ward practice in the state hospitals. All those planning to leave gave their reasons in the following order:

1. It is impossible to practice psychiatry in this institution.

2. Psychiatric research cannot be undertaken in this hospital.

3. The prestige of psychiatrists practicing on the wards in state hospitals is low among other medical men.

4. Better salaries or higher income can be secured almost anywhere else by a psychiatrist.

5. Working conditions and surroundings in the hospital are unpleasant and depressing.

In the long run, the problem of the doctor's qualifications is likely to be the most important one faced in staffing the state hospitals if our hospital is a sample. The ward physician carries out most diagnosis and formal treatment prescription in the state hospital, and the operating procedure of the institution necessarily assumes his professional competence in psychiatry. Everything we were able to determine about the doctor's functioning in the hospital, from present observation and past records of the institution, indicates that the doctor's attainment of psychiatric certification almost immediately removes him from the practice of psychiatry with the hospital patients.

The implications of the situation are clear enough, however, to need no great spelling out. National medical manpower statistics indicate that state hospitals all over the country are short 2,000 physicians in terms of APA standards. Certified psychiatrists are even more scarce, numbering only 4,048 for the United States in 1951. To serve a population of 5,710,150 people in South State in 1950, there were only 80 certified psychiatrists listed as practicing in the state.[9]

It is apparent, then, that none of the usual solutions offered to the medical staffing problem in the state hospital, such as increased salaries or better working conditions, can be applied to this yawning gap between need and supply. To remedy the situation we found in Southern State Hospital and that throughout the United States in the case of the physicians, a much more careful redesigning of the medical role of the hospital staff physician is obviously necessary. Medical care at this level is a scarce commodity and should be used accordingly.

Administrative Overload of Physicians;
Nonmedical Nature of Doctors' Duties

The second of the major problems centering around the physician in the hospital is the amount of his time consumed by nonprofessional duties.

In interviewing and working with the ward physicians, we found individual doctors carrying responsibilities for patients varying all the way from one doctor to 150 patients to one doctor to 1,200 patients, depending on a fluctuating group of conditions, such as leaves, illness among physicians, staffing of new services like pathology, amount of special therapy, and the resignation of physicians. Because of the turnover among staff physicians and the frequent transfers of patients between wards in the constant quest of space in the hospital, it was almost impossible to calculate accurately the average load of patients per physician.

Using the 212-day-year basis recommended by the American Psychiatric Association Committee on Psychiatric Hospital Standards and Policies,[10] we estimated that a staff physician at the hospital, by taking advantage of every available moment of his working time, could give each patient under his supervision about 4 hours of attention each year. Like any other average figure this one is not very useful, however. In practice, the physicians simply have to regard about 1,700 patients in the hospital (mainly those with senile disorders, the mentally deficient, and those with certain types of schizophrenia) as hopeless, to be checked only routinely for physical illness or injuries.

One of the main reasons for the restriction of the physician's time with patients is the administrative work connected with his patient responsibilities. Our time estimates show that in the case of nearly every physician about 60 per cent of his

time goes into paper work and correspondence, record reading and analysis, organizational and medical staff meetings,
assisting in surgery or other hospital duty of a nonpsychiatric
sort, conferring with auxiliary medical personnel, carrying
special responsibilities during the rotating officer-of-the-day
period for receiving service, and conferring and working with
other physicians and the Superintendent on the chronic problems of recruiting, training, and firing personnel. No more
than 40 per cent of the physician's time is available for his
ward rounds or for any treatment of the patients in the ward.

The outcome of this situation for the physician is that he
is usually under pressing executive responsibility for rather
routine administrative work. Most of the doctors we interviewed stated that they found this type of work frustrating
and unpleasant, and the majority of those intending to leave
gave the heavy load of administrative work which prevents
them from doing medical practice or research as one of their
primary reasons for seeking other types of employment.

The resistance which the ward physicians feel toward the
way the hospital organizes their services is undoubtedly one of
the main causes for their rapid turnover in employment. The
turnover rates we computed for ward physicians over the
period 1938 to 1950 [11] showed a median length of service of
these physicans of 1.5 years, with 12 of 31 physicians staying
1 year or less, 16 staying 2 years or less, and 25 staying 3 years
or less. Thus, 80 per cent of the ward physicians had spent
3 years or less in the system.

It is apparent that a great deal of the ward physician's time
must be spent in getting broken in and in stand-by performance and replacement training as he is preparing to terminate
employment. The turnover of physicians has further effects
which could be predicted by an experienced personnel officer.
The physician's mobility forces or permits those working

under him to develop procedures which will function in his absence (or preoccupation elsewhere). Much of the control over the patients exercised by the attendants is a consequence of the necessary delegation of the physician's responsibility for the patient to the attendant. If Southern State Hospital depended too greatly on a social organization which presupposed continuity of tenure in the physicians, it would be thrown into constant confusion because of physician turnover.

As in the case of the understaffing and overcrowding problem, the difficulty in this situation is circular. Because the work is unsuitably organized from the physician's point of view, the physicians tend to leave the hospital within a very short time. But the tendency of the physicians to leave aggravates the other problems of the hospital, tending particularly to create a self-sufficient organization of the attendants which controls much of the treatment of patients independently of the doctor. In addition, the mobility of the professional personnel through the system puts a premium on the keeping of records, which thus adds to the paper work confronting those coming into the system.[12]

Ill-defined or Conflicting Working Relationships

Partly as a function of the problems we have been describing, the ward doctor's relationships with his superiors and colleagues and the auxiliary treatment services in level II present a third set of recurrent difficulties. The more important of these difficulties as we found them can be divided into six groups, centering around the relationships of the physicians with (1) the Superintendent and Clinical Director, (2) the new nursing service staff, (3) social service, (4) occupational and recreational therapy personnel, (5) the psychology department, (6) attendant personnel in level III.

1. *Physicians and Superintendent and Clinical Director.* In terms of the formal organization of the hospital, the Superintendent and particularly the Clinical Director are supposed to provide technical assistance and counsel to the ward physicians. In practice, we found that, partly because of the excessive administrative load on the executive positions and the mobility of physicians, very little such assistance and guidance was given. This was not because efforts were not made to guide and counsel the individual physicians by the executives. This responsibility was taken quite seriously by both superintendents and at least one clinical director. The requirements of the doctors' jobs in the hospital were such, however, as to make any continuous counseling or guidance relationships between the physicians and their superiors almost impossible.

2. *Physicians and Nursing Service.* The organization of the hospital at present includes the new nursing directorate described above. The head nurse, or Chief of Nursing Service, is the line head of all registered nurses and the attendant staff, an organization patterned with some modification after that in general hospitals. Administratively, her position is somewhat superior to that of the ward physicians, in the sense that she is the head of the hospital's major group of working employees who perform the main medical auxiliary service in the hospital.

Our study of the relation of the physicians to the nursing service indicates that the present organization of the service is far out of line with traditional procedure in the hospital. The physician in our state hospital has typically controlled and managed the wards under his supervision, and all the older attendants are in the habit of reporting to the ward physician or to their charge and supervising attendants. The addition of a new supervisory staff of registered nurses since 1950 has meant that the authority line in the hospital has been split. During our study the physicians, nurses, and attendants were far from having worked out a mutually satisfactory interpretation of their relations. The physicians were generally pleased to have a larger staff of registered nurses in the hospital, but frictions were developing on several points over the functions to be supervised by physicians and those to be supervised by registered nurses. The experienced attendants were uniformly hostile to the nurses, whom they regarded as unnecessary supervisors. Since the attendant personnel must perform the constant custodial-maintenance work of the institution and the actual clinical supervision of patients, and since the physician is personally responsible for this work and the nurse is not, the physician cannot permit the nursing directorate to exercise complete personnel control on his wards. In practice, most physicians were forced to back the attendants rather than the nurses when the attendants resisted the nurses.

Since this situation clearly represented a split authority line, it was having bad effects on the morale of doctors, nurses, and attendants. From the physician's point of view it was at times a serious additional irritation in an otherwise badly organized system.

3. *Physicians and Social Service.* In Southern State Hospital, the social worker, who is perhaps the most valuable potential adjunct to the doctor's work in and outside the hospital, is practically nonexistent. The tendency of all the physicians, with one or two exceptions, was to employ the social service staff simply as specially instructed case-history stenographers. This situation is partly the result of the doctors' administrative overload and of the usual one worker to 710 patients ratio of social workers in the hospital. But it is partly a result of the failure of the hospital organization to define the role of the social worker properly in terms of modern

psychiatric practice and to allow at least a minimum personnel
and travel budget for a modern social work staff. The result
of this failure is that the social worker is unable to function to
help the doctor determine whether a patient is potentially
dischargeable to his family or relatives, to assist in any problems of rehabilitation for the patient, or to help evaluate the
success of treatment after discharge.[13]

Since the social work staff is so far below any minimum
effective level, the doctor actually has no alternative except to
treat this staff as secretarial rather than as treatment auxiliaries.
This naturally results in resentment on the part of the social
workers and has led over the years in Southern State Hospital
to relations between the physicians and the social workers
which verge on hostility. The physicians with psychiatric
training on the staff of Southern State Hospital were unanimous in regarding the lack of an effective social work staff as
one of the worst defects in the hospital's organization. But
none of them was individually in a position to do anything
about the problem.

4. *Physicians and Occupational and Recreational Therapy.*
Because of the general problems of their practice in the hospital, there were only six or seven instances in which the
physicians were making sustained systematic use of the occupational and recreational therapy personnel. In studying the
occupational and recreational therapy system in the hospital,
we found some good planning by the best modern standards.
The hospital has been fortunate in having a highly competent
person in charge of this therapy from 1949 until 1951, at
which time he was transferred to the central state board.
Much of the planning of this therapy, however, has been
wasted, because the hospital was unable to hire a director of
the program thereafter, and the therapy program still lacks
interpretation and integration into the professional and busi-

ness system work of the hospital. Moreover, the indicated authority position for the Director is not strong enough to secure necessary compliance from personnel.

At the present time the tendency of the physicians is to use the occupational and recreational therapy program largely in a common-sense diversionary way, to keep the patients active and exercised, and to leave much of the conduct and planning of this program to the fourteen or fifteen employees assigned by the hospital to occupational and recreational therapy. Here, as in the case of the other level II departments, the physician finds an auxiliary pattern which, being improperly organized, cannot function effectively in terms of modern psychiatric hospital practice.

5. *Physicians and the Psychology Department.* The present use by the physicians of the psychology director in the hospital is primarily that of a prescription psychometrician on 17 to 20 per cent of the incoming patients. He is used also as a teacher in the attendant-training program, and he practices a limited amount of psychotherapy under the theoretical supervision of the physician. In this hospital, the APA standards require twelve qualified psychologists to be assigned to the Admission and Intensive-treatment cases and between three and four to be assigned to the Continuous-treatment cases. As in the case of the social service department, the psychology department is so completely understaffed that it cannot be employed in routine testing, group psychotherapy, or other adjunct therapy now practiced in the better-organized mental hospitals. The physician cannot use the psychology services in this hospital, and this condition in turn makes the position professionally untenable for a competent psychologist.

6. *Physicians and Attendant Personnel.* While one can say in general that the ward physician in the hospital is handicapped at every point in his relations to the auxiliary profes-

sional services in level II, his worst problems actually occur as a result of the hospital's organization in level III. This organization will be discussed at greater length in the sections on the third level, but a few of the outstanding difficulties should be reviewed in connection with the physician's operations.

Our data show that with certain minor exceptions, the supervising, charge, and ward attendants form part of a social system which is able to control ward routines and to handle the flow of information about patients to the ward physicians. Since the attendants' social system is absolutely essential to the custodial-maintenance system of the hospital, it apparently cannot be eliminated, but the control established here by the attendants means that by and large these attendants have a great deal to do with both diagnosis and treatment of the mental patient, since the physician's overload and occupational mobility through the system make him dependent on the attendant for much information.[14]

The dependence of the physician on the attendant at this point represents what is perhaps the worst feature of Southern State Hospital: the least-educated, least-trained, lowest-paid, and generally worst-treated employees actually have the most to do with day-to-day patient treatment and symptom diagnosis. As the hospital is organized at present, much of this situation is apparently unavoidable. The attendant has the job of maintaining order and reasonable cleanliness, under conditions of work which would be regarded as almost intolerable by most employees in the United States. The attendant turnover rate is the highest for any of the groups in the hospital, and such order as does exist in the attendant system results from a fairly stable pattern of beliefs and expectations maintained by a nucleus of older employees. Those physicians experienced in the hospital's work deplore this system; however, they regard it as essential to the operation of the institution as it is organized at present, even though the system, as will be seen below, tends to block everything except the simplest type of custodial care for at least 90 per cent of the patients in the hospital.

CHIEF PROBLEMS IN THE DEPARTMENTS
AND SERVICES

Most of the serious problems of the second level in the hospital have been reviewed in connection with the ward physicians' work. In observing and interviewing at the second level of the hospital, we found a number of other recurrent problems, some of them general throughout the level, others peculiar to particular departments or services.

Two general characteristics strike the observer almost at once on contact with the personnel at this level, and they continue to be highly noticeable as the observer remains in the system. The first of these characteristics is an atmosphere of discouragement and cynicism about the jobs and the hospital as a whole. This is almost universal, particularly among the employees who have been working in the hospital for a year or more. The second characteristic is the lack of mutual discussion, communication, and teamwork on the working level.[15]

The general understaffing throughout this level of the hospital has had the result of restricting most of the departments to the essential routine administrative work. There appears to be little energy or time left for such cooperation as might occur between social service and occupational therapy, or with the nursing service and the other professional groups. Such relationships are not defined and worked out by the executive authority in the system on a continuous basis, although many efforts to do so were observed. Generally speaking, the work relationships are so ill defined throughout the second level between the departments and services that many employees seem honestly puzzled as to how they should regard one another. The salaries of the clerical office group are about one-third lower than those of most of the professional group, and there is general resentment of this on the part of the former. A peculiarity of the organization at this level is very noticeable in connection with the salary differential. The office personnel consider that the professional people are actually doing administrative or clerical work rather than technical medical work in spite of their titles. This is not officially true, but unofficially, or informally, it is quite true because of the administrative overload of the medical functions, resulting from understaffing in the professional positions. This leads to hostility between the two groups because of the salary differential.

The understaffing of professionals has been going on so long in this hospital that most of the older clerical and secretarial employees have developed a traditional attitude toward all professionals, including the doctors, which assumes that they are relatively functionless in the hospital but that they have softer and better-paid jobs because they were lucky enough to get college degrees and professional education. This attitude is masked, of course, but it is present, and it has very profound effects in determining what the professionals are able to accomplish.

Among the particular departments and services, with the possible exception of nursing service and the office staff, understaffing is probably the key problem. There are many examples of faulty functioning and of poorly organized services, but these seem to be mainly related to staffing which falls below minimum levels.

The social service department is both understaffed and budgeted inadequately for travel funds. The APA standards for hospital social workers would require 43 trained social caseworkers for Southern State Hospital. The higher New York standard indicates that the hospital should have 54 trained social workers and a budget permitting at least 3 months of travel status per year for 40 workers.[16] At the present time, the social service department has 7 employees, only 1 of whom holds certification from an accredited school of social work. These 7 handle an admission load which is now more than 1,000 patients per year. The social workers in Southern State Hospital are largely untrained, are too few, and thus do very little social work. Our time analyses show that approximately 80 per cent of the workers' job time is spent in collecting and writing up case histories on incoming patients, in routine correspondence with social agencies and patients' relatives, and in other administrative work developing from the intake process; the remaining 20 per cent largely on similar work involved in getting patients out of the hospital. It is impossible to apply in this hospital the modern concept of psychiatric employment of social workers as treatment and rehabilitation personnel.

The personnel turnover in the social service department is about what would be expected in view of the conditions of employment. From 1927 to 1950, the median length of service of social service employees was 1.3 years. Of 28 social workers, 9 stayed 5 months or less; 19 stayed 2 years or less; 25 stayed 3 years or less. Our interviews with the social service personnel leave little doubt that frustration and dissatisfaction with the position of the social worker in the hospital are the cause of much of the turnover. The social workers consider that they are treated in terms of rank and housing privileges less well than higher business employees on the business side of the hospital and the craft employees such as the electricians. Many of them state that their relations to the ward physicians are thoroughly unsatisfactory, in that their possible role in the treatment of patients is neither understood nor appreciated. Because of our familiarity with the views of physicians on the functions of social workers in the present organization of Southern State Hospital, we knew that there was some justice in the complaints about lack of understanding and appreciation. But to a majority of the physicians and particularly the younger or better-trained physicians, the social work function had more prestige and importance than any of the social workers realized. It was a comment on the communication structure of the hospital that so little was known by either of these groups—both essential in the treatment of the mentally ill—about the attitudes and problems of the other.

The newness of the psychology department in Southern State Hospital meant that many of its relations to the physician were not defined in many respects. There was some tendency on the part of the physicians to make increasing use of the department as a prescription testing service and as a source of occasional therapy for certain kinds of patients, since at the time of the study the department was placed for the first time in charge of an able and relatively permanent psychologist with a Ph.D. degree and training in clinical psychology. But there was also an observable tendency to absorb the psychologist's time in teaching duties in the affiliate nurse program and the psychiatric aide–training program. Further duties of an administrative or personnel character for the psychologist were just over the horizon, since many of the medical staff wanted him to be employed in screening attendants and other applicants for mental ability and psychological stability through tests and interviews.

Although he had been in the hospital only a short time, the psychologist was finding himself in a position not greatly different from that of the physicians. His professional status and prospects were in jeopardy. He had been promised a certain salary and emolument level equivalent to that of the lower physicians, but this was not forthcoming. His budget for assistants had been cut down and his time absorbed by new duties not contemplated when he was hired. He had been promised opportunities for psychological research with the patients, but when he set up two of his projects he found that the hospital's loose administrative control, its peculiar classification and assignment system, and the ward social organization prevented any reliable field procedure or even adequate separation of experimental and control groups.

Since neither the level of pay and emoluments nor research conditions for the psychologist were adequate, and his future prospect for being overloaded with nonprofessional administrative duties was excellent, he was already preparing to leave the hospital at the time the present study started. At the end of the study he had done so. But by this time, both the physicians and the psychologist had learned that a fully qualified psychologist could actually do very little in the organization of Southern State Hospital.

Occupational and recreational service in Southern State Hospital seems to be in excellent status as far as planning is concerned. In execution, however, the programs for occupational and recreational therapy for the patients suffer, like all the other second-level services, from understaffing and from the lack of communication between the departments and services. The relations with social service and the physicians are particularly problematic. Modern mental hospital practice requires the closest working connections and understanding between these three divisions, and we could find very little evidence of such connections.

From the medical-psychiatric and administrative points of view, one of the key divisions of the hospital is the office of the statistician or medical records librarian. The reporting of medical and psychiatric statistics in Southern State Hospital has been vastly improved during the years since 1951 as far as the collection of national statistics in terms of the Public Health Service standards is concerned. Sufficient funds for adequate personnel have never been available to this department, however, and the result has been that operational or executive statistics are particularly weak.

This division of the hospital should, but cannot, provide definite and useful data on the effectiveness of various therapy programs, on fluctuations in the intake and discharge of patients as ratios of the district population, on the variations in all treatment programs, space allocation to patients, personnel turnover, and many trend analyses to show past, present, and future needs for the hospital. In a mental hospital, statistics of this sort are of more than merely operational significance. They need to be kept because of their research importance in the field of mental health and because of the need for programming by state legislative and executive authority.

To the physicians, the possible function of this office as an operational statistics or research unit in the hospital was something beyond any probability. Such functions would of course require radical changes in the entire hospital, including improvement in classification and assignment, many more professional employees, and many changes in the wards to ensure that the data on which these statistics were based were up to date and conscientiously maintained. The main problem in any future functions of this sort for the medical records office lies in the wards, where the actual care and treatment of the hospital goes on, and in the relation of the level II system to these wards.

The patient records kept in the medical records library are based on two official classification systems, which will be considered in the following chapter. One system uses the nomenclature used in collection of hospital statistics in terms of the U.S. Public Health Service standards; the other uses that of the hospital's institutional classification of status and assignment of patients. But in work on the wards, the physician in Southern State Hospital and the ward attendants employ another system which is not reflected in any formal way in the medical records. The medical records department thus was not significant in operations. It tended strongly to be a place where formal reports of diagnoses and physical treatment records, as well as formal medical status reports, were filed or specially prepared for higher authority on the hospital board, and where records of routine administrative assignments of patients and administrative time books for the professional staff were kept.

For the physician there was, and in fact could be, little use of this department for the maintenance of any realistic operational statistics in his sphere of responsibility, and we found almost no attempts in this direction among the physicians.

CHAPTER EIGHT

Classification and Assignment of Patients
(Level III)

In Southern State Hospital there are actually three classification schemes for patients. The first is the scientific one employed in records and formal staff presentation. The second is the institutional classification, or patient-management system. The third is the informal system of patient classification used by the ward attendants and physicians in their daily work with the patients. The first and second systems are both official systems, although they are essentially unrelated to each other. The third system is unofficial and unacknowledged but is in fact closely integrated with the second system. In the over-all organization of Southern State Hospital, the second system seems to work at least in part as an intermediate or coupling system between the medical-psychiatric function of the hospital and the custodial-maintenance function.

Learning how to integrate the three systems is the first task which the new physician faces in Southern State Hospital as he takes up his duties on the wards. His textbooks and academic and residency training have usually centered around the conceptions of the official record diagnoses. In the state hospital institutional classification he often encounters something new as far as much of his formal training goes.

The clinical psychiatry in which the physician has been trained has developed mainly in private practice, specialized psychiatric research, and small psychopathic hospitals, usually attached to medical schools in America and Europe. Its categories are derived from, and assume, intimate personal knowledge of the patient. Institutional psychiatry, of the kind represented in state hospitals, has developed largely in these state hospitals and seems to represent in many respects an altogether different kind of growth.[1] When the types of classification used in state hospitals are compared with the categories of the revised nomenclature of the American Psychiatric Association, the differences in origin and effect of the two types of classification are quite striking.[2] The institutional system is essentially an operational device for the management of large numbers of patients from the point of view of their relation to an administrative organization. The APA classification is just as clearly the beginning of a scientific taxonomy developed by and for research and individual practice in psychiatry.

In his work in Southern State Hospital, the ward physician has the task first of fitting the clinical frame of reference into the hospital classification and then interpreting this joint product to patients, attendants, nurses, and social workers. Since these two systems of classification are devised for different purposes and many of their categories overlap, the individual doctor's interpretation of their relationship is often fraught with difficulties.

The gap between the official psychiatric diagnostic categories in Southern State Hospital and those of the hospital's institutional or operating classification can be compared in the following tables. These tables show the percentages of patients in the hospital as they appear in the two types of classification systems.

The general diagnoses in Table 2, with their refinements, are quite significant to the trained psychiatrist as guides in prescribing treatment and analyzing the course of illness for the individual patient. But the hospital classification with which the physician must work often mixes the patients in one sub-group of the diagnostic categories with those of others because of gross behavior resemblances. No matter how irrelevant these differences may be to technical diagnostic taxonomy, they are often quite important in the hospital's operations.

TABLE 2. PERCENTAGE OF SOUTHERN STATE HOSPITAL PATIENTS IN
EACH OF SIX MAJOR AMERICAN PSYCHIATRIC ASSOCIATION
DIAGNOSTIC CATEGORIES, FOR BOTH SEXES

Diagnosis	*Per cent*
Schizophrenic reactions	40
Affective reactions—manic	8
Mental deficiencies	10
Meningoencephalitic syphilis	4
Cerebral arteriosclerosis	6
Senile brain disease	4
Undiagnosed	18
All other	12

Some of the complexity of the typical hospital classifications can be seen in Table 3. Since an important part of the hospital classification scheme rests on segregation of the sexes and a different organization of employment and control, Table 3 is broken down into the percentage distributions of both sexes.

Historically, the institutional classification scheme used in the hospital was developed before the present system of psychiatric classification; it represents a pattern for the institutional management of incoming patients in terms of age, sex, and behavior patterns, rather than a scientific nosology. Many of these institutional categories cut across the official psychiatric diagnoses, as, for example, when one patient will be formally diagnosed as an agitated psychoneurotic, another as

TABLE 3. PERCENTAGE OF SOUTHERN STATE HOSPITAL PATIENTS IN EACH CATEGORY OF THE INSTITUTIONAL CLASSIFICATION SYSTEM, BY WARDS AND FOR BOTH SEXES *

PERCENTAGE DISTRIBUTIONS

WARD	NUMBER OF PATIENTS	BY GENERAL CLASSIFICATION			BY HOSPITAL WARD STATUS			BY PRIVILEGES OR DEGREES OF CONTROL			
		0 to 1 year— new cases	Old cases In hospital more than one year continuous treatment	Geriatric cases Continuous treatment	Employed Outside ward	On ward	Idle	Paroled on grounds	Chapel or parties	Disturbed and/or excited	Not specifically defined (un-diagnosed)

MALE—WHITE

WARD	NUMBER OF PATIENTS	0 to 1 year new cases	Old cases continuous treatment	Geriatric continuous treatment	Outside ward	On ward	Idle	Paroled on grounds	Chapel or parties	Disturbed and/or excited	Not specifically defined
11	44	100			11	33	55		10	4	86
12	102	15	85		35	15	50	30	35		35
13	108		100		22	9	65	13	18	12	57
14	42		100		100			100			
15	50	100			42	12	46	84	16		80
16	82		100		8	10	81			20	87
17	110	18	82		2	15	83	3		10	93
18	75	20	80		20	40	40	20		7	
20	150	10	47	43	5	15	80	20	8	13	59

I	43	11	89		36	23	77	4	27	9	64
II	50	6	94		20	28	36		26	2	68
III	54	13	87			9	71		13	31	56
IV	54	13	87			22	78	5		40	55
V	55	5	92	3		22	78	15	18	18	49
VI	56	7	91	2		28	72	10	20	46	24
VII	44	100				22	78	18			82
VIII	56	14	86			23	77	10	23	66	
IX	56		100		12	35	53		19	46	35
X	67	12	73	15	22	23	55	6	15	20	59
XI	57	5	30	65	3	17	80		16	9	75
XII	68	14	63	23	12	15	73		12	58	30
XIII	200	2	72			19	81	2	3		95
XIV	159	25	75	26	40	10	50	32	30	1	37

* Figures are rounded in columns on percentage distribution.

127

an excited paranoid schizophrenic, another as a manic-depressive in a strong manic phase. Informally, all three may be classified together in the table as "disturbed" or "excited" and treated accordingly.

One of the peculiarities of procedure in Southern State Hospital is that the institutional classification and diagnostic system seems to be far more important in the care, treatment, and discharge of patients than the official classification. Yet, the professional personnel must report and speak in terms of the official classification, while they and their subordinates are required to manage the patients and do most of the practical work of the hospital in terms of the institutional ward systems. This situation leads to a great deal of confusion, since the formal administrative action of the hospital proceeds in terms of quite deceptive labels. The official diagnostic terms must be used in the statistical reporting of the hospital, so that records kept of patients often reflect little of what is being done for them except to people who know what the formal terms actually mean in the institutional classification scheme. The phrase "continuous-treatment," applied to a patient in Southern State Hospital, almost always means in the institutional classification that he is receiving no psychiatric treatment at all. The diagnosis of schizophrenia in one of its subtypes in the APA classification may apply to a patient in almost any category of the institutional classification.

This situation is further complicated by the third classification used on the wards. The ward classification is completely unofficial in Southern State Hospital. It is keyed to the institutional classification but has an altogether different structure and execution from that implied in the institutional system. The ward classification distributes the patients in terms of their manageability and occupational utility on the ward and in the hospital work. Just as the APA categories may describe little of the patient's position in the hospital's institutional classification, the latter may give little information about the patient's status on the ward.

Our study of the composition of the wards in the hospital in relation to the two official classifications of the hospital showed that neither of these two classifications was employed in any apparent functional way in determining the composition of any one of the wards. As will be evident from Table 3, patients are distributed throughout most of the wards without much homogeneity even in the institutional classification. Young persons are placed with senile persons, and wards which are predominantly made up of psychiatrically deteriorated mental patients frequently house a group of patients who are comparatively in much better condition. On the male white ward in which many senile cases are kept, 10 per cent of the ward is made up of new admissions or convalescent cases. In terms of the official psychiatric classifications, comparatively light cases, some of them diagnosed as mild behavior disorders, are found scattered among stuporous catatonic schizophrenics, badly deteriorated hebephrenic schizophrenics, advanced cases of paresis, and the mentally deficient with psychoses.

This mixture of patients is of course contrary to the logic of any modern school of psychiatry, and it means in substance that little if any systematic group therapy or occupational or industrial therapy can be set up on the natural administrative unit of the ward in the hospital. At the same time this mixture of patients exposes the severely ill, mild, and intermediate mental patients to uncontrolled interactive relationships with one another, while it makes integrated professional treatment programs for the group impossible.

It was during our efforts to find some explanation for this mixture of patients that we began to see some of the elements of the hospital's third classification and assignment system. This system had been mentioned indirectly, and we had been given several hints about it by people we interviewed in level II; but the subject seemed taboo at this level. When we began to spend time on the wards, and when some of our observers on the wards gained the confidence of the attendants, however, the general pattern of the third system emerged as the most important and most thoroughly consistent of the hospital's classification and assignment procedures.

We had been told (as we usually were with any problem we brought up) that the mixture of patients on the ward was the result of the hospital's chronic understaffing and lack of space. This answer explained overcrowding in the hospital generally, but it did not explain the mixture. In pursuing the question further we found that in nearly every case the patients in reasonably good mental condition always seemed to do the housekeeping work on their wards. They also cleaned up after the patients who soiled, and they bathed and dressed and toileted the patients who needed these services.

In due course of time it became clear that the mild mental cases on all the wards were part of a definite work system of patients who performed most of the work of the wards under the supervision of the attendants. This work group was maintained without regard for the logic of the two official classifications, because such a group was necessary in the operation of the wards for the hospital as a whole. Once we had this clue, it was easy to see that it was the admixture of definite proportions of lucid patients in most of the wards for work purposes which produced what at first had appeared as a rather chaotic mixture of patient types.

When we suggested this explanation for the mixture to our informants for verification, they admitted that it was true and told us at first that this arrangement of working patients on the wards is a practical necessity for ward management, since the population of the hospital is badly distended and personnel in poor supply. But as we became more familiar with the wards, we found that this was only a partial explanation of the arrangement. The use of patient labor is tied in with the ward status system, and has many purposes and functions which are not simply the result of overcrowding of patients and small attendant staff. On the wards it serves as much to focus a definite system of patient management as it does to get physical work done. It is in this area of management that the hospital's informal or third classification system centers.

The organization of ward work defines a particular status for the attendant and a set of patients' working statuses underneath him; and these statuses in turn determine the position of all patients on the ward. The principle in this system, as we saw it, was that the ward attendant must give orders in the ward which will be obeyed. If his authority fails with the patients, there are no further levels of authority until the ward physician is reached. For most people, one element in authority is symbolized by supervisory rather than servile activities, and for this reason, although his job specifications require it, the attendant cannot clean up after patients.

In developing at this point a supervisory role which is not formally defined in his job, the attendant also creates the third classification system of the hospital. This system had developed far back in the hospital's history as a device which supported the authority of the attendant through his ability to determine privileges for the patients in return for work in the hospital and for obedience. And the patients in the working group serve the attendant in many ways that go beyond housekeeping. Some of them are lieutenants, spies, helpers with food service, and with minor therapy. As a group they appear to be essential in the present operation of the hospital.

It is this third classification system, necessary in the management of the ward, more than any other feature which produces the peculiar distribution of patients in our sample wards. A sufficient number of patients in the privileged, or working, status must be present to do ward housekeeping and provide the necessary authority pattern by which the attendant operates the ward. This is accomplished by assigning, if necessary, the needed proportions of the "right" sort of patient to wards which may be made up of badly deteriorated psychotic and senile individuals. The effect of this practice is of course that of altering the second, or institutional, classification scheme to conform to the requirements of ward organization set by the third system.

As will be shown below in the more detailed treatment of ward organization and social control, the social organization of attendants and patients has many other effects than those on classification and assignment. It is enough to point out here that the effects of living with deteriorated patients are obviously not those desired by modern psychiatry for treatment of the patients who are closer to normality and capable of maintaining good contact with reality. And it is also evidently not a desirable professional situation when the physician in charge must go along with the requirements of ward management and housekeeping without primary reference to desirable courses of therapy for the patients.

Over the many years of Southern State Hospital's history, an accommodation of sorts has developed between the two official systems of classification and assignment of patients and the unofficial ward classification and assignment. Examination of specific instances illustrates this accommodation.

CLASSIFICATION IN WARD SAMPLES

A superficial inspection of the designations of the various wards in the hospital would lead to the notion that Southern State Hospital possessed a satisfactory and, on the whole, rather scientific psychiatric classification system. But if we look at the sample of nine male white wards in Table 4 and consider some of the discrepancies lying behind them, it can be seen that the designations describe very little of what goes on in the wards.

TABLE 4. INSTITUTIONAL CLASSIFICATION OF A SAMPLE OF NINE MALE WHITE WARDS IN SOUTHERN STATE HOSPITAL

Ward	*Title*
G	Admission
H	Continuous-treatment
I	Continuous-treatment
J	Open
K	Convalescent
L	Continuous-treatment
5	Continuous-treatment
M	Disturbed
T	Geriatric

Closer examination of these wards shows the investigator that there are high percentages of patients on each of the wards who do not correspond to the ward designation. The Admission Ward carried a fluctuating group of 12 to 15 per cent of patients who had been in the hospital for over 2 years. The Continuous-treatment Wards actually held nearly all types of patients, but with a predominant group of chronic patients regarded as substantially hopeless, with an average stay in the hospital amounting to 9 years. Among these chronic cases were many cases which could have been classified as geriatric and thus placed in Ward T. The Open Ward, J, was inhabited mainly by the so-called "institutional cures," patients who are almost completely normal within the hospital but who cannot adjust to life outside the hospital. Among these patients, however, there were a minority of other patients who were regarded as convalescent, with some chance of leaving the hospital shortly. And the institutional cures were not all on Ward J. Rather, they were scattered through all the other wards, mainly as part of the patient working group.

The discrepancy that exists between the unofficial and official composition of these wards is not random, but in nearly all cases results from arrangements necessary in the hospital's operation. A wide distribution of the institutional cures is necessary, for example, because they are often essential to the attendant in supervising and caring for helpless older patients and violent and disturbed patients, as well as in the ward housekeeping tasks. A core of reasonably reliable patients is also necessary in management of the Admission Ward. Convalescent patients and patients with mild but stable and harmless mental conditions are distributed through these nine wards on much the same principles as are the institutional cures.

It takes only a very small amount of actual observation of the way these nine sample wards operate in Southern State Hospital to establish that for the overwhelming majority of the patients in these wards there is neither true medical status nor treatment in the general sense now recognized by modern psychiatry. The main purpose of the ward classification and assignment procedure is to ensure that Southern State Hospital's legal custodial and maintenance responsibilities are met. Since these responsibilities cannot be met on an individual basis over a 24-hour period for nearly 800 patients (a period which requires three shifts of attendants), they must be met on the basis of a relatively efficient system of authority with organization techniques for extending this authority widely enough to handle large numbers of people. It should be remembered that at times a few of the patients are extremely difficult to care for and control and are even dangerous,[3] and that the organization of the wards must take this into account.

Since the professional medical-psychiatric conception of treatment is based on the ideal and on methods of individual treatment of the patient and complete control and supervision of the patient by the responsible individual doctor, the professional conception is obviously incompatible with the actual working of the hospital classification and assignment system in these male wards.

A SAMPLE OF THE FEMALE WARDS

The incompatibilities are if anything worse in the case of a sample of fourteen female wards. On these wards the mixture of different types of patients is in some ways even more indiscriminate than in the male wards. In Table 5 below, it is evident that the distribution of the "hopeless" and convalescent cases does not conform to a clear-cut pattern. Only on the Admission Ward is the composition homogeneous, and even here there are dissimilar elements which are not indicated by the way the table is organized. Convalescent patients, who in Ward VII number 100 per cent, are not all of the same age, degree of disorganization, or psychosocial characteristics. The only thing these patients have in common is their newly acquired status as mentally disordered persons.

On all the other wards, among the female population, there is a mixture of new with old cases. On the whole, the homogeneity in the distribution of female patients is far less than among the male patients. On all wards except two (VII and

TABLE 5. PERCENTAGE OF EACH TYPE OF PATIENT IN A SAMPLE OF
FOURTEEN FEMALE WARDS

Ward	Convalescent	Continuous-treatment	Geriatric
I	11	89	0
II	6	94	0
III	13	87	0
IV	13	87	0
V	5	92	3
VI	7	91	2
VII	100 *	0	0
VIII	14	86	0
IX	0	100	0
X	12	73	15
XI	5	30	65
XII	14	63	23
XIII	2	72	26
XIV	25	75	0

* Admissions.

IX), there is a rather consistent combination of convalescent cases with chronic patients, and in at least six of these wards, the composition is further complicated by the inclusion of geriatric patients. In all wards, the chronic cases predominate, while the convalescent and new cases remain in a distinct minority. In the average female ward, 15 per cent of the patients are convalescent cases, while the remaining are either chronic or geriatric. This means that for the greater part of the average new patient's period of hospitalization there will be a constant interplay between nearly rational patients and chronically ill patients. As indicated before, those new patients who are not, at the time of admission, in an advanced state of disorganization must suffer the adverse consequence of association with deteriorated patients, and there are also reverse disadvantages for the deteriorated patients.

A noticeable difference between the organization and distribution of the male and female patients is that among the latter the senile patients are scattered over a larger number of wards than is the case among the males. On the male wards, while there is some scattering of geriatric cases, they are mainly located on one ward, while among the females they are found in varying numbers on six different wards, and in none of these wards is the concentration exclusively or heavily geriatric.

While the limitation of a male research staff handicapped us in close observation and in interviewing in the female wards of Southern State Hospital, we were able to determine that the processes of female classification and assignment are not different in principle from those of the male patients. The differences are those of degree and of general sex status. The authority system in the female wards was organized as explicitly as the male system in terms of custodial and maintenance considerations, but elements of coercion necessary for the males were clearly absent or minimal in the case of the female patients.

Cultural differences between the sexes seemed to account for differences in coercive patterns. The authority of the female attendants operated around a different pivot. They could and did perform many housekeeping tasks *with* the patients. We almost never saw this on the male wards. The job of attendant is one of higher status by comparison with outside jobs for women than is the case with the men attendants. Women do not lose status by performing such tasks outside the hospital provided the tasks are done in a family context, and neither the patients nor the female attendants saw anything out of the way in their performance within the hospital, even by a woman in a strong position of line authority. The most experienced female attendants we observed oriented their authority around a pseudomaternal relationship to the ward and used pseudofamily terms in thinking about and organizing the activities of patients. Housekeeping and the maintenance of some order in terms of superordinate and subordinate relationships are processes with which most people are familiar in their early family background, particularly under maternal supervision. If the pseudomaternal role, with its family connotations, is carried out skillfully, it can apparently achieve a much less irksome and more effective control of mental patients than the pseudomilitary system employed in the male wards.[4] The female wards and the patients were somewhat cleaner than those of the males, even in the wards with deteriorated patients, and the general tone of relationships was more harmonious.

But although the authority system was comparatively gentle and more subtly constructed on the female wards, we found that it was still organized primarily to maintain order and to get the work of the hospital done.[5] The lack of homogeneity in ward classification, with at times an almost random distribution of patients, showed, itself, that organized administrative therapy could not exist, and the harmony in the wards under the pseudomaternal authority emphasized "getting along" and not "getting well." There was in fact an undercurrent of quiet pessimism among the older attendants regarding the ultimate cure of most of the patients—an attitude which might be described as hopeless but kindly. We observed several instances in which patients seemed to pick up this attitude toward themselves from the attendant. The pressure of the ward system was in the direction of orderly behavior, cleanliness, and helpful conduct, backed up by firm authority and by an intricate system of rewards and penalties which could be invoked if this authority was questioned.

SOME VARIATIONS IN THE HOSPITAL CLASSIFICATIONS

The general scheme of patient distribution in Southern State Hospital reflected in the sample wards seems to result from a very old tradition in this and other state hospitals. This tradition, as was pointed out above, has developed around a common-sense method of patient classification which maintains the maximum degree of order on the wards of the hospital and at the same time gets the daily work of the institution accomplished. The main elements in the general scheme of classification are, first, the categories of the hospital's work and authority system for patients and attendants, and, second, the broad sociocultural differences between the state hospital patients. These latter include race, sex, and to a lesser extent, age. Whites and Negroes are segregated from each other, as are men and women, and there is some attempt, as can be seen from the sample wards, to separate age groups, though segregation by this criterion is not so clear-cut as it is by race and sex.

The work-authority elements and the sociocultural segregation of the patients are fixed conditions in Southern State Hospital which set limits to other kinds of classification schemes used or attempted by professional personnel in the hospital. The interplay between the professional schemes and these objective limits is extremely complicated. Some physicians were able to develop ways of classification which were at times in considerable harmony with modern psychiatric conceptions and yet realistic enough to operate within the limits or even to employ the limits.

Our interview data and observations, however, suggest that for the majority of physicians an adjustment eventually has to be worked out which is generally in harmony with the institutional limits rather than with any consistent professional scheme. In the past many physicians have come into Southern State Hospital, attempted to set up strict professionally oriented psychiatric classification and treatment, and eventually—because of the pressing need to routinize their enormous patient loads—have had to give in to the traditional system. This fact has become a part of the culture of medical personnel in Southern Staté Hospital and outside the hospital; it enters not only into the view the hospital physician takes of his job but into the opinions of his internal and external colleagues. The short career cycle of the average Southern State Hospital physician, the small percentage of certified psychiatrists practicing in the South State system, and the chronic difficulties in recruitment of both physicians and nurses obviously result partly from the negative pressure of the traditional classification and assignment system on professionals.

In some cases the professional attempts at patient classification and assignment had an outcome somewhat more insidious than the resignation of the physician. In these attempts a subtle verbal rationalization of psychiatric treatment and the ward work and authority system actually seemed to bring about a conscious adjustment between the professional and the system. Many of the younger physicians were highly conscious of the danger to their own professional integrity in this kind of adjustment. The danger of the adjustment indeed does seem to be great because of a number of forces over which no physician can have any control. The work environment of the physician has never had adequate administrative planning, from either the lay or the medical point of view. Things taken for granted in industry or in general hospitals do not exist in the state hospital. There is no provision for line and staff communication in the hospital on a regular basis, committee management is never seriously employed, grievance procedures do not exist, understaffing and overcrowding and high personnel turnover go along with communication blockage. An over-all audit of the Southern State Hospital social organization had never occurred, so that, instead of being subjected to functional administrative planning, the hospital has simply grown without any study of the effects of the growth.

This does not mean that the hospital is not organized. But it does mean that the physician cannot always know the organization. If he is to get anything done at all, he has to make his own discoveries in the hospital's custodial-maintenance system, develop his own system of communication, and then adjust his professional classification and assignment to what can be done. Since the physician's responsibilities always include massive numbers of patients, he is forced from a strictly clinical individual role into the role of a medical executive. And his capacity to act at all depends on his communication of his medical aims to the attendants on the ward. This communication he finds very problematic, and any physician's classification scheme must adjust to this fact. While the physician's particular scheme almost never has much effect on the attendants or patients on any sustained basis, it is at this point of communication that the physician himself seems to incur the greatest risk of being warped out of the medical-psychiatric functions into the custodial-maintenance functions of the hospital.

In establishing this point we made both interview and observation studies of classification procedures of particular physicians in the hospital and of those formerly employed there. Then we interviewed and observed in the wards where these procedures were, or had been, in effect, talking particularly to the older and more stable charge attendants. From these upper and lower perspectives on physician classification we were able to make some judgments on physician-attendant communication and on the effects of certain types of physician classification.

The classifications of the ward physicians varied considerably from one doctor to another, and over a year's period of time particular doctors changed their schemes. These classifications were affected by the doctor's own abilities and energy, his special medical interests, and his training and background, by his preferences among the different schools of psychiatry, and by the state of his knowledge of the hospital social organization. The physician's execution of his scheme was also dependent on the various schedules of personnel allocation during the periods of hospital operations. Some physicians were rotated over many different types of patients in many different wards; some tended to be assigned largely to one or two types of patients.[6] At times, shortages of personnel, illness, or vacation schedules among physicians would make one doctor briefly responsible for nearly a fourth of the patient population of the hospital and thus for nearly every type of patient.

Viewed from the perspective of the ward attendant or the patient, this variation in medical schemes appeared at first almost random. It seemed strange to us that the professional classification schemes, which must serve as the contact point or bridge between daily hospital patient management and the medical leadership in the hospital, should have so little consistency or continuity. But further acquaintance with ward operation suggested that there were two main patterns of rather consistent adjustment between ward organization and physician classifications. One pattern of adjustment was in effect between the attendant system and those doctors who attempted strict use of the clinical frame of reference and categories, and those who were experimenting with different combinations of custodial and medical classifications. This first pattern consisted of a tacit understanding among the attendants that the doctor was to be respectfully ignored whenever possible.[7] The physician's instructions were usually carried out to the letter but very seldom in spirit. The function of this attitude was that of insulating the operating work and authority system of the ward from authority which was random and unpredictable (or hostile, as is definitely the case with most trained psychiatrists) with regard to the principles of ward organization and ultimately with regard to the institutional classification itself.

A second pattern of adjustment between ward organization and the physicians' classifications was present when the physician employed a classification system which was in effect based on the ward social organization. These were the physicians who, in the opinion of the older attendants, "actually knew what was going on, and the right way to do things." In organizing their work, the physicians in this group defined their patients in three layers:

1. The convalescent and hopeful patients who show improvement and potentiality for discharge by adjustment to the realities of ward life. This adjustment is manifested in orderly conduct, willingness to do ward housekeeping and hospital maintenance chores, and a generally cooperative attitude on the ward.

2. The potentially hopeful group of patients who show general tendencies toward adjustment to the ward and are at least passively accommodated to hospital life.

3. The patients who have little prospect for improvement, who show little adjustment to the realities of ward life, who are uncooperative, often disturbed or excited, of little use in ward work, and sometimes dangerous to themselves or others.

In practice the attention and treatment of these physicians

was concentrated on the first of these categories, but with the idea that the passage of time would enable many of the patients in the second group to rise into the first grade and thus receive attention. This classification represents largely an adjustment of medical treatment to the system employed by the attendants in organizing work and behavior on the ward. Each of these three layers is associated with a graded series of rewards and punishments in the attendants' social system, and there is little conflict and a great deal of cooperation when the attention and procedures of the physician in charge become part of this system.

The second pattern of adjustment is perhaps the most usual one among the older physicians and among those with generally more state hospital experience in Southern State Hospital and elsewhere. In terms of modern psychiatric conceptions, of course, the type of medical classification employed here restricts most of the physician's attention to the group which probably needs it least. And the logic of this distribution of the physician's attention clearly implies that for the most aggravated mental cases it is useless to employ the physician at all. Only when the seriously ill patient—by a process in which he receives little personal assistance—gets well enough to move up into the top categories does he receive much attention from the physician. And the judgment of his progress must evidently be left to the attendant until he arrives at the top group. As will be seen below in the treatment of social organization on the wards, it is difficult to imagine a medical arrangement better calculated to strengthen and maintain the existing organization of patient management by the ward attendants.

CHAPTER NINE

Relationships of the Ward System
with the Upper Levels

For the patient in Southern State Hospital the ward where he lives is the only important part of the hospital. What is done in the ward for him and to him determines the effect of his hospitalization.

In preceding chapters we have outlined the job functions of the chief upper-level hospital personnel and the relation of the professional and institutional psychiatric classification operations used in the hospital. These two classifications in Southern State Hospital are, as we have suggested, tied in with yet a third system prevailing on the wards of the institution. The first two systems are formally recognized by everyone concerned with the hospital. The third is known to exist by the older employees in the hospital and by those outside the hospital who have considerable experience with the institution. But this third system is not recognized in any official way.

All three of these systems serve historically developed purposes and interests inside and outside the hospital, and each of the systems contributes in certain ways to each of the others. Although there are conflicts between the systems, they seem to be accommodated to each other, in the sense that elimination of one of them would require many changes in each of the others.

Most of the reforms proposed in the numerous investigations of Southern State Hospital in the years since its foundation have made the crucial mistake of concentrating their proposals on the two formally acknowledged systems, without taking account of the third, except perhaps as a flaw in the hospital. Yet an acquaintance with all levels of Southern State Hospital's operation makes it certain that the third, or ward, system is in an operational sense just as important in the hospital's stability and in its effect on patients as the other two. It is the ward system which deals with the Southern State patient on a daily basis, defines his behavior, carries out the daily supervision of his treatment, both physical and psychiatric, sees that he is fed, protects him from injury, provides a sanitary and orderly environment and most of whatever personal consideration, entertainment, or recreation is possible for him. These things done by the ward system obviously should have high priority in any organization for mental patients.

The formal organization of the wards as shown in the Organization Chart shows the formal authority line in ward management as operating downward from the Clinical Director (level I) through the Director of Nursing Service (level II), the general-duty registered nurses (level II), the attendant supervisors (level III), and ending in the ward charge attendants (level III). The charge is chief of the attendants on all shifts on the ward.[1]

For Southern State Hospital this is a relatively new arrangement and replaces, or rather attempts to replace, an older authority line which ran from the Superintendent through the ward physician and directly to the charge attendant by way of the attendant supervisor. At the time of our study the older authority line was the one employed in practice, since operating procedure on the wards was not adjusted in any way to the use of registered nurses. As was discussed above, the occasional presence of the nurse on the ward as a supervisor split the authority line from the physician to the charge attendant without contributing in any tangible way to the psychiatric job of either. This arrangement was causing a good deal of friction during all the time of our study. It was apparent that the hospital either should have had enough nurses to replace all the attendants or should not have attempted their employment on the wards at all. As it was, however, the problem was largely solved by the fact that the registered nurses were scarce and expensive (by hospital standards) and were used more appropriately in terms of their medical qualifications in the hospital's specific therapies (electroshock, insulin therapy) and in the two infirmaries. The nurses' oversight of the wards was something of a fiction.

As an administrative structure, the actual authority line between the ward physician and charge attendant is an oddity. The formal job definitions rigidly limit the range of decision of the charge attendant to minor nursing and housekeeping duties, and his pay is adjusted to this limitation. The attendant supervisors, who are placed in the formal line between the physician and the charge attendant, seldom perform (and seldom could perform, since there are only two of them) regular supervisory duties in ward operations. The formal functions of the supervisors seem to be restricted in practice to serving as staff clerks to the ward physicians for routine administration, including supplies, reports, and personnel and patient assignment.[2]

The professional and subprofessional personnel in level II, like the supervisors, are essential staff people with reference to the physician's line to the wards, without any defined line functions. Thus the formal line function of the physician runs directly to the charge attendant with no intervening delegated formal steps of responsible execution and supervision. The average physician's line and staff structure is shown in Figure 5, below, on the conservative assumption that he will be responsible for four wards, averaging sixty-five patients each.

Administratively the official position of the ward physician is that of an executive whose accountability embraces 296 people, since his line runs directly to each individual patient. Properly speaking, in administrative terms, the ward physician does not have a span of control in any official sense. This is because, in terms of formal job definitions, the charge attendants are not actually foremen or supervisors but rather orderlies and helpers in dealing with the patients on the ward. Formally, the physician's span of control in Figure 5 is a span of performance.

This formal definition of executive responsibility at the work level of the hospital would indicate a severe problem to any experienced administrator. When executive authority of any kind is diffused in this manner, no social system can accomplish any type of work at all. In the eighteen wards of Southern State Hospital which we analyzed, however, the informal organization of the hospital had long since closed and organized this gap in executive control by establishing a well-understood social organization for both attendants and patients.

In effect, this organization redefined the span of control of the ward physician to include, taking Figure 5 as an example, the twelve charge attendants as something approaching area supervisors or administrative assistants to the physician and to include the attendants as foremen in direct charge of the patients. This organization, in administrative terms, inserted two levels of supervision between the physician and the patient and thus permitted a practically inoperable system to operate, at least in a certain way.

The closure by informal organization of the administrative gap in the physician's job definition is a good example of the

Fig. 5. Span of Control of an Average Southern State Hospital Ward Physician

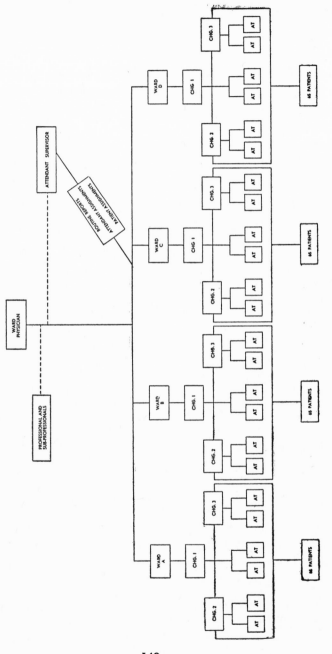

planless type of growth which has been pointed out as characteristic of Southern State Hospital. As far as we could determine from interviewing older professional and nonprofessional employees, the informal organization of attendants must have developed and consolidated somewhere between 1875 and 1890 as Southern State Hospital grew larger and more complex in its operations. In all this history we found little material indicating that anyone had studied the attendant organization or tried to determine its functional position in the hospital, with the exception of the Bruns Associates investigation. This study, which was a thoroughly competent administrative analysis of the state hospitals in South State, did in fact point out that one of the very few stable points in Southern Hospital's organization centered around a core of families with a hereditary relation to the hospital, whose members in each generation, having grown up in the hospital campus, found it natural to work there. The Bruns study found that these employees were the nucleus of an exceptionally loyal and stable group of supervisory and charge attendants, who were habituated to hospital employment. But the Bruns investigation did not explore to any great extent the type of organization which had been developed by these older employees and, particularly, the functional linkage which exists between this organization and the more formal aspects of the hospital.[3]

The informal organization of the wards is maintained and transmitted in its essentials by a core of about 18 per cent of the attendants. The annual turnover rate of this group is less than 1 per cent, as compared with 83 per cent for the remaining 82 per cent of the attendants. Seven out of ten of this core live on the hospital grounds, and six out of ten are married to other attendants employed in the hospital. Two out of each ten men in the core had fathers or mothers who had been employed in Southern State Hospital or other state hospitals. The median length of hospital employment for this core is 12 years, as compared with the median length of employment for ward physicians of 1.5 years, and a median tenure for the hospital superintendents of 2.6 years.[4] The core of attendants had completed a median of 8 years of school. The core employees hold most of the charge and supervisory positions in level III, although a few of them are ward attendants. In the direct work of Southern State Hospital with its patients, these core attendants are almost the only career employees in the medical part of the hospital.

FUNCTIONS OF THE INFORMAL WARD ORGANIZATION

The main function of the informal organization on the wards for the attendant is to set up a system which permits him to adjust personally the requirements of psychiatric treatment, as represented by the hospital's formal classification on the one hand, with the requirements of daily patient management on the other. This adjustment involves a definite organization of interpersonal relations between the attendant and his fellow attendants, between the attendants and the members of the two upper administrative levels, and between the attendants and the patients.

The system includes patterns of expected behavior and ideas for the attendants in relation to patients and to the upper-level professionals in the hospital. These patterns are justified by an ideology centering around the attendant's functions in the hospital, and the entire system is held together with considerable solidarity, or in-group feeling, against patients and the professionals, who are out-groups. The system is a complete social organization, with an ideology and a tradition at least seventy years old. It can be considered as a type of culture in the hospital, with its own functionaries, legends, and justifications.

Toward the hospital patients on the wards, the attendants' system operates primarily as a set of behavior controls, backed up by a system of rewards and punishments. Toward the professionals in the hospital, and particularly toward the physicians, the attendants' culture operates both cooperatively and defensively. Among the attendants themselves the system of organization is maintained by informal but organized training and by the regular elimination of attendants who do not conform to the roles defined for them.

In our material on ward organization a number of general points seem to stand out. One of the major points, as we have mentioned above, is that the hospital's formal organization has defined an impossible span of control for the ward physician. Essentially this means that the hospital's formal organization has avoided the problem of defining daily patient management and supervision on the ward and left a gap which had to be filled in the hospital's operation. The attendant's functions have not been delegated to him at all but have grown up by default.

The second major point is related to the first. The formal system of the hospital defines the attendant and pays him more or less as equivalent to a general hospital orderly. But because of the administrative gap, the attendants in Southern State Hospital have always had far more important nursing responsibilities than those of any general hospital orderly. This mixture of low status and serious responsibility is resented by every one of the old attendants to whom we talked, and it is immediately sensed and resented by most new employees. It was obviously blocking and inhibiting creative activity for most attendants and had in fact become a definite part of the negative attitude toward the upper levels and any innovations which we found characteristic in the wards. In the ideology of the attendants about their jobs, this situation was translated into statements like the following, taken from our case records:

This place would go to pieces if it weren't for the attendants. But we never get any credit or recognition.

The doctor spends 5 minutes a day on my ward and doesn't know one patient from the other. But if I try to tell him anything he puts his foot in my mouth.

I've worked here 20 years, and I've learned a good deal about mental cases and helped a few of them. But the doctor always takes the credit for anything good, and I get the blame for anything that goes wrong.

That bunch in the front office [the level I and II personnel] sit around on their ———s all day and read reports and write letters and diagnose the cases at long range, but we're the boys who have to handle the problems.

Statements of this sort are part of what the new attendant hears almost as soon as he comes on the ward, and they are given freely to investigators who show any sympathy.

A third major point on the attendant's ward organization is that he is in fact faced with an extremely difficult and unpleasant job, with many potential personality strains. To the person who has never made more than a conducted tour of a state hospital this point needs special emphasis. The state hospital must take all kinds of patients, from the seriously to the mildly ill. Many of the patients have troublesome chronic physical ailments, and among these are many partially debilitated senile persons. Incontinence, both of feces and urine, is a characteristic symptom or phase in several types of mental illness. Behavior of the various patients on the wards of the state mental hospitals almost always runs the scale from hyperactivity to complete listlessness. With any large number of mental patients, there is always the risk of dangerous violence at unpredictable times. And the average number of patients on most of the Southern State Hospital wards is near eighty.

Familiarity with the daily environment of the attendant demonstrates very quickly that the individual working in this atmosphere must make adjustments not required of people in more ordinary occupations. The attendant does not even escape this atmosphere periodically and retire to an office, as do even professionals closely associated with treatment. He must live with it for his entire shift.

In making his adjustment to his job, the attendant's first need is obviously for order and control of his ward environment, and secondly for some psychological support while he performs his job. The in-group of attendants with its culture meets both these needs and is probably essential, both in helping the individual attendant organize his work and in maintaining his personality balance.

A fourth major point about the ward organization is that the upper-level professionals in the hospital seem markedly distant and unsympathetic toward the attendant and have as a whole little real comprehension of the character of the attendants' organization, of its real problems, or of its function in the hospital. Most of them are of course aware that this organization exists, but their tendency is to regard it as "something to fight" or "to educate" the attendant away from. A small minority of the experienced professionals did see and understand something of the functions of the attendants' culture, and they were attempting two types of solutions to the problem. One solution was that of raising the status of the attendants by special psychiatric aide training, with concurrent elimination of attendants who could not qualify in this training. It was recognized that this program would take many years to realize, since the budget of the hospital allowed no adequate salary revision for the higher positions. The other solution proposed was the use of intensive treatment "teams" made up of psychiatrist, social worker, psychologist, nurse, and attendant, the teams to be assigned in different proportions to admission, continuing treatment, geriatric service, and perhaps to special therapeutic efforts.

Both of these solutions had merit, but neither squared with some of the things we felt to be true of the ward management problem. The psychiatric aide–training program has had considerable vogue recently in mental hospitals in the United States but without any clearly demonstrable sustained success, except in a very few cases.[5] Some of the reasons for this doubtful picture were evident in the administrative structure of Southern State Hospital. The functional position of the psychiatric aide in the program would still be kept firmly in level III. Nothing in the training program would permit him to rise in any way into competition with the higher positions in level II. The hospital was in fact able to offer not even a really substantial salary or emolument improvement on completion of the training program, and there would obviously be little status improvement. The program was contradictory, since it aimed ultimately at producing people equal in responsibility to registered nurses but also at keeping them in a position below the status of registered nurses in the hospital. This point was often profanely discussed by the Southern State Hospital attendants when we talked with them. Their opinion of the program was cynical in the extreme, except in the case of a few of the women charge attendants who envied the nurses their status and welcomed anything approaching it. The future of psychiatric aide training in Southern State Hospital did not appear at all hopeful, at least during our study, both because of lack of realism in the program in terms of the hospital's status structure and job requirements, and because of the exterior recruitment problem for all medical professionals in the United States. In South State even the profession of registered nurse, which enjoys vastly better working conditions, pay, and status than anything proposed for the psychiatric aide, is unattractive to most of the best-qualified young women.[6]

The psychiatric treatment team concept seemed to us almost unworkable, mainly but not entirely because of the very small professional staff in the hospital. Another serious obstacle was evident in the fact that the team concept obviously implies definite status in treatment for each of the team members. In Southern State Hospital, we found that even the upper-level professionals felt that their treatment role was unessential in the view of most of the physicians, and this was even more true of the attendants. The probability that a psychiatric team would work across these decided barriers was very low indeed in the hospital. Moreover, it was also obvious that the entire organization of the hospital would have to be changed if the team were used. No team members really work continuously on the ward except the attendant.

In pursuing the views of the level II professionals toward the attendant organization on the ward, we found not only distance and lack of sympathy among these professionals but also considerable amounts of hostility. The avoidance between the two groups was marked, both inside and outside the hospital. Level III knew and resented the attitude of level II. In the case of level II personnel there was less in-group solidarity and a much less clearly observable culture, partly because of their larger annual turnover when compared with the core of older attendants, partly because of their professional diversity. But almost every member of the level II culture shared the pattern of lack of sympathy, avoidance, and some hostility toward the members of level III. The members of level II who remain in the hospital perpetuate this general attitude and practice various procedures to maintain it. Level II personnel who cross the barrier to level III, except in line of business, are disciplined in many ways, some delicate and some heavy-handed, but all of them ultimately effective in blocking any real communication or mobility across the barrier. In its effects and persistence throughout our study, and in the devices by which it is maintained, this barrier can be compared in many ways with the interracial barriers in the old South. It is close to a caste system in its effects.

The existence of the barrier between levels II and III in Southern State Hospital is the major reason for the poor future prospects not only of the psychiatric aide program and the team plan but of any continuous and efficient program of cooperation for staff members of Southern State Hospital. The barrier itself defines the upper and lower levels as two more or less antagonistic groups. Level II is the level on which creative planning and organization occurs in the hospital; in terms of the formal organization chart this is the level to which it is restricted. But the primary face-to-face work of the hospital with its individual patients goes on in level III. Unless these levels are linked together in a close relationship of mutual respect and understanding of each other's problems, planning and action in the hospital can obviously have no firm basis.[7]

Some of the reasons for this barrier between levels II and III are not clear unless one is thoroughly familiar with both sides of the barrier. It is at the barrier that Southern State Hospital makes the translation of most of its formal medical-psychiatric functions into more or less explicit custodial-maintenance functions.

This is a translation which the conscientious professional in level II does not like to face because of its implications for his own position and his professional ideals. His repudiation of the personnel in level III is partly the result of a strong desire to dissociate himself from the massive and largely untreated psychiatric problems he knows are dealt with by level III. This is not merely a problem of psychologically insecure individuals; it is rather one forced on any professional, whether a physician, psychologist, registered nurse, or psychiatric social worker, who goes to work in level II of Southern State Hospital.[8]

That this attitude of the professional further aggravates the difficulty of communication in the hospital is clear enough throughout our interview material. But it is also clear that there are distinct limits on what the professional can do about the situation as long as Southern State Hospital remains in its present organizational form.

THE ATTENDANT'S IDEOLOGY

As a worker in the hospital, the attendant who remains on the wards is faced with a group above him who are his superiors and leaders but who are overtly or covertly somewhat antagonistic to the job he has to perform, who are oriented generally toward a frame of reference both in the formal psychiatric and institutional classifications which often has little relation to his job on the practical level, and with whom he has little informal or formal communication, either personally or professionally.

The attendant's ideology and the practices of his social system are adjusted to this situation in the two ways we have indicated above in the treatment of the classification problem in the hospital. Where the physicians or others in level II meet him on a strictly formal psychiatric basis and attempt no translation of the psychiatric frame of reference, or where these level II personnel are experimenting with various combinations of approaches to classification and assignment, the attendant adjusts as much as he is able by ignoring the orders he receives, particularly those which interfere too extensively with traditional ward routines and practices. But where the physician or other level II personnel conform to the basic requirements of ward management as the attendant sees them, the relation of the attendant to his superiors is much more cooperative and is marked by a certain amount of spontaneity.

In the attendant's ideology, the actual running of the hospital is accomplished by the ward organization of which he is a member. The level II professionals are necessary for certain limited purposes—mainly those having to do with the physical care of patients. Among these professionals there are some who understand this situation and do not interfere in ward management but, rather, act in ways which reinforce the attendants. Other level II professionals, however, are without proper understanding of their roles and must be watched carefully to see that their orders do not destroy vital ward routines.

To the majority of the attendants, most of the group in level II are somewhat academic and cold people who have little personal interest in either the attendants or the patients. Their personal contact is brief and usually businesslike, as when the physician makes his ward rounds, or when the special team of physician, nurse, and supervisor appears on the ward to administer shock therapy. The attendant feels that the level II personnel know very little either about individual patients or about what goes on in the ward. It is part of the cross which he has to bear in his work but a very important part, too, of his conception of his own importance. He takes a good deal of pleasure in joking with other attendants about this situation, and he often finds satisfaction in doing what he can with his job in spite of his supervision, or in remedying what he considers grave faults in this supervision. In general, he considers that on a psychiatric basis he himself knows more about mental patients than anyone in level II, with a few very rare exceptions. In his opinion, he and the other attendants are the only ones in the hospital who actually look after the patients, care for them daily, or do anything personally for them.

The attendants' ideology as it focused on the level II professionals included a definite group of conceptions about mental illness which were regarded by the attendants as more realistic and useful in dealing with patients than those involved in the two more formal frames of reference used by professionals.

Our efforts to get a satisfactory idea of the attendants' conceptions of mental illness proceeded along three lines. First, in interviewing them specifically on the problem we asked them for expressions of opinion on the curability of mental illness of various types, and we asked related questions on their conceptions of the functions of the hospital in the treatment process. Second, we kept a series of running observations on the actual practices of the attendants as related to their conceptions. Third, our informants who were employed as attendants at various times in seven wards kept a detailed record of these conceptions and their appearance in ward operation. We were particularly interested in this problem, since much of the current literature on ward attendants suggests that most of them hold views which are contradictory to modern psychiatric conceptions.

In putting the material from these three sources together, we found that 86 per cent of the attendants with 10 years or more of service in state hospitals were in almost unanimous agreement on certain conceptions of mental illness and that this agreement was reflected consistently in ward operations. The more important of these conceptions, as they were expressed to us, are as follows:

1. There is a difference between incoming patients and those who have been in the hospital more than a year. Nearly half the incoming patients are not seriously ill, are curable, and will leave the hospital "for good" within the first year. These people are benefited by the hospital and owe their cures to hospital treatment.

2. Of the remainder, about half have something seriously wrong with them, which is probably permanent and in all likelihood something in the family (hereditary), but it is something they can learn to live with eventually. These people will probably be discharged within the year, but they will be recommitted again once or twice before they become stabilized. The hospital is good for these people but not completely successful in curing them.

3. The remaining one-fourth of the incoming patients are incurable, because they have inherited weak or distorted minds or are degenerating with old age. These patients will have to stay in the hospital for the rest of their lives. The best that can be done for them in the hospital is to make them comfortable and treat them in a kindly manner. Some of them will adjust fairly well in the hospital and will make good workers if they are supervised, but the majority are too listless or feeble for this.

4. Most of the resident patients on the ward who have been in the hospital for 2 years or more fall into the third group, and the wards have to be managed in a way allowing for this fact.

5. Most of the patients, whether in the hopeful or hopeless

groups, may tend to become disturbed or excited at times. The more dangerous of these patients need to be kept on special wards, as do chronic escapees and those committed as criminals. The treatment of mental patients on the ward must be organized at all times to take account of the possibilities of escape, excitement or disturbance, and attack on the attendant or other patients. This organization cannot be effected without the use of certain patients as helpers.

6. Electroshock therapy is the best treatment for most disturbances of mental patients. It is not only good for the patient, but it helps the other patients by cutting down on disturbance in the ward. It is a good substitute for stronger measures of patient management like wristlets, wet packs, the camisole—and such things as a bar of soap in a sock.

7. Most mental patients behave better and are more treatable if they know that they have a certain position and certain duties on the ward. It is the job of the attendant to place the patient in his position and keep him there. There should never be any question in the minds of the patients about who is running the ward. The maintenance of this situation requires the attendant to keep social distance from the patient and to see that as much of the work on the ward as possible is done by the patient.

8. Mental patients are sick people and deserve help and sympathy.[9] This is a sincere attitude, but it is qualified by the universal notion that firmness and strong discipline are part of the help needed by all mental patients.

These conceptions of the attendants are those neither of laymen nor of psychiatric professionals. They are the product of the position of the attendant in Southern State Hospital and are interrelated functionally both with level II above him and with level IV below him. Their function, as we have indicated above, is that of permitting the attendant to organize his personal relations to level II, while at the same time he deals with the concrete problems of managing the patients in level IV. The functions of his conceptions of mental illness are those both of defining the nature of his job and of justifying the job, in a technical and moral sense. These functions become clear as one studies general hospital system on the wards, and as one gains knowledge of the intricate processes in particular wards.

The material that follows sketches the more general or common elements in the attendants' classification and management of patients.

GENERAL FEATURES OF ATTENDANT CLASSIFICATION AND MANAGEMENT

In the experienced attendant's classification, the patients in Southern State Hospital are divided into three groups: (1) the cooperative patients, to be given the most privileges, who may be used for work in the ward, for helping with other patients, for surveillance of patients, and for protection; (2) the neutral patients, who may be given limited privileges, and who are generally neither cooperative nor uncooperative; (3) the uncooperative group, who have no privileges, and who may be potentially dangerous or disturbing.

From among the first group the attendant draws his assistants and helpers, without whom ward management would be impossible. This assistance is not provided in the hospital's formal organization, but, according to the attendants' belief, the average hospital ward would be completely unmanageable without it. By using his social position, the attendant is able to make it worth while for this group of patients to obey his orders and keep him informed. These patients aid him in the management of the neutral group, and they protect him from and enable him to handle the patients in the uncooperative group, as he finds this necessary.

The authority of the attendant in the operation of his control system is backed up by both positive and negative power. This power is an essential element in his control of the ward. He can give the patient privileges, and he can punish the patient. The privileges consist of having the best job, better rooms and beds, minor luxuries like coffee on the ward, a little more privacy than the average patient, going outside the ward without supervision, having more access than the average patient to the attendant's companionship or to professional personnel like the physicians, and enjoying such intangible but vital things as being treated with personal kindness and respect.

The punishments which can be applied by the ward attendant are suspension of all privileges, psychological mistreatment, such as ridicule, vicious ribbing, moderate and sometimes severe corporal punishment, or the threat of such punishment, locking up the patient in an isolated room, denial or distortion of access to the professional personnel, threatening to put, or putting, the patient on the list for electroshock therapy, transfer of the patient to undesirable wards, and regular assignment of the patient to unpleasant tasks such as cleaning up after the soilers.

This working system of patient classification we have represented on the general organization chart in level IV as three sublevels of patient status, each accompanied by a pattern of privileges or penalties. As the patient experiences the hospital, it is as a member of one of these three groups, as defined by the attendants on the wards:

1. Patients with special and outside privileges
2. Patients with limited privileges
3. Patients without privileges

The privilege classifications are part of the attendants' control system, but to the patient they are primarily definitions of what he does in the hospital, including definitions of his relations to the attendants, to the other patients in his particular status, and to the patients below or above this status.

The system is by no means evident to casual visitors to the wards. Interview material suggests strongly that it is not thoroughly understood by many of the professionals in level II. The system does not stand out clearly until the observer has spent enough time on the wards and gained enough intimacy with the patient-attendant organization to see the connections which actually exist between isolated examples of behavior. And such access is almost impossible for anyone in the upper levels of the hospital. Inquiry or observation by these line superiors does occur, but it is so limited by the diffuse administrative control span and personnel shortage and turnover in the upper level that it produces no visible results in the form of knowledge in level II. Such inquiry usually only increases mutual suspicion between the members of the two systems.

Once the characteristic patterns of the patient organization are understood, it is easy to see that all these patterns have great significance in determining the effect of the hospital on the patient. In the long run, only those formal medical orders which can be applied without any general disturbance of the ward social system will be put into effect, a fact which often reduces or even eliminates the physician as a factor in the experience of the patient. In a time sense, the attendant always has close to 24 hours' advantage of any of the upper-level personnel. The hierarchy of patient status establishes a system of relations among the patients themselves which may have many treatment effects uninfluenced by professional control; one of the most obvious of these is that the upper group of patients monopolizes access to the attendant (and thus to the doctor), to recreation on the ward, and much recreational therapy activity in the hospital. This group maintains the monopoly vigorously by sarcasm, ridicule, physical threats, and sometimes physical punishment directed against lower-status trespassers. This exclusion is also at times an exclusion from a group which the lower-status patient desires to join. Many of these lower-status patients are of course in much greater need of attention from the attendant and physician than are the members of the upper group, and this exclusion blocks their mobility into a position where they can secure such attention.

In general, patients with special or outside privileges are distributed throughout most of the different wards in the hospital. There seems to be a tendency for them to cluster, however, on certain wards, one of which, male Ward 14, has the status of an "open" ward, where patients are free to come and go almost at will. Generally speaking, the special-privilege patients can go unattended about the grounds and can go to work or to the canteen at will. Much of the hospital's housekeeping and maintenance work is done by them, and although they are not forced to do this work, most of them apparently prefer to work. Within this top group there seem to be two subdivisions, the first with almost unrestricted privileges, the second enjoying these privileges but in a probationary status. The group is not psychiatrically homogeneous, either in professional or institutional terms. It includes a few patients in almost every psychiatric classification, and a large number of patients (the institutional cures) who are regarded as probable life-long residents of the hospital. Mixed with these last, however, are a number of patients who are considered convalescent and expected to leave the hospital within a year or less. Since these convalescent patients are also present in the group below the privileged patients, the latter cannot be regarded as made up entirely of patients who are convalescents.

The next lower group of patients, those with limited privileges, consists largely of patients who are candidates for the top group or whose condition has stabilized into a mildly cooperative or predictably neutral balance. These patients cannot leave the ward at will but must always be supervised and leave the ward only at scheduled times. Their privileges are confined to the negative one of being subjected to a minimum of the control techniques of the attendants,[10] and to the opportunity to get away from the ward at appropriate times. This last may seem a small privilege to the outsider, but it is of great importance to the patient, who must otherwise remain shut up in a ward which is almost always oppressive and dismal. The trips outside for the second group may be to the canteen, to church, or to hospital recreation. In all these cases, the patients are accompanied and supervised by attendants; occasionally by designated therapy personnel.

The third group of patients, those without privileges, are strictly custodial inmates, whose position is even more circumscribed than that of most penitentiary prisoners. These patients may receive visitors and may be permitted to leave the ward on special and irregular occasions. This group is quite heterogeneous on a psychiatric or any other basis. It includes patients who are almost completely stuporous, some who are clearly mentally deficient, some who are passive and listless, senile and deteriorated largely through physical aging, some who are frequently disturbed, and some who are nearly always uncooperative. Of these a few are potentially dangerous to the attendant or to other patients, and some of them are given to occasional or regular incontinence. Other patients have hallucinatory or delusional symptoms which force them to nag or pester anyone who will listen, and many who will not.

Members of this last group, very frequent on the wards we observed, are often subjected to treatment by both attendants and other patients which is little short of brutal. After observing the cumulative effect of this nagging and pestering on the human beings exposed to it hour after hour on a daily basis, we were able to understand some of the reasons for this treatment. But the effect of the natural defensive reaction on the part of attendants and fellow patients was of course that of closing for these patients an avenue which a trained psychiatrist could have used for treatment.

But among the patients without privileges there is another group—the newly admitted patients—who are there because there has not been sufficient time for them to be placed in the ward system by the attendants and other patients. Their status is indeterminate for the time being. Subject to a variety of intricate interactional processes on the ward, the newly admitted patients will ultimately be classified in one of the other two general patient statuses or remain permanently in the group without privileges.

The interactional processes which determine the movement of the new patients into more or less permanent hospital categories are not generally highly visible, but they operate constantly. The patient placed in this lower group will have different experiences in different wards, depending on the way the attendants manage the ward, the type of patients in the other two groups, the patient's own social or ethnic background, and his own configuration of personality or psychiatric symptoms at the time of commitment. In general, however, he runs considerable risk of being typed and permanently placed in the thinking of the upper patients and attendants in terms of his initial symptomatology and social background. If this does occur, and if the judgment is adverse to his progress, he has an additional problem beyond that of overcoming his illness. The additional problem is one of finding ways to get around the various sanctions of the ward social system which tend to keep him isolated from medical attention and from fairly normal social interaction, and under authoritarian management of both upper patient groups and attendants.

The over-all pattern in which this variable process of early ward patient classification occurs is a relatively simple one from the administrative point of view. The chief focus of the attendant system is on maintenance of order in the ward. The patient systems below the attendants function to bring about the same focus. To the attendant and the members of the upper patient systems, those actions on the part of the new patient which show probability that his mental condition will not lead to unpredictable outbursts of anger or fits of excitement are regarded as signs that he is potentially a good patient. The patient who dutifully executes the orders of the attendant and cooperates as indicated with members of the upper patient group is likely to become a candidate after a few weeks for the limited privilege group. He can now leave the ward under supervision for special occasions. If he continues to show this sort of improvement, he ultimately qualifies for the top group of patients.

In this top group of privileged patients, the patient has a new and gratifying status—one which approaches at times that accorded to normal persons. But the new status is subject to controls by the attendant which are as stringent as those elsewhere. If the patient breaks the working rules of this upper group—becomes insubordinate, forces too much intimacy on the attendants, shows disturbance—whether justified or not, he can be disqualified instantly and sent back down to the lower groups. This is not usually done directly by the attendant but requires official action by the ward physician, since it involves suspension of privileges.

In the usual case of this kind, such things as impudence, insubordination, and excessive familiarity are translated into more or less professional terms, such as "disturbed" or "excited," and presented by the attendant to the physician as a medical status report. The doctor must then officially revoke or modify the patient's privileges on the ward or work out a transfer to another ward where the patient has to begin all over to work up from the lowest group. A "good" doctor in the attendants' culture is one who does not raise too many questions about these translated medical terms.

In summary, as the ward system seems to work generally in Southern State Hospital, there is good reason to believe that this system, rather than formal hospital operating procedures and directives, is what usually prescribes the treatment a particular patient will be receiving at a particular time. Direct individual attention to most of the patients by the professional staff seemed to be the exception rather than the rule; and even such attention as did appear to be individual often was filtered in administration and evaluation through the ward system. Professional functions were largely those of administration. In general, the physician, nurse, psychologist, and social worker had to depend on the attendant for continuous information about the patients. Most of the treatment of the patients in the wards we studied was dictated by the status they came to occupy in the organization of patient status under the attendants in the ward.

CHAPTER TEN

The Ward Control System in Action—Ward 30

The general pattern in the ward organization which has been discussed is an abstraction from the processes that go on in the wards themselves. In the given ward there are many concrete details in status and in the modes in which status is won, maintained, and lost. Ward 30 is selected here to illustrate some of the important details in attendant control. This ward represents the highest probability of treatment for the average male patient coming into Southern State Hospital. It is neither the oldest nor the newest of the wards in the hospital, and neither an admission ward nor a maximum-security [1] ward. We have changed only those details in the following material which would permit specific identification of people and events.

The floor plan for Ward 30 (Figure 6) shows an arrangement of space typical of Southern State Hospital's wards.

Ward 30 is on the second story of a building built in 1919 of yellow common brick. The exterior of the building is well constructed, though the lower sills of the windows around the ward are damaged and rotted in places, both from weather and from damage by occasional patients who use the window for urinary purposes, and occasional disposal of buckets of mop water. The windows are covered on the outside with special wide-mesh security screening.

The interior of the ward is designed on a triple-wing plan

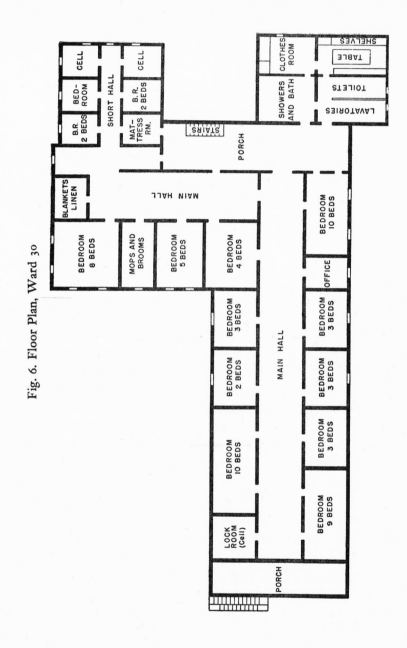

Fig. 6. Floor Plan, Ward 30

which places the office of the attendants near the intersection of the two main halls and the short hall leading to baths and toilets and ending in a supply-storage area. The interior is painted a light gray, illuminated by eight light bulbs in the hall and bulbs in each of the rooms. The light is generally poor throughout the main halls, partly because the wiring of the ward is inadequate, partly because of the ward's high ceiling. The ward is clean and usually very well kept but pervaded with a faint odor from the bodies of the patients and from disinfectants, which must be constantly used not only in housekeeping but in cleaning up after the soilers. There is a faint but persistent smell of urine. Sixty-three men give a crowded feeling to the ward. Most of them are sitting; one or two recline against the wall, seated on the floor. One group stands around listlessly.

The bedrooms shown in the floor plan were in some cases designed for single patients. Most of them throughout the hospital, as well as in Ward 30, have had to be converted into dormitories for two or three men. The general rule is that two to three patients sleep in rooms intended for one patient; seven or eight men sleep in small dormitories intended for three to six men. All doors to these rooms have peepholes.

The rooms are quite different from each other, both in their formal and informal uses. Three of the dormitory rooms have steel wire screen doors opening into the ward interior. Patients who have been troublesome are locked in these rooms during the night by the attendants. Such confinement is regarded as light and temporary. In addition to the locked dormitories, however, there are three cells or "seclusion rooms" for the highly disturbed or dangerous patients. In these cells there is no furniture except for the radiators. Windows are tightly boarded up, with ventilation only through the door.

While a few of the other rooms on the ward are provided

with security doors, they are usually left open at night. These rooms are reserved for the privileged patients and are regarded as part of the privileges. A radio for the patients and two extra benches are kept in one of these rooms opposite the attendants' office. Subject to the attendants' occasional changes in the arrangement, two of the three informal cliques of intimate friends among the privileged patients on the ward have usually arranged to sleep in the same dormitory together.

Four showers and one bath tub, one urinal, five toilets, and four lavatories make up the toilet facilities for Ward 30. At the time of our study, most of the patients were allowed one regular bath per week and were to shave at the same time. This rule could be altered for special reasons, necessarily in the case of the soilers, but also occasionally as a special privilege. Both the toilet facilities and the clothes room and closets were forbidden territory except at authorized times to most patients. A selected group of patients, however, was allowed in the clothes room and, under certain circumstances, in the mop and broom room.

THE STATUS SYSTEM ON WARD 30

The social organization of Ward 30 is made up of six status levels. These are represented below in Figure 7.

Each of these levels is defined by a system of partly informal but definite rights and duties. The first three levels are command or authority levels, in which the ward physician corresponds to the executive (first level); the charge attendants to supervisors (second level); the attendants to foremen (third level). The group of privileged patients are the work level (fourth level) for both the ward and the hospital. The patients in the fifth and sixth levels represent as a group the object of this authority system. The command and work levels

Fig. 7. The Status System, Ward 30

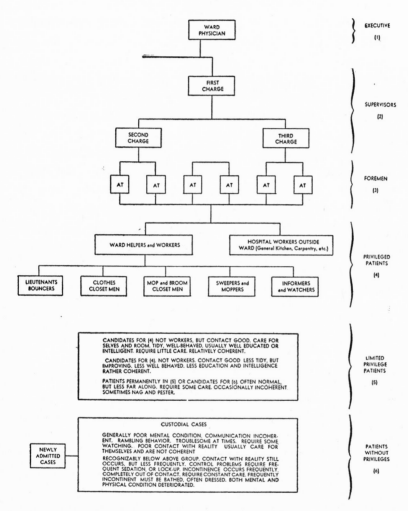

WARD PHYSICIAN

FIRST CHARGE

SECOND CHARGE

THIRD CHARGE

AT   AT   AT   AT   AT   AT

WARD HELPERS and WORKERS

HOSPITAL WORKERS OUTSIDE WARD (General Kitchen, Carpentry, etc.)

LIEUTENANTS BOUNCERS

CLOTHES CLOSET MEN

MOP and BROOM CLOSET MEN

SWEEPERS and MOPPERS

INFORMERS and WATCHERS

CANDIDATES FOR (4) NOT WORKERS, BUT CONTACT GOOD. CARE FOR SELVES AND ROOM. TIDY, WELL-BEHAVED. USUALLY WELL EDUCATED OR INTELLIGENT. REQUIRE LITTLE CARE. RELATIVELY COHERENT.

CANDIDATES FOR (4). NOT WORKERS. CONTACT GOOD LESS TIDY, BUT IMPROVING. LESS WELL BEHAVED. LESS EDUCATION AND INTELLIGENCE RATHER COHERENT.

PATIENTS PERMANENTLY IN (5) OR CANDIDATES FOR (6). OFTEN NORMAL, BUT LESS FAR ALONG. REQUIRE SOME CARE. OCCASIONALLY INCOHERENT. SOMETIMES NAG AND PESTER.

CUSTODIAL CASES

GENERALLY POOR MENTAL CONDITION. COMMUNICATION INCOHER-ENT. RAMBLING BEHAVIOR. TROUBLESOME AT TIMES. REQUIRE SOME WATCHING. POOR CONTACT WITH REALITY USUALLY CARE FOR THEMSELVES AND ARE NOT COHERENT

RECOGNIZABLY BELOW ABOVE GROUP. CONTACT WITH REALITY STILL OCCURS, BUT LESS FREQUENTLY. CONTROL PROBLEMS REQUIRE FRE-QUENT SEDATION, OR LOCK-UP. INCONTINENCE OCCURS FREQUENTLY. COMPLETELY OUT OF CONTACT. REQUIRE CONSTANT CARE. FREQUENTLY INCONTINENT MUST BE BATHED, OFTEN DRESSED. BOTH MENTAL AND PHYSICAL CONDITION DETERIORATED.

NEWLY ADMITTED CASES

EXECUTIVE (1)

SUPERVISORS (2)

FOREMEN (3)

PRIVILEGED PATIENTS (4)

LIMITED PRIVILEGE PATIENTS (5)

PATIENTS WITHOUT PRIVILEGES (6)

function to provide management, care, and treatment from initiation through execution for the fifth and sixth levels.

Except for a minority of patients (about 1 per cent) of special interest to the ward physician or to other professional staff members in the hospital, the members of this ward system are occupied primarily within the boundaries imposed by their statuses. These status limits are part of a system which has two primary functions: (1) to accomplish the daily housekeeping, cleaning, and physical care of patients on the ward; (2) to organize patient behavior in routines which hold the ward to a secure level of orderly or neutral conduct.

The primary figure in terms of authority is the ward physician, Dr. Baker. All his decisions are essential in any actions in the ward. These decisions involve such important things as privileges, release, transfer, and any kind of significant treatment, and must be made by Dr. Baker, or in his name. Dr. Baker is forty-five years old. His M.D. degree is from South State Medical School, and he has been employed in Southern State Hospital 8 years. He has completed one year of residency in South State Medical School's psychiatric hospital in psychiatry and neurology.

Dr. Baker, during our year's period of observation, was responsible for an average of four wards in the hospital, totaling 397 men. On his daily rounds, he spent a daily average of 45 minutes in Ward 30. During this time he conferred with the charge attendant in the office—usually the "day charge," Mr. Albright, who is informally chief of the charges and thus of all the ward attendants. There is some familiarity in the relation of the day charge and the physician on a workaday basis, but this familiarity is limited and cautious on Mr. Albright's part and reserved on Dr. Baker's part. There is a rank and prestige difference between their positions which does not permit too much intimacy; their relation is analogous at many points to that of an infantry company commander to one of his platoon sergeants.

After conferring with Mr. Albright about ward operations and particular patients and going over records in the office, Dr. Baker then calls an average of seven patients into the office. He talks to the patients and may examine or treat them for particular physical conditions. Perhaps the majority of patients seen in this way are those with physical symptoms, such as fever, sore throats, skin disorders, headaches, or chronic back difficulties. The older patients provide a full quota of chronic illness on Ward 30. Dr. Baker may also see one or two psychiatric patients who are on specifically psychiatric therapies, such as those proposed for or terminating electroshock or insulin treatment.

Since many of the patients are anxious to see the doctor on his rounds, the attendants must act as mediators between the patients and the physician if the latter is not to be swamped. On Ward 30, it seemed to be generally true that patients without physical symptoms who fell into the two lower privilege groups were almost never permitted to talk to the physician unless Dr. Baker himself asked for them. The persevering, nagging delusional group—who were termed "worry warts," "nuisances," "bird dogs," in the attendants' slang—often tried to break through the attendant-mediator but were always quite summarily dealt with when they tried.

The next figure and decision point in the organization of Ward 30 is the charge attendant for the ward. While each leader of the three shifts of ward attendants is called the "charge" attendant and is generally an attendant with some seniority, the real management of the ward and acknowledged leadership is always given to the "day charge," Henry Albright. Henry Albright completed 8 years of formal schooling. He is fifty-nine years old and has been employed at Southern State Hospital for a total of 18 years. Prior to employment he served one enlistment in the regular army. His mother was employed in another of the South State hospitals after she was widowed, and when Henry was ten. The other two charges acknowledge and conform to Mr. Albright's leadership in many informal ways. All matters seriously affecting ward discipline are referred to him for discussion, or for confirmation if they have involved action. One of his important functions is to make certain that each shift of attendants understands Dr. Baker's orders, and that a consistent policy is followed in the ward in relation both to the doctor and to the patients. Mr. Albright has a fund of experience on the ward and with mental patients which the other charges and attendants draw on constantly, and any questions regarding reports and requisitions are always referred to him. He himself handles and signs the majority of all reports and requisitions on the ward as the day charge.[2]

In Ward 30, under the informal leadership of the day charge, the three charges act as representatives and deputies of the physician through the ward's 24-hour cycle and provide the next regular level of command in the ward's structure. Carl Knight, the second charge, is a member of the older attendant group, sixty-one years old, and a close friend of Mr. Albright. The third charge is a Millville College student. The afternoon and night shifts both make considerable use of students, who are thus able to attend college classes in the morning. Although the turnover rate for most of the students is high on Ward 30, as it is elsewhere, a small number of these students do stay on through their 4 years of college. Harold Scott, the student charge, has worked in Southern State Hospital for 2 years, a year of this time on Ward 30. Scott is planning to teach English in high school after he graduates, and, at twenty-four, is the youngest man among all the attendants on this ward.

On Ward 30 the large general annual attendant turnover has its effects mainly on the attendants below the charge level, and of the three shifts, mainly on the third, or night and early morning, shift. This incidence of turnover is both cause and effect of the importance of the day charge and his crew of two attendants in the maintenance of continuity in ward policy in Ward 30. In the course of a year, we saw six men come and go in the second and third shifts of attendants under the charges—a turnover for these positions of 100 per cent. During this period Mr. Albright's group did not change; it is clear that sheer continuity and stability tended to reinforce the natural informal authority of the day charge's position and to maintain the system of patient statuses organized around this authority.

The position of the charge attendants is symbolized and reinforced by a system of etiquette and certain arrangements of social space on the ward. The sets of keys carried by the attendants function as one of the central emblems of this system. The charge set is handed to each charge as he takes over on his shift, and they are often not used by attendants even when they are substituting for the charge attendant. The feeling about the charge keys as a set is that they should be used only by the charges, although the other sets will open the same doors. When the charge is on duty, he alone sits behind the desk in the office. Only on the charge's off days does either of the two attendants below him use the desk. When the charge is in his office, the office itself and a zone of about 6 square feet outside the office is off limits to all except the top group of ward helpers among the privileged patients. The other patients neither stand nor sit in this zone. Even the privileged patients may be sent away with abrupt authority if the charge or his attendants desire it. Obedience when this order occurs—usually in a parental form, such as "run along, now"—is instantaneous. The privileged patient is privileged precisely because he understands the meaning of this social space and other aspects of the attendant's position. Above the office door a sign is lettered: "Patients Are Not to Enter the Office Unless Called For."

TRAINING AND SUPERVISION FOR THE INFORMAL WARD SYSTEM

Throughout the time of our observation there was a number of persisting relationships among the group of charge attendants and attendants which involved a status system among the attendants themselves. This status system had both supervisory and training functions. Albright and Knight both clearly thought of themselves and of the two attendants under Albright as different from Scott and from most of the other attendants. One aspect of this difference was that Albright and Knight and Albright's attendants were "permanent" on the ward, whereas the other charge and most of the other attendants were "temporary." Others of the permanent group were scattered strategically about the hospital.

Over a long enough period of time the feeling of solidarity between the members of the permanent group could be seen as the basis of a number of personnel operations among the employees of Ward 30. Albright and his two older attendants, along with Knight, kept up a constant though unobtrusive observation of all the other attendants and particularly of the new ones coming on the ward. When either of these two charges saw, or had reported to them, any behavior on the part of these attendants which violated the codes of procedure on the ward, some kind of action on the part of Albright or

Knight usually followed immediately. Scott cooperated with the other two charges but took no direct part in their actions.

Both the observation and actions of these two older charges were focused on ensuring that the new attendant—and all attendants in fact—understood and could carry out the proper role of an attendant. This was not a formal procedure. The organization of Southern State Hospital has never included a systematic familiarization and training plan for new personnel on the wards, just as the administrative line to the ward allows no formal supervision. But there is an informal training and supervisory procedure which is quite definite.

This procedure is carried out by the senior charge attendants and their fellow senior attendants in many ways and with many effects not known to the professional administrative heads of the ward and the hospital. The continuous inspection by Albright and Knight of the other attendants in Ward 30 and the actions they undertook from time to time were designed to accomplish one major purpose. This was to maintain the structure of statuses on the ward by ensuring that the attendant behaved appropriately and required appropriate behavior from those below him. If the attendant failed in some important aspect of this behavior he was warned, and if he persisted after the warning he was eliminated.

The processes by which this elimination was accomplished were all of an informal nature. The formal organization of the hospital gives no authority of the discharge type to ward personnel, with the exception of the physician. The most usual method of elimination was the simple one of going to the attendant supervisor and informally requesting the offender's transfer to another ward. Since the attendant was already in the status of a rejected person by the older attendant group, the transfers we witnessed were in every case to wards regarded as more undesirable than Ward 30. The effect was that the attendant was discharged from the hospital, since those transferred in this manner always resigned.[3]

As this system worked out, the high turnover among new attendants was not surprising. Since the pay and working conditions for the attendants in general were poor, and since the prestige position of the job was the lowest in the hospital, most of the new attendants who came to Ward 30 admitted that they regarded their jobs as stopgaps until they could get something better. Some of those among the remainder who had more permanent intentions were eliminated because they could or would not conform to the pattern determined for the attendants. Those remaining were the ones who could get no other employment or who found the pattern agreeable.

The attendants who passed inspection by the senior attendants were the ones who learned quickly a role for the attendant which was essentially that of foreman over the fourth-level group of patients. This role is pivotal for the entire informal organization of the ward status system—as for the entire hospital. It is here that the direct, personal contact of the hospital with its patients is maintained. In outline, the problems in the role are not greatly different from those of the foreman in industry,[4] but they differ in details. The essential problem for the industrial foreman is that of harmonizing a management system and a work system which have very often conflicting characteristics in structure, personnel, and culture. The attendant's problem is similar, but he has the additional handicap of working with a ward system which is not formally recognized by upper management and in turn with an upper management which is separated from him by strong communication barriers.

The training of the new attendant for his role must be largely covert; in the special culture of the wards it is the responsibility of the senior attendants. In the practical situation faced by the new employee on the wards in Southern State Hospital, this training is all that is available to him.

The upper administration in Southern State Hospital has been historically without much interest in the welfare, training, or adjustment of the attendants as a group. The evidence for this is plainly written in the hospital's personnel policy, or rather its lack of personnel policy for the attendants. The hiring and placement procedure is perfunctory. Familiarization and job indoctrination are haphazard and unorganized.[5] The hospital has no grievance procedure except the naive and outdated one of complaining to immediate supervisors. We could find no evidence that the upper administration had ever taken any interest in exit interviewing of attendants leaving the hospital—an indifference which is strange indeed in view of the high turnover rate among the attendants.

As the new attendant comes into the hospital he does not encounter a planned, supervised familiarization program until he comes under the informal and unrecognized one of the senior attendants on the ward. Prior to this he has received a physical examination and hand-out material describing the attendant's duties and ward procedures. He is told to read the attendant's manual and the hospital rules and regulations, but he usually is not provided a copy of the latter. Finally he is informed that he can turn for guidance and instruction to attendant supervisors, ward doctors, charge attendants, trained attendants, and "practices, principles, and policies" established on the ward. With this indifferent preparation he is sent out to the wards. The new attendant may come on as the shift changes and find himself perhaps assigned without training or instruction and completely alone on the night shift in charge of seventy or one hundred patients, some of whom may be homicidal and all of whom appear frightening to an inexperienced man.[6] He is more fortunate if he arrives on his job at first under Carl Knight's supervision on Ward 30, since he will have the company of an experienced attendant and some instruction of an elementary sort.

Where the new man on Ward 30 has had time to consult his manual for attendants, he has learned that attendants in Southern State Hospital are to provide complete physical care of patients, to carry out instructed treatment of patients, to clean and maintain the patients' surroundings, to manage clothing and supplies, and watch the patients. They are also to maintain good relations with visitors and public. These duties are to be carried out under certain guiding principles:

1. The attitude toward the patients should be one of patience, courteousness, gentleness, with firmness only as necessary.

2. Harsh words or orders to the patient are not permitted. No curse words to a patient will be permitted.

3. Calling the patient names, like "crazy," "idiot," or "dumb," or doing anything to humiliate the patient is forbidden.

4. Under no circumstances will any employee be allowed to strike a patient or in any way abuse him.

5. Show friendliness to the patients. Introduce them to other patients. Find out what the patient likes and try to follow that in helping him adjust.

6. Patients are not to be punished for any reason. Misbehavior on the ward is never to be used as an excuse for keeping the patient on the ward and denying him the privilege of entering the usual activities off the ward, except in such cases as where the patient has proved himself dangerous.

7. Patients' records are confidential, and should be shown only to authorized personnel. Don't gossip.

As his on-the-job training proceeds, the new attendant finds that many of these formal rules are either contrary to ward policy or are not specific enough to cover his work, and that they require certain alterations. But he learns from the senior attendants that the formal rules are always to be respected in appearance at least.

The first modification in the formal practices and principles of the attendant's job which must be taught the new man is that in Ward 30, the patients do all the work except for the most dignified medical work, such as giving injections and posting records. During his first few days on the ward he hears a verbal description of the organization of the patient work system and its functions in the fourth level and sees this system in operation under the experienced attendants.

The new attendant learns that the work system of the ward begins at the fourth level with the top group of privileged patients. There are two divisions in this group of working patients. One division works outside the ward in hospital maintenance, the kitchens, and elsewhere. The other division is of more direct importance on the ward. These ward helpers and workers, as they are designated, have many functions in the ward, centering around the five positions indicated as lieutenants, clothes-closet men, mop-and-broom-closet men, sweepers and moppers, informers and watchers. The first and last of these positions are often combined in the ward, but there are some patients who tend to act mainly as lieutenants for the attendants in getting work supervised and who are always ready to help with a violent patient, but who do not inform or check up on other patients in a general sense. And there are others who do little supervision, avoid contact with violent patients under any circumstances, but who regularly supply the attendant with information about what is said and done by patients who may be out of the attendant's sight. The informers and watchers serve an important informal function in the general ward security and in providing continuity between shifts of attendants. The outgoing shift members do not always pass along all important facts about the day's happenings on the ward, but the informers and watchers are sure to tell the incoming shift about anything at all unusual. Information of this type is important in the care of mental patients.

A fairly frequent example of such information is the reported observation that "Old Simpson is fixing to pitch a good one," turned in by one of the informers who had observed signs that Simpson's behavior is building toward a violent outburst of excitement, in which he may be dangerous. Such excitement may be dealt with by sedation or even by some sympathetic attention if it is perceived in time. Knowledge that it is imminent may make the difference between a smoothly running and a violently disturbed ward. In dealing with a large group of adult men, some of whom are strong and vigorous and most of whom are of doubtful mental status, the experienced attendants know that continuous surveillance and information from some of the patients are essential, and they reward their informants with suitable privileges.

The principle in handling the working group of patients which the new attendant will learn from watching the senior attendants is that of maintaining a firm superior-subordinate relationship. This relationship is to be maintained with all patients on the ward, but it involves a special problem with the working group, which interacts continually with the attendants. If the problem is properly handled with the working group, this group in turn will manage many of the relationships with the lower groups of patients in the ward status system.

The superior-subordinate relationship in Ward 30 is kept up, the new attendant learns, by two basic props: one is the maintenance of a strict social distance between the attendant and all patients; a distinction between their statuses which may be graded slightly to allow for different patient status but which is always there. The other prop is the employment of the system of rewards and punishments which is available to the attendant as the ward manager. Strictly speaking, the superior-subordinate relationship and the reward and punishment system are themselves the two essential aspects of ward status, since both of them can be defined for any individual in terms of his position in the ward status system. The attendant learns that his ability to place or remove a patient in the three major privilege groups is the essential ingredient of his power to command behavior and keep order in the ward. And as the ward is organized, he can routinize his job in no other way.

During the new attendant's learning process the senior attendants are quietly watchful of his progress. The guidance they provide is very seldom explicit but is constantly present, both verbally and by precept. One teaching technique is of course by example. Another is by means of illustrative teachings or stories of attendants who learned quickly how to "handle" patients by the approved techniques, or of attendants who did not learn and came to disaster. When the attendant was new, the teaching was elementary, but if he stayed on he learned more of the senior attendants' conception of mental illness and of the importance of the attendant and his unrewarded position in the hospital. Ultimately, if he became accepted, he learned too that there were ways to handle doctors, nurses, social workers, and psychologists, some of whom were unable to understand the needs of Ward 30 and were likely to expect things in the way of treatment which were impossible.

The examples, verbal instruction, and illustrations always centered around the key problems of teaching the new attendant to maintain his appropriate social distance and to apply the reward and punishment system skillfully, primarily with the fourth-level patients at first, and then with the fifth- and sixth-level patients.

The primary logic that lies back of the Ward 30 status system is rather quickly grasped by the adjustable new attendants. The patients who are in the best mental condition and physical health get the most privileges. The grading of the privilege system reflects and expresses the maintenance needs of the ward as it is organized under the attendant's authority. The top group of patients consists of those who are in excellent contact with reality, look after themselves well, are usually relatively intelligent and energetic, and are thus able to work. The next group below them, fifth level, are generally inferior in all these characteristics, but they are able to look after themselves, and many of them will improve in mental condition and move into the fourth level. In terms of ward management, the fifth-level patients in Ward 30 could be described as a potential source of ward or hospital workers, but presently neutral in the management of the ward, with the exception of a few episodic delusional cases in the lower part of the level. And these patients were mild "nuisances" rather than difficult or dangerous. If their symptoms became bothersome they would be moved back down to the sixth level.

The sixth level is made up of the patients who are least useful in ward work, who have as a whole little contact with reality, who are the least intelligent and energetic. Some of them are periodically violent and dangerous. As a group they have the worst illnesses, both psychiatrically and physically. Many of them are incontinent and must be bathed and changed frequently by the attendants and lieutenants. These patients, viewed as a management problem, make most of the work for the ward.

In operation of the ward, the working-level patients in the fourth level do most of the work which must be done for the sixth-level patients and in return are given most of the privileges of which the ward is capable. As a group, the fourth level are the aristocrats of Ward 30 patients. They have relative freedom to leave the ward, they live in the best rooms and those having the fewest number of men. Most of them have their own clothing, rather than the free state clothing. They can carry money with them and may possess radios, watches, and jewelry. They sit in preferred seats at the dinner table. Within the limits of the authority system they have relatively pleasant and continuous interaction with the attendants, and they receive the major amount of attention from all personnel above them. They are the only patients on the ward who can usually invade the off-limits zone outside the attendants' office and even go inside to talk. Such limited recreational facilities as dominoes, checkers, and cards as are available on the ward are more or less confined to the fourth-level patients, because their contact level and relationships with one another permit group games and prevent loss or scattering of cards and dominoes, such as occurs in other levels.

A few of the improving fifth-level patients are occasionally permitted to play by fourth-level patients, but this is an exception rather than a rule and usually marks a new probationer for the fourth level if it continues. A clique of fourth-level patients on Ward 30 have monopolized for their domino and card games a certain spot where the two main hallways come together and give the strongest combined light in the ward for night playing. No other patients are allowed here by the clique or the attendants. Regular recreation available to all patients is confined to the movies shown once a week on the ward and to the planned recreation for the entire hospital which the patients may attend under supervision and which is usually scheduled two or three times during the week. With very few exceptions, however, most of the daily recreational activity, and particularly that involving group participation and play, was limited on Ward 30 to the fourth-level patients.

The fact that the patients in the best mental and physical health receive most of the privileges means also that they get the most attention and the most considerate treatment. They also enjoy the greatest immunity to the hospital's penalty system, since the penalties are in many cases defined by exclusion from privileges.

The attendant learns that his power has a strong base in the fact that he can move any patient in the fourth level back to the fifth level or transfer him to another ward where he may have to begin at the sixth level. Something of what this power means, both to patient and attendant, becomes clear as one sees the confidence with which the experienced attendant issues orders to his helpers and the speed with which they are obeyed. Even more impressive is the fact that most of the work of the fourth-level patients in Ward 30 is done without any orders at all.

By following the rules laid down by the senior attendants and maintaining the existing organization of the fourth-level patients, the new attendants who stayed on Ward 30 were soon able to manage the ward by themselves on occasion. Throughout most of the days on Ward 30 the system of organization on the ward functioned to maintain a tidy and clean, though perhaps socially stagnant, ward. There were always a few interruptions of this routine, however, which occurred once or twice a week, and which activated the punishment system.

Ward 30 uses no "mechanical" restraints, such as camisoles, straps, or restraint sheets; and only under very special circum-

stances and with medical permission are the "belt and cuffs" [7]
used. These items were and still are in use in some state hospitals as punishments, and their passing is still regretted by some of the older Southern State Hospital attendants.

Ward 30 still has the stronger disciplinary resources, however. When any patient—chiefly members of the sixth level, with an occasional member from the fifth—is rude or insubordinate to the attendants or to a worker carrying out the attendant's orders, or when the patient picks a fight with another patient or becomes violently aggressive in general, he may be placed in one of the ward seclusion rooms, or special cells. In theory, this seclusion is carried out by the attendant and his lieutenants for the patient's own good and to give him an opportunity to cool off. But in most cases of disturbance we witnessed this was not exactly the spirit in which the patient was incarcerated. In addition to its outright use in ward discipline for unruly patients, the threat of seclusion was often employed by the attendants or working patients to secure discipline. The new attendant learns to give medical, rather than disciplinary or punitive reasons for this seclusion, a procedure made possible by the fact that seclusion is under certain rare circumstances necessary in psychiatric treatment.

Another strong disciplinary device used on Ward 30, and one of much wider significance in the maintenance of order, makes use of the hospital's electroshock therapy (EST). This therapy is under strict medical administration by the professional team of ward physician and nurse, who come on the ward twice each week with the attendant supervisor to give the treatment.

Patients who are to receive this treatment are selected by the physician and by the first charge attendant. On the day before the shock team is scheduled, the charge attendant makes out the EST List, as it is called. He lists for treatment those patients he feels need the treatment because they are "acting up," are causing trouble, have become disturbed, or show strong evidence of becoming disturbed or violent. In addition to these patients, there are three or four patients who are on the list more or less routinely for what is called in the ward "maintenance therapy." These are patients who have had a continuous history of violence or disturbance on the ward since admission until they are put on a shock series which may last for as long as 3 months. The amnesia and disorientation produced in these patients by the shock treatment keeps them quiet and prevents their disturbing or hurting the other patients and upsetting the ward routine.

On all the lists for shock made up by Mr. Albright or Mr. Knight there were always several patients who were on the list for insubordination to the attendants or to a ward helper or for having fought each other. If both the patients in the fight were in the fifth or sixth levels, both were shocked. If one of the patients was in the fourth level and the other from the lower levels, both were held responsible, but the fourth-level patient was usually given admonition and temporary loss of some privilege, while the lower-level patient was put on the shock list. The probability of the punitive use of shock treatment varies inversely with status in Ward 30, except for a few patients selected by Dr. Baker for individual attention.

On Ward 30 it was evident that two concepts of the use of shock therapy were both being used. The formal purpose of the treatments was medical and therapeutic, but they depended for their execution on the cooperation of the attendants. They were thus open to uses which were disciplinary rather than therapeutic. In the last analysis, the physician had to take the attendant's word for it that the patient had been acting up, since the physician spent little time on the ward.

To an observer who had been on the ward during the week it would be clear that two or three patients were on the list because they had responded with normal resentment to actual ill treatment by an attendant or another patient, or because they had objected to the hospital food by refusing to eat it. The sixth-level hallucinatory and delusional "worry warts" were particularly likely to be put on the shock lists. One senior attendant said frankly that he put one of these patients on the list to give himself and the ward a rest from a particularly boring story.

The rule on Mr. Albright's list was, however, generally that any patient who deviated too far from his position in the status system was put on the shock list and told why. This was not done in a spirit of deception. Mr. Albright considered sincerely that any patient who did deviate from ward routine was thereby showing signs of mental disturbance. The maintenance of the system of ward statuses required the elimination of such deviation. Furthermore, as Mr. Albright said, the shock treatment was good for nearly all mental patients because it kept them from worrying so much about themselves and actually improved their physical health.

The new attendant who kept his eyes on the effects of shock therapy in Ward 30 could see for himself its effectiveness as a threat in maintaining order. Most of the patients who had been on the ward more than a few weeks were afraid of the treatment; those who had not experienced it were if anything more afraid of it than those who had. For most patients the threat of being put on the shock list had an instant effect in bringing their conduct into line with the requirements of their position in the ward.

The source of the patients' fear of shock therapy could not in fact have come with their personal experience of the therapy, since amnesia for this experience is almost complete.

But among both patients and attendants there is widely circulated knowledge of the administration of the treatment and its effect on the patient. This knowledge is based on the fact that some of the patients in Ward 30 have assisted the shock team in the administration of therapy to patients, holding them down, and helping to strap them in bed, or watching them after they have quieted. The administration of shock on the ward is often carried out in full sight of a group of interested onlookers. The patient's convulsions often resemble those of an accident victim in death agony and are accompanied by choking gasps and at times by a foaming overflow of saliva from the mouth. The patient slowly recovers without memory of the occurrence, but he has served the others as a frightful spectacle of what may be done to them. Moreover, in the early disorientation and vacuity of his state of recovery he is obviously upsetting to the other patients. Patients who have not seen shock treatment are provided with detailed descriptions by those who have.

In addition to the specific knowledge about shock therapy in Ward 30, there is a fearsome mythology that also circulates among some of the patients and attendants. Most patients and attendants are persuaded that the treatment is probably beneficial, but there are said to be risks of broken backs, mortal heart attacks, and brain injury from the convulsions. Tales are told of old men who were killed by the strain of the treatment and of patients who could not get well under the treatment and who had to be shocked so many times that both mind and body disintegrated completely. Since no explanation of shock therapy is attempted by the professionals or the attendants, while the treatment itself is not concealed, some such mythology is to be expected. The mythology of Ward 30 has grown through the years and plays a strong part in the disciplinary effectiveness of shock therapy in the ward social system.

Considered as a total social system over a long-enough period of time, Ward 30 could be regarded as a definite structure with laws of its own, supported and enforced by a system of rewards and punishments. The new attendants who learned this system and conformed to its laws remained and were ultimately accepted by the senior attendants, at least provisionally, as one of their own number. During our observation, no man remained on Ward 30 more than a week or two if he habitually permitted any deviation from the appropriate behavior on his part or that of the patients. Control of the ward by the senior attendants was informal and indirect, but it was almost completely effective because of the relative stability of the attendants in their jobs and their absolute authority to reward and punish patients and any new attendants.

The fate of the patient coming into Ward 30 depended very largely on the operation of the ward status system as far as he was personally concerned. If he was still reasonably lucid at the time of his commitment and automatic placement in the sixth level of the ward, and if his intelligence and physical health were unimpaired, he was often able to define the ward situation accurately and move upward through the fifth level and into the fourth level. Incoming patients who were unable to define the situation properly could not achieve this mobility and often remained permanently in the lower-status groups. Such permanent placement lowered the probabilities of any consistent interest or attention in them by the attendants, the more advanced patients, and the professional personnel. And as the patient remained in the lower level for a longer and longer period of time, there was an apparent tendency for the upper patients and attendants in the ward to type him permanently as incurable and to offer resistance to such efforts as he did make to move into a higher status.

As Ward 30 was organized, the fourth-level patients were grouped in a fashion which excluded all the fifth-level patients from personal association, except for an occasional probationer. The fourth-level patients regarded themselves literally as mentally sound and the patients below them as "crazy people." Such phrases were used continually by the fourth-level patients, and by the attendants as well, in speaking of the lower patients. Every day on the ward produced at least two or three incidents in which members of the fourth level repulsed members of the lower groups who attempted to converse or play dominoes or cards with them. The attendants, who understood this situation if they remained on the ward, never assigned any patient from the fifth level to work with the various groups of fourth-level patients unless this patient was acceptable to these latter. In this sense, the fourth-level patients, rather than the attendant or the doctor, ultimately determined upward mobility in the ward for the majority of patients and thus the actual discharge potentiality for the average patient in the hospital.

CHAPTER ELEVEN

Getting Out of the Hospital

In the general hospital, the departing patient is free from complications in legal status, has a family and usually a job to return to, and has suffered no loss of social status in the community. He is a free citizen, with little or no adjustments to make in the community. His period of hospitalization has only temporarily immobilized him and has not seriously interfered with his social role, his family unity, and social position in the community. These conditions are not true of the discharged Southern State Hospital patient. His period of hospitalization is anywhere from ten to fifty times longer than that of the person who has been hospitalized for physical disease.[1] Many of his social relations have been permanently severed, and his status in the community has undergone a radical transformation.[2] If he returns to his family, there is a great likelihood that he will be received with anxiety and even hostility. He may not, and often does not, have a family to which he can return.[3] Too often the family life itself is so chaotic and impaired with dissension that it would precipitate another breakdown should the patient return there. Moreover, mental patients have nearly always lost jobs they may have had and hence are confronted with the sometimes difficult task of securing employment without assistance or retraining. Problems of this kind do not occur to this degree in patients with physical diseases and therefore impose no special burden upon the administrators of general hospitals. However, in mental hospitals, the problems should be faced squarely and met if patients are to be discharged from the hospital. In Southern State Hospital they are not met or even acknowledged.

In order to understand what is involved in getting a patient out of the hospital, it is necessary to go back to the time at which the patient first entered Southern State Hospital. When the patient first arrives at the hospital the social service department undertakes to secure information on the patient's family and occupational background. Included in this information is a record of the family's apparent attitude toward the patient, its financial standing, and its potentialities for taking the patient back. Unless this information is obtained it is difficult to formulate plans for the eventual disposition of the case. Patients cannot be arbitrarily turned out of the hospital. There has to be some responsible person or agency to whom the majority of patients can be sent.

The condition of the hospital's statistics on patients permitted us to make only rough estimates of the trends in the hospital's patient discharge and related movements of the population. The gross facts are as follows:

Over the 16-year period 1936 to 1952, about one-fourth, or 2,875, of the patients among the 11,509 first-admissions died either in the hospital or while on furlough. Another 480, or an average of 30 per year, remained in the hospital. A net 1,200 patients were transferred to other institutions, for the aged [4] or the tuberculous. Discharges for all reasons (Recovered, Improved, Unimproved, Unascertained, Without Psychosis) averaged about 49 per cent of first-admissions. Another 12 to 15 per cent did not return from furlough and were dropped from the books of the hospital. The trend in patients remaining in the hospital population is irregular but apparently toward a slow increase in the number, with an average of 70 per year remaining in the period 1947 to 1952 as compared with an average of about 12 per year in the 1936 to 1947 period. These 70 continue to add to a net load of patients already in the institution, which amounted to nearly 3,000 by 1952.

The chief means, in order of importance, by which the hospital has relieved itself of the load of incoming patients are through discharges, furloughs, deaths, and transfers to other institutions. The furlough is second in importance to the discharges for all causes, but furloughs consume a major amount of the energy which the medical-psychiatric staff is able to devote to getting patients out of the hospital.

Over the period 1936 to 1952, furloughs from the hospital averaged about 24 per cent of the first-admissions. The average rate of return from furloughs, however, is very high, fluctuating between 67 and 98 per cent of those furloughed. The poor showing of furlough procedure in Southern State Hospital is clearly related to the completely substandard position of the social service department in quantity of personnel.[5] But it is also related to a lack of contact which this centralized hospital will always have with its patients' communities.

Many of the problems of getting patients out of Southern State Hospital are obvious from the foregoing treatment of the internal professional and ward systems. The relation of the internal process of custodial classification and care and the getting-out process of discharge and furlough shows the same discrepancy between practice and theory which is present throughout the other medical-psychiatric systems of the hospital.

There seems to be little clear relation between the patient's condition on his entry into the hospital, his treatment, and the manner in which his discharge will be handled. Among the professional staff and attendants we found an unmistakable cynicism about the hospital's ability to cure the average patient. This cynicism is based on the covert knowledge of all hospital personnel that the patients are not actually getting the kind of treatment and attention presupposed in professional psychiatry as represented by the hospital's formal records or its chart of organization. Since ultimately the clinical director and physicians are the persons responsible for discharge of all patients, they have an understandable reluctance to discharge patients. This situation, more than any intrinsic merit in the procedure itself, accounts for the widespread use of the furlough in the hospital, as opposed to the outright discharge. The furlough permits the problem to be postponed without being solved, and, what is more important, transfers legal responsibility for the patient from the hospital to the relatives.[6]

Looking at the furlough process in a common-sense way, we find about four steps involved.

1. The initial movement which sets the getting-out machinery in action comes from the medical staff. When a doctor makes a decision to permit a leave of absence or furlough, the decision is based upon his own personal opinion about and experience with the patient.[7] There is no completely objective set of standards by which to judge whether one patient is in better mental condition for a furlough or leave of absence than another. Generally the ward social position of the patient has been the guide for making decisions, though there is some variability in standards of judgment from one doctor to another. These variations result from differences either in rationally constructed conclusions or else in individual knowledge of the patient and his social environment for purposes of furlough. In the latter case, the doctors differ according to their work habits and methods of discharging their duties. Theoretically, it would be possible for such variations to exist on a much greater

scale. If a doctor, for example, held to a strict professional view of the psychological condition of his patient, and considered possible harmful consequences of a leave of absence, then he could easily decline permission for a number of leaves on the grounds that leaves could have unfavorable effects either on the patient or on other persons in the community with whom the patient might come in contact. Of the community possibilities, the doctor usually has no knowledge beyond that in the patient's sketchy social service case history.

2. The second step is for the doctor to serve official notice of his decision to the social service department. The social service department is charged with the obligation of locating the relatives and inducing them to accept responsibility for the patient. Sometimes this requires the writing of a formal letter to the family in which it is indicated that the patient would greatly benefit from a visit at home.

3. The location of relatives by the social service department is actually a third distinct step in the getting-out process and involves several alternative modes of approach:

   a. Sometimes it is not necessary to communicate in writing with the patient's family, relatives, or friends, because the family has been instrumental in getting the furlough. That is, some families, upon visiting the hospital, immediately perceive a distinct change in the behavior of the patient and undertake to convince the doctor of the advisability of a furlough or leave of absence. In such cases the social service department finds it unnecessary to go through the customary motions required to complete the furlough process. Since the family is already at the hospital, all that is necessary is to fill out the usual documents, and the patient goes home. Even here, however, there are variations. In the main they are two:

(1) The patient may be furloughed without the knowledge of the social service department, in which case it tends to confuse the members of this department. Whether or not the doctors should bypass the social service department is a question that is not, as far as we know, officially determined. But it is certain that only one method should be employed.

(2) The patient may be furloughed with the knowledge of the social service department and proper records made by this department. In this case there is at least an official continuity in the relations between the patient and the official agencies set up for formal disposition.

b. At other times it is necessary to make arrangements with the patient's family by correspondence before the patient can be furloughed. Families are not always favorably disposed toward reception of their committed relatives, and as a result it is necessary to induce them to come to the hospital and take the patient home. Since there has been no systematic attention to the problem of placement during the patient's stay in the hospital, this may or may not produce tangible results. Sometimes the family replies that it is in no position to accept the patient at that time, and frequently the family will take charge of the patient for a short period of time (usually about 2 weeks to a month) and then return him to the hospital.

c. Not all patients have families to which they may be sent, and it is therefore necessary to make arrangements with other outside agencies before the patient can be furloughed. The usual procedure in such cases is to furlough the patient to a friend or employer; however, these arrangements are comparatively rare.

4. The next main step in the furlough process is to transfer the patient into the custody of the person or persons who have indicated their willingness to assume responsibility for the patient. At this point it is necessary to fill out a document called "Authorization for Absence from Hospital." On this record are affixed the signatures of the person or persons in whose custody the patient is placed, the attending physician (the doctor in charge of the patient), and the superintendent.

This completes the last step in the mechanics of furloughing patients, nearly all of which, in Southern State Hospital, proceed in an atmosphere of complete uncertainty as to the condition of the patient's background and often as to his present symptomatology.

Just as Southern State Hospital has no preliminary procedure for evaluating, caring for the patient, and working with his family as he comes in, the hospital lacks any general machinery for following him up once he has been discharged. With the rarest exceptions, the discharged patient and the patient who remains successfully on furlough must make out with whatever aid they can find from friends or relatives in taking up again the strands of their lives which have been disordered by mental illness and commitment to a distant and impersonal institution.

CHAPTER TWELVE

Conclusions

I should like to summarize in this chapter what I believe to be the salient points in the organization of Southern State Hospital and to outline as briefly as possible the relationships between the recurrent problems in this organization and the development of the mental health program in South State. The chapter is based not only on the field material from Southern State Hospital but also on my study of all institutions in the South State Hospital system in comparison with other state systems in the United States. On the basis of this material I have tried to reach some definite conclusions on the nature of the state hospital problem and have ventured to propose measures which I think may lead eventually to solution or some reduction of the problem. It should be stated plainly at the outset of this chapter that these conclusions and proposals represent my own interpretation.

In the over-all view of Southern State Hospital one fact seems to stand out: from the time of its foundation the hospital has been defined as an institution which must carry out two contradictory and essentially unrelated functions. One of these functions was that of treating the mentally ill. The other was that of serving as a more efficient poor farm, with more centralized organization. The isolation of the hospital, its self-contained industrial and agricultural functions, its general low staus, and its constitutional responsibility for the indigent insane are all facts which speak plainly.

One of the curious things in the history of attempts to improve the numerous abuses in Southern State Hospital and its sister hospitals has been the failure of reformers to ask whether a large-scale, centralized, and partly self-sufficient institution is in fact able to function effectively in the treatment of the mentally ill. These features of the hospital were perhaps once conducive to a short-run economy in the care of paupers, but what relation do they have to modern concepts in the treatment of mental patients?

As far as we can determine, this one question was not asked in any way that called for a decision. Through the years, Southern State Hospital kept on growing planlessly, adding a building now and then, a few more personnel when the budget allowed, but changing very little in its basic design, even after it acquired the more dignified title of "Hospital."

In the meantime, and almost always in places other than state hospitals, scientific knowledge about mental illness was slowly developing. Some of this illness, like paresis and involutional melancholia, showed remission with physical treatment techniques like fever therapy and insulin or electroshock treatment. But the large and important classes of mental disease, like schizophrenia, manic-depressive psychoses, senile psychoses, and the psychoneuroses and psychosomatic disorders, showed much less specific response. Instead, research has indicated more and more certainly that attack on these latter would require a long chain of preventive, treatment, and rehabilitation activities on the part of medicine and its auxiliaries in addition to physical treatment. The attack on these mental diseases came increasingly to be seen by advanced psychiatry as involving treatment in the community environment of the patient, with hospitalization reduced to a phase, rather than a center of treatment.

In this development, the psychiatrist began to see himself

as one who must exercise control in the treatment process over the patient's relationship to family, community, and job. He thus required knowledge of all these sets of personal relationships and some direct and indirect control over them. And ultimately, psychiatry as a discipline would have to move from individual control to a complete prevention, treatment, and rehabilitation program in all the communities of the United States. This would demand close and continuous relations with the community families, schools, churches, welfare and health institutions, and occupations.[1]

The position of the centralized state mental hospital with reference to this newer development in psychiatry is dubious indeed. Jones, Grimes, Stanton, and Bateman among psychiatrists take the view directly or by implication that the hospital itself may be creating difficulties in treatment and rehabilitation.[2] Lemkau among public health physicians considers that the hospital blocks support for effective mental health programs.[3] Moreover, much of the effort exerted by psychiatric leaders to establish larger psychopathic units in general hospitals, more community psychiatric centers, and outpatient clinics is essentially directed toward preventing or shortening any patient's experience with the state hospitals.[4] Finally, and perhaps indicating more decisively than anything else the attitude of modern psychiatry toward the state mental hospital, is the very small percentage of certified psychiatrists or other trained psychiatric personnel practicing therein.

The fact that most professional psychiatrists will not accept the conditions posed by the state hospital is beyond dispute in Southern State Hospital and elsewhere in the country. In 1950, less than 16 per cent of the certified psychiatrists in the United States were employed in state hospitals, and most of these were administrators who did not practice on the wards. In South State, of the eighty certified psychiatrists in the state in 1950, only three were employed in the state hospitals, and only one of the three was in actual ward practice. In Southern State Hospital none of the ward physicians was Board-certified. Eighty-four per cent of the specialists concerned with psychiatry in the United States are not practicing in the agency which treats eighty-five per cent of the resident mental cases in the country, and in Southern State Hospital the rejection, except for the medical executives who did not practice on the wards, was complete.[5]

That the general physician also rejects the state hospital as an area of practice is evident in the fact that in 1950, with resident patients in the hospitals numbering over 600,000, only 1 per cent of the 203,000 physicians in active practice were employed in the hospitals.[6] In Southern State Hospital, about 10 per cent of the positions authorized and budgeted are not filled.

For the other main professional specialties in the state hospital the picture was similar or worse. Of the 382,047 graduate nurses in practice in 1950, only 1.3 per cent were in state mental hospitals,[7] and of 2,253 trained psychiatric social workers in the United States in 1950, only 507, or 22 per cent, were employed in state hospitals.[8] Accredited clinical psychologists in 1949 practicing in the state mental hospitals numbered 100 out of a total of 3,600, or about 3 per cent.[9] In Southern State Hospital, over the past 30 years, there have been on the average no qualified regular employees in psychiatric social work and clinical psychology.

If Southern State Hospital is considered as a case study in the relationship of state hospitals and modern psychiatry, it appears that the modern concepts of psychiatry are in the main unworkable in the hospital. Since it is centralized and large, Southern State Hospital concentrates a large number of patients in one community. Except for the patients from Millville, who make up 14 per cent of the patients in the hospital, those committed to Southern State Hospital come from communities which may be from twenty to one hundred miles away.

As a result of this concentration of large numbers of employees and patients, Southern State Hospital must be administered in an impersonal fashion with minimum allowance for personal peculiarities on the part of staff, patients, or relatives. Standard operating procedure is necessarily inflexible, and administrative routines dominant.

The hospital has no close and continuous contact through its personnel with the communities of a majority of its patients. A system of public relations activities and education in the communities (except for Millville) on a regular and personal basis is therefore impossible. No realistic or permanent industrial placement rehabilitation or community volunteer aid can be achieved for a majority of the patients without an impracticable and inequitable burden on this source in Millville. Interpretation of any role for the families of patients in treatment, maintenance of family contact, or development of community understanding of the patients cannot be designed as routine parts of the intake treatment and discharge process. In most cases, even such elementary relationships as visiting of the patients by the family are reduced by travel distance and cost. Finally, it is much easier for both family and community to forget a patient housed in another community.

From the technical psychiatric point of view, all these features of Southern State Hospital obviously represent a distortion or alteration in the modern therapeutic role of the psychiatrist as concerned with intimate treatment and rehabilitation of the mental patient. And all of them derive fundamentally from the initial mixture of purposes in the foundation of the hospital.

But in addition to the incompatibility with modern psychiatric treatment coming from the size and location of the Southern State Hospital, there is another consequence of the mixture with deadly effect on the possibilities of modern psychiatric treatment. This is the tendency in the local communities of South State to dump into the hospital the residual welfare, mentally deficient, and other types of problematic individuals for whom the community does not provide. An unknown, but very large, percentage of the mentally deficient, the old, and the sick poor are in Southern State Hospital only because there are no programs in special education or chronic illness care in the local communities of South State.

In the ward social system in Southern State Hospital this group of patients usually goes into the sixth level. Their presence has much to do both with the need for the ward social organization and with the stagnant and hopeless atmosphere prevailing throughout most of the wards. There is no evidence in Southern State Hospital that they are treated psychiatrically or that they are regarded seriously as psychiatric cases. But there is evidence that they absorb great amounts of medical time and skill in the treatment of their physical problems. This, again, further and decisively diminishes the possible psychiatric functions of the hospital.

IDEAL AND PRACTICAL MEASURES

All the human problems of Southern State Hospital that we have attempted to outline in the present report are directly or indirectly the result of the failure of those concerned with mental health to see and act upon the growing incompatibility of centralization, large size, and the residual welfare responsibility of the hospital with the spirit and most of the techniques of modern psychiatry.

Because the basic form and characteristics of the hospital were accepted, the medical accommodation to the custodial-maintenance system of the hospital was necessary. The deceptive shift of psychiatric classification into the institutional classification and finally into the ward classification occurred. The span of control of the physician to the ward charge was left undefined, because to define it would have been to admit what actually went on and would have made any further pretense of psychiatric treatment impossible. The bad and unsympathetic relations and lack of communication between levels II and III now became functional and necessary in hospital organization, since level III performed a job which had to be done but which was in flat contradiction to the professional ideals and theoretical functions of level II. Thus for every professional failure and frustration in level II, there was one reliable scapegoat in the attendant in level III—but only as long as level II personnel kept from formal admission of the still unsolved problem with which he dealt.

It may be argued that the problems of Southern State Hospital are the result of unusually poor financing in this particular state and that if the American Psychiatric Association ratios were achieved in staffing most of the problems of the hospital would be reduced. This argument should have careful consideration.

To begin with, the literature on state hospitals in the United States indicates that Southern State Hospital is not unique in its basic problems and probably not in its internal structure. This seems to be the case in Illinois, Ohio, Michigan, and in other states where the hospitals have been better supported than they have in South State. For the United States as a whole, the survey of Deutsch, the continuing analyses of governmental survey groups, and the testimony of those working in the hospitals themselves show the same pattern of problematic internal administration, difficulty in manpower procurement in all specialties and in nonspecialist positions, poor relations with the public, and generally unsatisfactory relations with state legislative and state executive authority.[10]

Secondly, the American Psychiatric Association standards at present begin by assuming that the state hospitals as they now stand should be left more or less intact. This is qualified by the reservation that when newer hospitals are constructed they should be built nearer the communities of the patients and preferably near medical schools. How both these aims are to be accomplished is not specified.[11]

The APA standards seem to us to begin by assuming that the form and population, including the centralized location, large size, and residual welfare definition of the state hospital, are to be taken for granted. The standards therefore can be regarded as an acceptance of the basic form of the hospital as the mechanism for treatment of the mentally ill.

In the light of the present study and in view of the history of the state hospitals in the United States and South State, it seems to us that these standards do not reflect the real position of American psychiatry today. The first psychiatric operation in setting standards should be that of determining the basic desirable form of treatment for the mentally ill in terms of the current scientific conceptions and data of psychiatry. Our opinion is that the desirable form evidentally is not an isolated, concentrated, large, and impersonal institution, in which patient and practitioner are alike divorced from the normal environment of the patient. In accepting this institution, the professional must accept a situation in which medical energy is absorbed in a constant round of custodial and physical care, and worse still, in purely administrative tasks.

Far from being too high, as some of their critics have insisted, it seems to us that the APA standards are too low. They are too low in the sense that they have not insisted on a complete redefinition of state treatment of mental patients to bring this treatment into line with the modern philosophy and technique of psychiatry. A complete application of psychiatric standards would probably require the abandonment of the central hospital institution and the creation of new, localized institutions.

That such a step will be undertaken is of course too much to hope for with the present tremendous investment of capital, interests, and habits in the state hospitals of South State. Yet it is clear from a study of the problems of Southern State Hospital that in the long run the abandonment of the state hospitals might be one of the greatest humanitarian reforms and the greatest financial economy ever achieved by South State.

Before proceeding to our final conclusions on the problems of Southern State Hospital, it is desirable to present the outlines of this ideal solution, even though it cannot be regarded as practical at present.

THE IDEAL PATTERN OF STATE CARE

The present problems posed by the isolation, centralization, large size, and welfare responsibilities of the state mental hospitals in South State suggest that the ideal mental health organization should be kept in the local communities. There it should be financed jointly by state and community, in a pattern analogous to that already employed for secondary education, and should be under the direction and standard-setting control of a central state commission for mental health but with local boards of mental health.

The organization of the decentralized hospitals should be

set up to deal with prevention, treatment, and rehabilitation in continuous relations with the patient's own community. Hospitalization should be treated as an episode in these three phases. The model for this local organization, with a balance of psychiatrists, psychologists, and social workers, is already substantially completed in the present clinics and psychopathic hospital units [12] recommended by the APA, with the difference that there would no longer be a large, expensive centralized state institution to siphon public funds, attention, and responsibility away from the locality. Family, visiting-nurse, and foster-home care in the locality itself could substitute for much of the present ward care. Rehabilitation and occupational placement of patients as part of treatment could be related directly to the community from the beginning.[13]

When the decentralization of psychiatric treatment is carried out, the new local institutions should be divorced sharply from responsibility for mental deficiency, indigent illness, and the chronic physical disabilities of old age. This can be accomplished, for the older people, probably with some ultimate saving to the state and certainly with greater humanity, by the development of resources now present in the South State communities in the Old Age Assistance, Old Age and Survivors Insurance, and Federal rehabilitation programs. Funds from these programs, with small supplements, can be used to support home-care and visiting-nurse services and to supplement supervised care in private nursing homes along with realistic vocational retraining. The administration of such care should be the responsibility of employment, welfare, and health authorities, not of the psychiatric hospital. The mentally deficient who are not clearly psychotic should be defined as education, welfare, or rehabilitation responsibilities in the community, and the responsibility for their care placed where it belongs in joint state and local programs.

At present, in Southern State Hospital, the situation is clearly the reverse of the proposal above. Instead of dealing with specific mental illnesses, the hospital deals with many types of problematic people, some mentally ill, some not— at a considerable distance from their communities. It is residual, as an institution, to these local problems. The result is severance of the hospital's control over needed prevention, treatment, and rehabilitation areas, the swamping of psychiatric functions with these residual cases, and the development of the present problematic internal hospital organization as an adjustment to confused institutional purposes.

POSSIBLE REORGANIZATION OF THE HOSPITAL

An alternative to the drastic step of abandoning the centralized state hospital may in fact exist. Such an alternative would require two primary changes.

The first of these changes would be that of eliminating the conflict in the basic definition of the hospital's functions at both state and local levels of government. The basic step in this definition is that of preventing by whatever means are necessary the present use of the state mental hospital as a solution of welfare and mental deficiency problems in the local communities. The power to take such a step has never rested in South State in the hands of those charged with responsibility for the state mental hospitals. The lack of such power has perhaps contributed more than anything else to the basic difficulties of the hospitals. But such power does exist in state and local government, and it will have to be exercised to bring the hospitals into a position where they can improve their own internal structure.

Redefinition of the hospital's function by appropriate authority will sufficiently reduce the population size and responsibilities of the hospital to permit the second of the two primary changes to be undertaken.

This second change will require thorough alteration in the administrative organization of the hospital. As a redesign of the hospital, it will meet many of the problems in the institution. But it cannot be stressed too strongly that the second change will not be effective unless the population of the hospital is reduced by the previous step.

The second change requires in substance a change in the internal administrative structure of the hospital from what is termed a *scalar* to a *parallel* organization. In its essentials, this change involves running the hospital as a system of linked auxiliary services under over-all medical supervision, rather than as a simple line and staff organization, in which these services are discharged by delegation of commands to subordinates. Such a reorganization, assuming the accomplishment of the first change, should bring the form of the hospital into greater harmony with the nonauthoritarianism and insistence on individual spontaneity of modern psychiatry.

To make the purpose of this second change clear, we might begin by considering the hospital's problems of executive action and communication, which are the heart of any organization's operation.

The arrangements of status inside Southern State Hospital which lead to the barrier between the professional and working levels of the hospital can be seen as blocking both executive action and communication. Yet those arrangements cannot be broken down as the hospital is presently organized without destroying the vital distinction between the standards of the professional and the custodial situation on the wards. Even if the barrier between levels II and III were abolished by administrative action, the present social and occupational differences between the people of the two levels would speedily restore it. What is called for, if the present hospital form is retained in South State, is a direct attack on this one problem.

But before the attack can be successful in Southern State Hospital, the institutional psychiatrist will have to develop specifications for the 24-hour social situation of the institutionalized patient which are in harmony with modern psychiatry. In Southern State Hospital this problem has not even been seriously posed, and by default it has been "solved" by the ward organization.

The studies of Stanton and Schwartz in a private hospital where staff actually exceeds the APA ratios in quantity and quality show that the ward organization of what they term "the other 23 hours," is of the most crucial importance. And they do not regard the problem as entirely solved in their hospital.

It is clear enough that in Southern State Hospital some provision must be made for care of patients. But from the point of view of modern psychiatry no therapeutic results can be expected unless every aspect of this care is organized to bring the patient back to normal functioning in the outside world. This general view developed by psychiatric leaders like White, Sullivan, Myerson, Bryan, and the Menningers [14] makes it plain that no medical treatment of the mentally ill can work in any other way on the basis of present knowledge of mental illness.

But there are a number of problems which must be faced in this knowledge of mental illness. One of these problems is that the etiology of much mental disease is not known, and prevention, treatment, and rehabilitation are therefore not always certain. Among other things, this means that our entire society still lacks the main elements of a firm public health approach to the problem of mental disease: simplicity of techniques and cheapness of application.[15] Even those mental diseases which are in fact treatable and subject to remission must receive during their course some individual attention from competent professional personnel, within an environment where every obstacle to recovery is eliminated.

Given the present probabilities for mental disorder in the population and the massive existing population in the state hospitals, these specifications for treatment by modern psychiatry pose a problem of great magnitude. Since professional psychiatric training is expensive and time consuming, it is inherently scarce, even in the United States. Yet the present basic knowledge in psychiatry is not generally at a level permitting treatment on anything but an individual basis. The need for psychiatric personnel is thus immeasurably greater than supply.

Judging from the history of American state hospitals and those of South State, including Southern State Hospital, these institutions cannot be regarded as efficient organizations of this scarce psychiatric supply. In the case of Southern State Hospital, there is reason for the suspicion that the hospital itself destroys much of the effectiveness even of the small number of professionals employed there.

The problem in Southern State Hospital is that of finding a type of organization which will extend professional control into 24 hours on the ward and which will also extend the control far outward beyond present limits into the intake and discharge processes.

From an administrative point of view, Southern State Hospital is attempting to solve this problem by a structure in which the psychiatrists and generally the medical personnel occupy the positions of greatest prestige, income, and control and are essentially superior to a series of subordinate positions in levels II and III of the hospital. The examination of this formal structure shows that it is organized in an almost completely authoritarian manner. Nurses, psychologists, social workers, technicians, and the attendants are departing from this formal structure at any point where they initiate action with implications for patient treatment. Such initiation is at least formally confined to the superintendent, clinical director, and ward physicians.

Instead of employing a set of relatively autonomous auxiliary professionals and subprofessionals in its control of the internal and external relations of Southern State Hospital, the present leadership therefore necessarily works with subordinates who are supposed to follow orders and who are paid and treated in keeping with this subordination.

In the next level below, the subordinate definition as applied to the attendant is even more complete, with any initiation of action or spontaneous activity restricted by severe regulations in the formal organization.

The result of the hospital's authoritarian organization as it appears in our interview material is a progressive constriction of spontaneity and lowering of job morale as one descends the administrative hierarchy through level II. Below the barrier, in level III, the constriction of spontaneity is almost complete. And the kind and quality of personnel who are willing to accept this constriction are now present in the system.

On the basis of the present study, we feel that the cause of the inadequate executive control and communication in Southern State Hospital rests primarily in this constriction of spontaneity in the subexecutive and work levels of the hospital. This in turn results from an administrative design which places too much responsibility on one centralized, large institution and, within the institution, on one inherently scarce type of manpower. There are secondary causes at work. The problem in Southern State Hospital is worse than it should be because of the failure to provide enough personnel and facilities. More physicians, nurses, social workers, psychologists, consultants, technicians, statisticians, and others are needed. But the history and internal problems of this hospital and of similar hospitals throughout the United States suggest to us that the problem of understaffing and poor financial support are symptoms and not causes of the problems of these hospitals.

The primary cause behind these symptoms is an organization which cannot give strong status in the treatment of mental patients, first, to those who deal with the patient during the 24 hours on the ward—the attendants; and second, to those who deal with the patient's family and community in the intake and discharge processes—the social workers.

In administrative terms, failure to give strong status to these functions means that the executive can rely on none of the motivation, spontaneity, creativeness, and participation in a central shared purpose which is required by any organization to get work done. As Barnard and other students of the executive process have shown, the executive cannot function effectively in any situation without having around him a well-motivated system to execute both the spirit and the letter of his delegated authority.[16] And the constriction of responsibility and status in the operation of Southern State Hospital has long since destroyed any such possibility.

The present form of the organization of Southern State Hospital then appears to be itself an obstacle to those concerned with strengthening the psychiatric function of the hospital. This strengthening can occur only when the psychiatrist is able to delegate to first-class trained personnel the management of the patient on the ward on a 24-hour basis; and when he can also make this delegation to similar personnel in the hospital's intake, discharge, and rehabilitation processes. And the necessity for delegation will still exist if the present supply of psychiatrists is doubled or even quintupled.

The management of patients on the wards and the management of the hospital's external relations in intake and discharge are both functions requiring the highest levels of personal capacity, independent action, motivation, and training on the part of personnel; and the most continuous formal and informal communication, both between these personnel and between these personnel and the ward physicians.

The status relationships and constrictions in the hospital's present definitions of the jobs of attendants and social workers have been and are now such as to make it impossible for the hospital to find and keep personnel of the desirable quality and training. The result is that the existing levels of personal capacity, motivation, and skill at the disposal of the physician in the hospital are far below the requirements for any effective psychiatric treatment or rehabilitation.

The analysis of job specifications and salary levels in the present organization of Southern State Hospital for the attendants and social workers—the key positions through which the physician operates—shows that the attendant's job is conceived as formally about equal in status to that of a common laborer in the outside society. The status of the social worker within the hospital is formally somewhat below that of the registered nurse and about equal to that of a secretary in business or industry.

Status differences of this order cannot be changed by minor personnel procedures, such as moderate salary raises, improvement in fringe benefits, grievance procedures, or physical working conditions. If these jobs are to be staffed at the necessary level of quality, some changes in the entire organizational plan of the hospital are essential, because the present status differences are a part of this plan. The attempts at improvement in Southern State Hospital, such as the use of the team concept in treatment and the psychiatric aide–training program, have both faltered at the level of execution. In the case of the team idea, the present status differences have blocked communication between team members, because the authority organization of the total hospital is not consistent with equalitarian team procedures. The aide-training program fundamentally seeks only to improve the attendant's efficiency in carrying out orders from his superiors and presumes an educational level and status permanently far below that of most of the level II professionals. In terms of his real functions it is unrealistic.

An examination of Southern State Hospital's internal and external systems, which, it will be remembered, have grown up without much over-all planning, suggests that the major problem of applying modern psychiatric science can be met by two changes: one external, the other internal.

The desirable external changes have been partially indicated above. They include the redefinition and refinement of the hospital's intake responsibilities to eliminate or reduce the strictly mentally deficient, residual welfare, and geriatric patients.

The internal changes include two steps. One of these is a redefinition of two particular functions in the hospital; the second, an over-all increase in budget in all categories. If all the indicated changes are accomplished as they should be, the increase in budget should represent a large net saving to the state within 10 years.

The redefinition of functions within the hospital involves the two key functions of ward care and community contact for patients. In one of these functions, that of ward care, our material suggests that a radical change is necessary if this function is to serve the psychiatrist. In the other function change may be somewhat less radical.

The first and most outstanding of these changes should center around the need to improve the hospital at the main patient-contact point: the level of ward organization. Analysis of the attendant's job from any point of view shows that he bears a tremendous responsibility in ward management and that if this function breaks down, improvements elsewhere in the hospital are irrelevant. Comparative data on mental hospitals which we have cited above show that not only in Southern State Hospital but elsewhere in American state hospitals this function has been problematic throughout their history. Our material suggests that this is primarily because of the fact that the function has not been properly weighed and located in the organization of the hospital and has been traditionally staffed in a way which may destroy the treatment effectiveness of the hospital.

The redefinition of the attendant's job should be complete. It should be relocated in the hospital's administrative status structure. The redefinition should not take any form resembling the present psychiatric aide–training programs, all of which are designed, throughout the United States and clearly in Southern State Hospital, to create high-class hospital orderlies. It should be designed instead to attract and hold men and women who are of the highest possible type, recruited, trained, and treated in a way calculated to maintain high morale for an important and difficult job. The minimum specifications in qualifications and salary for these jobs should be such as to attract and hold college graduates, with training in the base sciences of psychology, sociology, anthropology and with special technical training in psychotherapy, group management, and medical nursing and administration. The attendants' positions should be set up with adequate lines of promotion to administrative positions equivalent to those of the ward physicians, and they should live off the grounds of the hospital without any of the so-called "emoluments" or food and living quarters provided for attendants at Southern State Hospital. If they eat on the hospital campus, they should eat with doctors, nurses, and other present level II personnel. They should appear and be heard during every decision point for every patient in the intake, treatment, and discharge process. Their status should be superior to that of the registered nurse and equivalent to that of the highly trained psychiatric social worker, nurse supervisor, and psychologist, and their relation to the hospital psychiatrists personally should be much closer than that of any of these personnel.

Such orderlies as the hospital must maintain should be under the direction of these attendants, and the attendant should not be confused in any way with the graduate nurse. The functions of all three are quite different. As a subexecutive in charge of the application of psychiatric science to a large annual load of patients, the attendant is functionally equivalent to a supervisor of nursing service in a general hospital, and he should never be ranked as a general-duty nurse.

The next most vital redefinition should be that of the social worker, and, following changes in the attendants' positions, changes in those of the social workers should have the next priority. Changes here are less radical in their requirements, since national standards are now clearly pointed in the necessary direction. The social worker must be given rank and treatment proportional to her responsibilities in the hospital's basic functions. Her service must be defined as essentially a relatively autonomous auxiliary service to the psychiatrist, and, like the attendant, she should be heard at every decision point in the relation of the patient to the hospital. Her abilities and capacity determine the effectiveness of the hospital in the intake and discharge process, and more than any other staff member she relates the hospital to family and community. Her present role will require redefinition for higher status and salary than those of any personnel under the psychiatrist himself, as well as a line of promotion leading to a chief of social service, equivalent to that of the ward physicians.

Both attendants and social workers should be represented on the superintendent's staff through directors of their respective services, with the present Directorship of Nursing Service for graduate nurses eliminated from the formal chart of the organization and assigned to staff position. The position of attendant, required to meet the special problems of the state mental hospital, has little relation to the position of registered nurse, trained primarily for general hospital duty, for physical illness, and this should be recognized in the hospital's basic organization. The failure to make this distinction has resulted in endless problems in Southern State Hospital.

Other changes in the hospital will of course be necessary as an adjustment to those suggested, but we are concerned here only with the main changes which now appear necessary. The acceptability of the hospital to highly trained psychiatrists and to research psychologists should be sufficiently improved by these changes to solve some of the chronic manpower supply problems in these specialties. That the relocation of attendants in the hospital's administration will itself represent a problem in training and manpower recruitment is unfortunately true. But in the light of what we have seen, this seems to be a minimum condition if effective psychiatric practice is to exist in Southern State Hospital.

With the general reorganization of present subordinate line positions in Southern State Hospital, many of the problems of the application of modern psychiatric science which we feel are inherent in the present structure of the institution will be eliminated. The change in status of the attendant and of the social worker will replace the psychiatrist's present almost nonexistent control of the ward and of the patient intake and discharge process with a capable and responsible administrative organization. A group of highly trained psychiatrists, which will probably always be relatively small in numbers (though larger than it is now), can then operate the state hospital with maximum effectiveness, because they will be delegating work to well-paid and competent auxiliaries instead of to poorly paid, untrained, and resentful subordinates.

The suggested reorganization amounts to a shift upward of the hospital's basic treatment services into a parallel status in the level just below the hospital executive system (level I). This shift brings about a fundamental redefinition of Southern State Hospital's administrative organization as a cooperative system of services, organized as an institution-wide team under the leadership of the psychiatrists. Until this complete redefinition of the position of fundamental treatment personnel in the total organization of the hospital is accomplished in levels I and II, the functional relationships in Southern State Hospital probably will remain as we found them: undefined or rigid, defensive and often hostile, and at almost every point presenting obstacles to any sustained progress in the care of the mentally ill.

APPENDIXES

References

CHAPTER ONE

[1] *Twelve Facts about Mental Illness* (New York: National Association for Mental Health, 1952), pp. 1-2. The prevalence of mental illness in the population of the United States is estimated, at 6.5 per 1,000, as of 1953. In 1952, 250,000 persons were admitted for the first time to mental hospitals in the United States. During that year, new admissions and readmissions to these hospitals totaled 390,000. Exclusive of veterans' hospitals, the number of patients in mental hospitals in the United States in 1954 was approximately 700,000. See *Care of the Long-term Patient* (Washington, D.C.: Department of Health, Education, and Welfare, 1954.)

Commitment to a mental hospital is not a problem of the few but of the many. If, as has been estimated, the average person's chance of being committed for insanity is one in twelve, the risk of being a member of a family in which such a commitment becomes necessary is certainly much greater. If we include a father, mother, one sibling, a father- and mother-in-law, a spouse, and two children as making up an average family group, it is clear that there are eight chances in twelve, or three in four, that some one of them will be committed. The average person, therefore, has much higher than an even chance of becoming more or less directly involved in the suffering and difficulties attendant upon commitment to a mental hospital.

The best discussion of the general problems of hospitals and mental illness is given in Chapter I, *Training and Research in State Mental Health Programs* (Chicago: The Council of State Governments, 1953); and throughout *The Mental Health Programs of the Forty-eight States* (Chicago: The Council of State Governments, 1950).

[2] Estimates made in 1951 of private mental care showed that a good private sanitarium might charge from $75 to $150 per week. Some institutions, even at these figures, do not provide an individual doctor of one's choice, but rather a staff doctor. In nearly every case professional fees are extra. Electroshock therapy costs between $5 and $10 but is often more. Psychiatrists' fees range from $25 to $150 a week. General examinations average about $30, and nearly all supplies are extra. See *When Mental Illness Strikes Your Family*, Public Affairs Pamphlet No. 172 (May, 1951), pp. 12–14.

[3] Myerson, Abraham, "Theory and Principles of 'Total Push' in the Treatment of Chronic Schizophrenia," *Am. J. Psychiat.*, vol. 95 (1939), pp. 1197–1204. Myerson's research was based on the use of every element in the patient's daily environment to push him out of psychotic isolation. This included general medical measures, exercise and games, diet, vitamin therapy, friendliness and sociability in dining atmosphere, grooming, and the development of a good psychological attitude toward necessary discipline. The therapy required an environment rigidly tailored to the patient's least symptom and closely supervised by the medical staff.

[4] This is reported in Barrabee, Paul S., "A Study of a Mental Hospital; the Effect of Its Social Structure on Its Functions," unpublished Ph.D. dissertation, Harvard University, Cambridge, Mass., 1951.

[5] Later reported in Galioni, E. F., F. H. Adams, and F. F. Tallman, "Intensive Treatment of Back-ward Patients—a Controlled Pilot Study," *Am. J. Psychiat.*, vol. 109 (February, 1953), pp. 576–583.

In terms of our own research experience, we found this particular study to be perhaps one of the most significant ever conducted in a state hospital.

⁶ See, for example, the discussion of basic problems in these statistics in Kramer, M., H. Goldstein, R. H. Israel, and N. A. Johnson, *An Historical Study of Disposition of First Admissions to a State Mental Hospital: The Experience of the Warren State Hospital during the Period 1916–50*, Public Health Monograph No. 32, Public Health Service, U.S. Department of Health, Education, and Welfare (Washington, D.C.: U.S. Government Printing Office, 1955). See also *Proceedings of the Second Conference of Mental Hospital Administrators and Statisticians* (Washington, D.C.: Federal Security Agency, Public Health Service, 1953), particularly pp. 1–26; 28–31; 51–62; 66–74.

⁷ This comparison was suggested originally by the very stimulating paper by C. A. Bonner, "Mental Hospital Employees, Their Importance in Future Mental Hospital Betterment," *Am. J. Psychiat.*, vol. 105 (April, 1949), pp. 669–672.

⁸ Much of this literature is reviewed in Schwartz, Charlotte Green, *Rehabilitation of Mental Hospital Patients*, Public Health Monograph No. 17, Public Health Service, U.S. Department of Health, Education, and Welfare (Washington, D.C.: U.S. Government Printing Office, 1953).

⁹ Weinberg, S. Kirson, *Society and Personality Disorders* (New York: Prentice-Hall, Inc., 1952), Chapters XVI, XVII. Weinberg reported on his research in detail in a paper read at the University of Chicago in 1947. The study by A. H. Stanton and Morris S. Schwartz, *The Mental Hospital* (New York: Basic Books, Inc., 1954), was of particular importance.

¹⁰ Rowland, H., "Interaction Processes in a State Mental Hospital," *Psychiatry*, vol. 1 (February, 1938), pp. 323–337, and "Friendship Patterns in a State Mental Hospital," *Psychiatry*, vol. 2 (May, 1939), pp. 326–373.

¹¹ Dunham, H. Warren, and Bernard N. Meltzer, "Predicting Length of Hospitalization of Mental Patients," *Am. J. Sociol.*, vol. 52 (September, 1946), pp. 123–131.

[12] Bateman, J. F., and H. Warren Dunham, "The State Mental Hospital as a Specialized Community Experience," *Am. J. Psychiat.*, vol. 105 (December, 1948), pp. 445–448.

[13] Compare here the observation of Kramer and his colleagues that there is no control in present reporting techniques which will permit this effect to be measured (Kramer, *et al., op. cit.*).

[14] Dr. Dunham served as research consultant to the present project during 1952.

[15] Bateman and Dunham, *op. cit.*, pp. 447–448.

[16] Weinberg, *op. cit.*, Chapter XVII.

[17] Lemert, E. M., *Social Pathology* (New York: McGraw-Hill Book Company, Inc., 1951), Chapter 11. Dr. Maurice Grimes has published a study of this aspect of the hospital which is the most creative to come to our attention. More than any other physician in the field of psychiatry, Dr. Grimes (a former director of the mental hospital survey for the American Medical Association) senses the need for a broader attack on the problem of the hospital than that through the one discipline of medicine. His work is so original, in fact, that it has been most unjustly neglected. See his *When Minds Go Wrong* (Chicago: published by the author, 1951), particularly the final chapter outlining the ideal treatment for the mentally ill.

[18] Barrabee, *op. cit.*

[19] This ranking is computed from Tables 20 and 26, *The Mental Health Programs of the Forty-eight States.*

[20] References to the special studies of these investigators, appearing in *Psychiatry* originally, are in the combined report of their research (Stanton and Schwartz, *op. cit.*). The analysis by the authors of the institutional problems in their private hospital (Chapter 7) and of personnel problems (Chapter 9) may be compared with those in the present report. The similarity of these problems strongly suggests that many of the serious problems of the state hospital are inherent in the nature of mental institutionalization rather than simply in the financial difficulties of the state hospitals.

[21] The penetrating study by Dr. Greenblatt and his associates of the organization of three hospitals in Massachusetts has provided new and significant evidence for the existence and effects of this special social organization. See Greenblatt, Milton, Richard York, and Esther Lucile Brown, in collaboration with Robert W. Hyde, *From Custodial to Therapeutic Care in Mental Hospitals* (New York: Russell Sage Foundation, 1955). The case study of Southern State Hospital was finished before publication of the first report on these Massachusetts studies. Since these studies were conducted independently of each other, the convergence of the Greenblatt research findings in hospital social structure on some of the findings of the Southern State Hospital study has been gratifying.

CHAPTER TWO

[1] The study by Kramer and his colleagues of the Warren State Hospital experience with patients is one of the most reliable available, for several reasons. Two of the main reasons are the length of the reporting period for which statistics are available, and the comparative accuracy and care with which these statistics have been kept in the case of this hospital.

In Southern State Hospital it is not possible to make reliable trend studies in first admissions, discharges, or any other type of statistics. The reasons for this are that the categories used in reporting statistics have changed in meaning, many of the patients are not diagnosed until they have left the hospital (that is, they are never really diagnosed), and, in an unknown percentage of cases, readmissions are given new admission numbers because of lax administrative control.

Using the decennial census civilian population of Apr. 1, 1940, as the standard population on the Warren first admissions, Kramer and his colleagues calculated an annual age-adjusted first-admission rate for all mental disorders. This rate increased for Warren from 51.6 per 100,000 population in 1916 to 1925 to 76.5 in 1946 to 1950 (an increase of 48 per cent). All age groups showed increased percentages through the years, with the age group seventy-five years and over showing the largest increase, of 126 per cent. In the functional psychoses, age-adjusted rates increased from 16.5 in 1916 to 1925 to 28.0 in 1946 to 1950, an increase of 70 per cent. Admission rates for mental diseases of the senium in the early period were 9.1; in the later 18.1, an increase of nearly 100 per cent. The study shows that the patients coming into Warren State Hospital have a higher probability of leaving the hospital alive in the later than in the earlier period, but evidence that this is because of the effect of the hospitalization itself is not conclusive, since data on the possible changes in the character of the contributing population are not available. See Kramer, H., H. Goldstein, *et al.*, "An Historical Study of Dispositions of First Admissions to a State Mental Hospital: The Experience of the Warren State Hospital during the Period 1916–1950," Public Health Monograph No. 32, Public Health Service, U.S. Department of Health, Education, and Welfare (Washington, D.C.: U.S. Government Printing Office, 1955).

See also Malzberg, Benjamin, "Rates of Discharge and Rates of Mortality among First Admissions to the New York Civil State Hospitals," *Mental Hygiene*, vol. 37 (May, 1953), pp. 619–654, and the discussion by R. H. Felix, "Uniform Mental Hospital Statistics" (mimeographed, U.S. Public Health Service, National Institute of Mental Health), presented at the National Governors' Conference on Mental Health, Detroit, Mich., Feb. 9, 1954.

[2] See Deutsch, Albert, *The Mentally Ill in America* (New York: Columbia University Press, 1949).

[3] *The Mental Health Programs of the Forty-eight States* (Chicago: The Council of State Governments, 1950), pp. 30–33.

[4] An interesting feature of the advanced psychiatric ideas of Rush and Tuke is their association with quite primitive and inaccurate concepts of physical medicine. Rush, for example, believed firmly in the practice of blood-letting therapeutics, as did other physicians of his time. The notion that modern psychiatry, with its newer terms, such as *milieu therapy* and *total push*, and

its emphasis on "interpersonal relations," has in fact developed something really new in the philosophy and practice of mental treatment needs examination by a competent medical historian. See Hamilton, Samuel W., "The History of American Mental Hospitals," in *One Hundred Years of American Psychiatry* (New York: Columbia University Press, 1944).

The reader may with profit compare the substance of the ideas of Tuke, Rush, and Pinel, and even those of the ancient Greek physicians with the treatment conceptions set forth in any standard psychiatric textbook today. This is not to imply that the antiquity of some modern psychiatric ideas is discreditable. But it does suggest that if these ideas are empirically correct, they must wait in their application until the social sciences perfect techniques for the scientific control of treatment environments. At the present time it is clear enough that neither the psychiatrist nor the social scientist has anything approaching such control.

[5] Deutsch, *op. cit.*, Chapter VI.

[6] The historian, Richard Shryock, has shown the same general trend in the understanding and treatment of the tuberculosis problem in the eighteenth and nineteenth centuries. See his *The Development of Modern Medicine* (Philadelphia: University of Pennsylvania Press, 1936), pp. 312–313. Some of the common problems in human care throughout the world which are involved in the treatment of mental illness are surveyed by Maxwell Jones in his *Rehabilitation* (Geneva: World Health Organization, 1952).

CHAPTER THREE

[1] The survey by H. M. Hurd *et al.*, *The Institutional Care of the Insane in the United States and Canada*, Vol. III (Baltimore: Johns Hopkins Press, 1916) shows that Southern State Hospital had not been established 10 years before it was badly run down and in an unsanitary condition. It was also overcrowded.

[2] These hospitals were recommended to meet the committee's strong demand that earlier attention be given mental disease.

[3] Though the blame was placed on the legislature, it is quite

difficult to determine just who would have advised the legislative body on the correct organization. If blame must be placed, it should probably rest on the executive branch of the state government and on the hospital superintendents. The habit of placing the blame for all the shortcomings of the state hospitals on the legislature is so firmly ingrained in South State that it becomes almost a ritual at times. One reason for this is obvious. This scapegoating permits the blame to rest on a great many individuals, many of them with a short term of office, and thus diffuses the responsibility for medical and political leadership in a fashion which makes it impossible for it to be pinned down. We found early in our study that until 1950, the medical and lay administrators in the South State system had never developed any system-wide plan for the hospitals, even in many clinical areas. We were told that this, too, was the fault of the legislature.

[4] U.S. Public Health Service, Washington, D.C., 1943.

[5] Gammon, Ralph, *A Survey of the Mental Institutions of South State* (Washington, D.C.: U.S. Public Health Service, 1950).

[6] "Infancy," rather than being nonexistent. Modern psychiatry does have certain partially tested theories of etiology and can achieve a number of empirically demonstrable results from certain operations. It has developed what Malamud terms a *broad foundation* of treating the patient's personality by study of his life problems, his historical background, and his social and psychological needs. Readjustment of his environment and reeducation of the patient may at times be quite effective. See Hamilton, Samuel W., *One Hundred Years of American Psychiatry* (New York: Columbia University Press, 1944), pp. 310–311. At the time the state hospitals were set up, psychiatry was not even sure of this modest foundation. Even at present this base cannot be compared with medical achievements in the control of infectious diseases, with general surgery and pathology, or with chemotherapy. The scientific position from which the psychiatrist can conduct treatment or on which he can ground his recommenda-

tions for the organization of treatment is obviously somewhat different from that of other medical specialists. See Felix, R. H., and Morton Kramer, "Research in the Epidemiology of Mental Illness," *Public Health Repts. U.S.*, vol. 67 (February, 1952), pp. 152–160.

[7] *Constitution* of South State, Article X, Section 6.

[8] Deutsch, Albert, *The Mentally Ill in America*, 2d ed. (New York: Columbia University Press, 1949), Chapter V.

[9] Dr. S. Weir Mitchell, at that time a leader in the medical profession, criticized the institutional physicians in the hospitals in his address of 1894 to the American Medico-Psychological Association as professionally isolated and lagging in their development of truly therapeutic institutions (see Hamilton, *op. cit.*, p. 167). Fifty-five years later, another leader in the medical profession leveled almost identical charges. See Proceedings of the First Annual Institute of the American Psychiatric Association, *Better Care in Mental Hospitals* (Washington, D.C.: American Psychiatric Association, 1949), pp. 62 ff.

A review of the professional status of the state hospital by the Council of State Governments in 1953 confirms this. See Chapters 1 to 6, *Training and Research in Mental Health Programs* (Chicago: 1953).

CHAPTER FOUR

[1] The American Psychiatric Association standard, which theoretically determines the rated capacity of the hospital, allows 70 square feet for each sleeping patient and 40 square feet of dayroom space. Actually, the "rated capacity" used above, as taken from the records of Southern State Hospital, refers to a standard of 40 square feet of sleeping space, and this, of course, usually is cut down by placing mattresses on the floor to accommodate the excess patients in many wards. In the fall of 1952, Southern State Hospital was 60 per cent below the 70-foot American Psychiatric Association standard. *Capacity* has always been a flexible term in state hospitals. See Supplement No. 1, July, 1952,

to *Standards for Psychiatric Hospitals and Clinics* (Washington, D.C.: American Psychiatric Association, Mental Hospital Service, November, 1951).

[2] There is a wide and confusing variation in these figures over each 12-month period. The over-all turnover rate annually for employees (arithmetic mean) is 68 per cent for the period 1949 to 1952. And the rate varies for certain official and unofficial groups in the hospital in many ways which will be considered in later chapters. During 1951 to 1952, the turnover rate in attendants as a group was about 80 per cent. But the senior attendants had the lowest turnover rate of any group in the hospital. In the figures given in Chapter Four, the reader should keep in mind that personnel quotas refer to "positions authorized and filled sometime during a year," not to a permanent employee group.

These excessive turnover rates are the rule rather than the exception in most state hospitals. S. K. Jaffary has reported rates for Illinois institutions as high as 100 per cent over long periods. See his *The Mentally Ill and Public Provision for Their Care in Illinois* (Chicago: The University of Chicago Press, 1942), pp. 27–38. See also Blain, Daniel, editor, Proceedings of the First Mental Hospital Institute, *Better Care in Mental Hospitals* (Washington, D.C.: American Psychiatric Association, 1949), Section 4. For the United States as a whole, in 1949, state hospitals all averaged high turnover rates as compared with other places of public employment. The turnover of physicians was 28 per cent; graduate nurses, 34 per cent; social workers, 17 per cent; attendants, 55 per cent. See *The Mental Health Programs of the Forty-eight States* (Chicago: The Council of State Governments, 1950), pp. 156–157.

[3] Sampling was necessary in studying the attendants in general because of their large number and their rapid turnover. Our intensive study was concentrated on the group of relatively permanent attendants.

[4] Ten per cent more of the attendants was made up of college students—an atypical group because of Southern State Hospital's

location near Millville Liberal Arts College, with 4,000 students. A miscellaneous group of occupations was represented by the remaining 5 per cent, who included a grocery clerk, mechanic, leather goods worker, etc.

[5] See Note 1, Chapter Two, above for references to statistical studies of this accumulation.

[6] This point will be taken up again briefly in the concluding chapter. The relation of medical authority and the usual line and staff authority in Southern State Hospital is a critical problem.

[7] Our only way of determining the facts about these job developments was to interview the older employees and former employees. Administrative records in the hospital are often deliberately deceptive, since historically the superintendents have had to smuggle necessary jobs into the hospital under other classifications than those needed. Milkmen and occupational therapists have been masked under titles such as Attendant and Clerk-typist. This practice indicates a lack of communication between the executive branch of the state government and the real needs of the hospital executives. It has also led to endless confusion in the relations of line supervisors to one another in level II, as when the psychologist finds himself without a secretary because she has been required by the Director of Nursing Service to attend a meeting of attendants because she is officially employed as an attendant, rather than as a secretary.

CHAPTER FIVE

[1] This type of commitment was provided in the *South State Revised Civil Statutes* of 1920. These voluntary patients must be discharged at the end of 90 days, or within 3 days after giving notice to the Superintendent in writing of their desire to be released. More than three-fourths of the commitments of this type to Southern State Hospital, according to the Social Service Department, are of persons desiring treatment for chronic alcoholism.

[2] Article 1, Section 15, *Constitution* of South State, as amended

in 1935; Article 31930–1, Section 1a, *South State Revised Civil Statutes,* 1925. The superintendents at Southern State Hospital tried to encourage this type of commitment to avoid the use of the indefinite term *jury commitment.* This represents a medical effort to get around the generally unpleasant and unnecessary use of juries in "insanity trials." At the time of our study, Southern State Hospital was one of the only three remaining state mental institutions in the United States requiring trial by jury for permanent or indefinite commitment.

[3] This action may be carried out by referral by a jury in the county in which Southern State Hospital is located.

[4] This type of commitment is of doubtful legality in South State.

[5] In Southern State Hospital this function is taken over by a special field representative, to whom the social service worker introduces the relative.

[6] The prospects for such tests are really not this good, since it has been very difficult to secure competent psychologists in Southern State Hospital. Psychological testing is essentially a prescription service in this hospital, not a routine practice with each incoming patient.

[7] This percentage is computed on first admissions in Southern State Hospital for the same year over the past 15 years.

[8] The social service department and other workers in the hospital continually attempt to give the discharged patients this service, but for reasons which will appear below they are unable to do so on any effective sustained basis.

[9] These duties are given in more detail in Chapter Ten.

[10] System II is perhaps more important in the organization of the hospital than this statement indicates. Personnel in this system perform much of the hospital's unofficial public relations activities. The social workers and clinical staff, for example, are a vital element in relations with patients' families. Also, the social workers and clerical staff carry out a vast amount of interagency correspondence and management in behalf of patients. All mem-

bers of this level are essential in in-service training programs in the hospital, since by experience and educational qualifications they are capable of serving as instructors. At the time of this investigation, both attendant-training and nurse-training programs were being carried out by members of this system.

[11] *Health Manpower Source Book,* Section 1, Physicians, Preliminary (Washington, D.C.: Federal Security Agency, Public Health Service, May, 1952), p. 20. This restriction has become part of the official position of the American Psychiatric Association. See Point 3, "Fundamental Principles," *Standards for Psychiatric Hospitals and Clinics* (Washington, D.C.: American Psychiatric Association, Mental Hospital Service, 1951).

CHAPTER SIX

[1] One common bond between the office clerical employees and junior executives and the business group clerical employees and junior executives is their jealousy of the status and of the higher salaries paid to the professional group. The salaries of the registered nurses, for example, are almost a third higher than those of the executives immediately below the Business Manager.

[2] In 1930, the Bruns Associates investigators reported on the employees as follows:

A very large number of the employees have been there several years, have intermarried, and really know no other home. This results in a tolerance of working and living conditions and of wage rates that would otherwise be impossible. It also builds up a loyalty to the service that would be difficult if not impossible to attain under different circumstances. Despite these valuable features, this type of organization has its own weaknesses, the most serious of which is that in the absence of a well-understood formal structure, it tends to continue the bad traditions and precedents as well as the good, and makes the absorption of new employees a difficult matter.

After a lapse of about 20 years, we were unable to find that there had been much change in this situation. Perhaps the main improvement was that better jobs outside the hospital had drained all but a residue of the older attendant group out of the hospital. But this drainage had not benefited the hospital, since the present organization actually still requires the older attendant type for its operation.

[3] This failure is aggravated by another type of barrier which seems to exist between the social workers and physicians on the team. Ninety per cent of the social workers felt that they had no standing with the physicians, that their work was not used or appreciated. Most physicians seem to use the social workers mainly as case-history stenographers. Though some of the physicians understood quite well that there were more effective uses of social workers, they also had to have completed case histories for the records.

[4] In practice, we have found that most Southern State Hospital superintendents have worked hard to carry out this obligation, which is probably the most difficult task laid on them, or on any class of institutional heads employed by the state. We have some reason to believe that the superintendents who work at this problem the most vigorously have taken on a man-killing job—and one which they cannot carry out successfully, given the nature of the institution. The Superintendent is continually torn between his obligations as a professional man and as an institutional executive.

[5] Conferences on budgetary and fiscal matters, space finding and utilization, and personnel matters in the business and medical organization of the hospital, and inspection of equipment took up another 50 per cent of the superintendent's time. About 10 per cent was devoted to correspondence, and another 10 per cent to miscellaneous paper work. This schedule left the superintendent with about 10 per cent of his day to devote to medical problems, including an occasional hasty inspection of the wards and

attendance at the medical staff meetings dealing with particular patients.

[6] Even in what is one of the best mental hospitals in the United States (Boston Psychopathic Hospital), Paul Barrabee found that the attempt to organize the hospital along totally therapeutic lines threw the hospital into administrative confusion. See Barrabee, Paul S., "A Study of a Mental Hospital; the Effect of Its Social Structure on Its Functions," unpublished Ph.D. dissertation, Harvard University, Cambridge, Mass., 1951, Chapters I, II, III.

[7] In each of the cases of long tenure since 1900 we were able to interview enough employees who had worked under the superintendent to be certain that the practices of their administrations were of a distinctly military character.

[8] The Medical Director of the State Hospital Board considered this problem the first and most acute in his administration of the system. See also *Better Care in Mental Hospitals*, Proceedings of the First Mental Hospital Institute (Washington, D.C.: American Psychiatric Association, 1949), Section E. Testimony in these proceedings leaves little doubt that the superintendency of Southern State Hospital is not atypical in its difficulties.

[9] This lack was the most frequent complaint of all personnel in the system. In the case of the upper-level professional people this was expressed in a frustration over failure to be able to perform necessary services to their clientele and in anxiety over loss of professional experience and standing. In the case of the lower-level personnel, such as the attendants, it was expressed in terms of immediate personal resentment that "one's efforts aren't appreciated." Modern personnel studies like those at the Hawthorne works of the Western Electric Company suggest that this difficulty is one of the most serious any social organization can have. See Homans, George C., *The Human Group* (New York: Harcourt, Brace and Company, Inc., 1950), Chapters 3 to 5.

[10] Such a personnel situation is, of course, intolerable. The details of a study made during the past year by the personnel

department of the hospital over the 11-month period from January to December, 1952, showed 528 resignations out of a total number of positions of 651. Of this group of 528, a total of 447, or 85 per cent, resigned to take "better jobs." About 8 per cent of the 447 quit inside the first 24 hours; 20 quit inside 30 days; and most of the remainder quit within 90 days.

[11] The American Psychiatric Association standards for 1951 are higher. See *Standards for Psychiatric Hospitals and Clinics* (Washington, D.C.: American Psychiatric Association, 1951, revised).

[12] This particular clinical director resigned after about 14 months of service.

[13] There is good argument for assigning research to a fourth special officer in the mental hospital. The range of research projects in modern psychiatry includes every specialty from biochemistry to the latest theories in psychoanalysis and group dynamics. The recent developments in anthropology and sociology require research using complex statistical techniques. The evaluation and supervision of this research require a competent administrator with an unusual background in biology, medicine, and the social sciences. It seems likely that a fourth function will emerge here in the further organization of the Clinical Director's duties.

[14] As one example, the consulting surgeon in 1951 pointed out that consultative medical services to the Southern State Hospital had never been organized in any systematic way.

[15] We are speaking here only of the internal therapeutic problem. The hospital is even less favorably organized to accomplish external therapeutic, or rehabilitative, relationships with family and community required by modern psychiatric milieu therapy.

[16] Our interview data leave no doubt of this frustration and irritation. In the cases of two of our clinical directors, who spent about a year each in the position, professional frustration was clearly the main complaint. Several superintendents have seen and reported on the difficulties of the Clinical Director.

CHAPTER SEVEN

[1] This superiority is indicated by the double line on the organization chart in Figure 2. The social rank of the physician outside the hospital is also higher. [See the evaluations for the United States in North, C. C., and Hatt, P. K., "Jobs and Occupations: A Popular Evaluation," *Opinion News* (Sept. 1, 1947), pp. 3–13.]

[2] Among these connections are the new position of chaplain and responsibility for certain routine and special service functions, such as provision of drugs, laboratory, radiology, neurology and pathology department, the white and colored infirmaries, and the organization of exterior medical-consultative services. Except for the position of chaplain, which was too new to repay analysis, these connections are tangential to the hospital's main psychiatric function. Such material as we did gather shows that these connections have at least the common problems of poor administrative control, communication blockage, and understaffing, and cannot generally be considered of any outstanding assistance to the resident physician in his job.

[3] The term *affiliate* means that the hospital was affiliated with complete nurse-training schools elsewhere to give a 12-week course in psychiatric hospital nursing to be started in the fall of 1952.

[4] The psychiatric aide training program was separate from the affiliate program, directed toward the attendants, with a 2-year program leading to a certificate as Psychiatric Aide. It was being conducted in cooperation with a state junior college. About ten students will graduate in 1953, and another thirty are enrolled.

[5] See *The Mental Health Programs of the Forty-eight States* (Chicago: The Council of State Governments, 1950).

[6] *Standards for Psychiatric Hospitals and Clinics* (Washington, D.C.: American Psychiatric Association, 1951), p. 10. These standards require one psychiatric social worker for each 80 new admissions each year, and one to each 60 patients on convalescent status or family care. The ratio in Southern State Hospital during

most of its history has been between one to 500 and one to 900, and very few of these workers were trained.

[7] The remaining two were graduates of recognized foreign medical schools but were not licensed to practice medicine in South State.

[8] As a rule American psychiatrists certified in their specialty do not practice in state hospitals. The percentage in all these hospitals of diplomates among members of the staff in 1947 was only 16 per cent. These were mainly administrators. See *Patients in Mental Institutions, 1947* (Washington, D.C.: Federal Security Agency, 1947), Table 4, p. 12.

[9] Even in New York there were only 480 psychiatrists to serve a population of 14,830,192. See *Health Manpower Source Book*, Section 1, Physicians (Washington, D.C.: Federal Security Agency, U.S. Public Health Service Publication No. 63, Preliminary, May, 1952), p. 26. See also *Building America's Health*, Report of the President's Commission on the Health Needs of the Nation, vol. 2 (Washington, D.C.: Government Printing Office, 1952), pp. 183–185. This shortage also applies to physicians generally. The state hospitals in the United States are estimated to need 2,000 more doctors. See *ibid.*, vol. 2, p. 193.

[10] *Standards for Psychiatric Hospitals and Clinics*, p. 7.

[11] This period was selected because of relatively reliable records kept during that time.

[12] One superintendent remarked that he thoroughly regretted the amount of time his physicians had to spend in keeping records of their work and in analyzing administrative reports. He pointed out, however, that much of this would be unnecessary if it were not continually necessary to have some kind of record for the men who would succeed them. "If they ever stayed," he said, "they could keep most of it in their heads."

[13] These are functions which require training and initiative. Properly speaking, they are not performed under the physician's direction at all, but as an independent auxiliary service to him. See DeWitt, Henrietta B., "The Function of the Social Worker

in the Total Treatment Program in a State Mental Hospital," *Am. J. Psychiat.*, vol. 105 (October, 1948), pp. 298–303. See also Dr. A. H. Eichert's comments on this paper, indicating the effectiveness of DeWitt's concept of auxiliary service in the use of social workers in his hospital.

[14] In actual fact certain types of patients on the wards play an active part in diagnosis and treatment.

[15] The employees at this level are sociable and friendly with each other on an informal basis. The reference here is to cooperation and communication on the level of job performance. Without executive coordination in level I, this cannot be expected.

[16] *Better Care in Mental Hospitals*, Proceedings of the First Mental Hospital Institute (Philadelphia: American Psychiatric Association, 1949), pp. 153–159. See also *Annual Report* (Albany, N.Y.: Department of Mental Hygiene, State of New York, Mar. 13, 1950), pp. 204–210. The figure of fifty-four for Southern State Hospital assumes the ratio used by New York in calculating the rural case load for New York State.

CHAPTER EIGHT

[1] See the analyses of William Bryan in *Administrative Psychiatry* (New York: W. W. Norton & Company, Inc., 1936), and of Maurice Grimes in *When Minds Go Wrong* (Chicago: published by the author, 1951).

[2] Compare the categories used in *Diagnostic and Statistical Manual* (Washington, D.C.: American Psychiatric Association, 1952) with those used by Bryan and Grimes in the works cited in Note 1. Both Bryan and Grimes were technically trained psychiatrists, but they employed a different frame of reference when discussing procedure with hospital patients. There is of course very little doubt that behind these two types of classification a deeper problem exists: the relation of psychiatry to two types of clientele—one dependent, institutionalized, and of relatively lower social status; the other independent, uninstitutionalized, and of relatively higher status. Redlich points out the power-

ful effects of social definitions, over which neither psychiatrist nor patient has explicit control, in developing a somewhat coercive definition of "adjustment" as "normal" for the first of these groups, and a more permissive one of creativity, spontaneity, and fulfillment of potential for the latter. See Redlich, F. C., "The Concept of Normality," *Am. J. Psychotherapy*, vol. 6 (July, 1952), pp. 551–576. See also Schaffer, Leslie, and Jerome K. Myers, "Psychotherapy and Social Stratification," *Psychiatry*, vol. 17 (February, 1954), pp. 83–93.

[3] The danger and difficulty of handling mental patients have been exaggerated. But it is well not to fall into the opposite error and ignore the potential danger and difficulty entirely. In every private or public mental hospital today, the mentally ill must usually be handled in relatively large numbers. Some of the treatment for all the patients has to be determined by the extreme possibility of violence to self or others which is present in only a small fraction of patients. Control or surveillance must always exist in such care. This is precisely the reason why the organization of this control should never be left without professional planning—as it has been in Southern State Hospital.

[4] On two of the male wards, however—both under charge attendants with more than 10 years of experience—there was an organization which resembled that of the female wards. In these male wards, the charge attendants clearly played a rather gentle pseudopaternal role, and with a good deal of success as far as the apparent tone of relationships went in the ward. In neither case, however, was there any particular reluctance to employ punishment if necessary.

[5] The attendant, male or female, has a formidable reward and punishment system to back up his authority, which will be considered below. Among other devices the female attendants could and did use the extreme ones of seclusion and shock listing.

[6] It will be remembered that the Clinical Director usually handles physician assignments. The high mobility and uncertain administrative functions of the Clinical Director's position often

resulted in very lax supervision of the physician assignment function. Junior doctors habitually received the worst wards and the heaviest routine loads, since there was an informal seniority system at work. Some doctors received lighter loads in consideration for infirmary assignments or special duties, such as pathology, which were sometimes not regarded by the other doctors as justifying relief.

[7] It should be emphasized that this was not done in a spirit of spite or with the idea of hurting the doctor's work. The feeling tone of the attendants in this matter was one of tolerant pity for the doctor who was strictly "psychiatric" (and of outstanding suspicion if he happened to be psychoanalytically oriented). With the doctors who were experimenting, there was a feeling of watchful patience until they got over it and settled down.

This situation is not so damaging to medical authority as might be supposed. Many of the doctors who were "strict" or who were experimenting, were highly respected on the basis of their skills in various aspects of physical medicine, and all of them were respected in a general way. The attendant view of this group as institutional psychiatrists, however, was that while they were undoubtedly highly intelligent and educated men, they simply did not understand as yet what could and could not be done with patients in Southern State Hospital.

CHAPTER NINE

[1] In theory each shift of attendants is under a Charge Attendant, but all three shifts are usually supervised by one of the senior charge attendants, who is the informal supervisor of the ward (and, at times, of two or three wards). The chief charge is usually the first day-charge, who informally controls all shifts. He is almost without exception the attendant best acquainted with the ward physician, who usually makes his rounds during the day-man's shift. In Southern State Hospital the third, or night, shift is generally supposed to have at least two attendants on duty with the charge, but turnover and shortage of personnel often

reduce this shift, as they often reduce the other shifts, to one man.

[2] The Supervisor is clearly outside the individual line system of the physician to the ward for any regular supervisory functions. But in the hospital as a whole, the supervisors are informally much more important than this statement indicates. Informally they are very close to the Superintendent, and at the same time their informal relations and functions in connection with the ward social system are intimate and far-reaching, because they are part of the senior attendants' culture. Administratively speaking, however, they are of no supervisory utility to the doctor in his relations with the charge attendants.

[3] See Chapter Three.

[4] The only positions in the hospital with comparable average length of service were some of the business office positions, many of which were filled with former attendants who had risen to them over relatively long periods. The route into the business side of the hospital is almost the only line of promotion we could find for the attendant.

[5] All programs increasing state hospital standards actually seem to increase personnel recruitment problems when higher standards are set. See Kline, Nathan S., "Characteristics and Screening of Unsatisfactory Psychiatric Attendants and Attendant-applicants," *Am. J. Psychiat.*, vol. 106 (February, 1950), pp. 569–574. *Cf.*, also, the discussion in *Training and Research in State Mental Health Programs* (Chicago: The Council of State Governments, 1953), pp. 96–104. The aide–training programs work best in mental hospitals with an adequate over-all personnel division. Southern State Hospital had nothing which could be considered a division of personnel.

[6] This is a general situation throughout most of the United States. See *Building America's Health*, Report of the President's Commission on the Health Needs of the Nation, five volumes (Washington, D.C.: Government Printing Office, 1952) vol. III, Table 271, and vol. II, pp. 122–123. Like physicians, nurses are in essentially inelastic national supply.

[7] The surprising success of the Stockton, Calif., program for "back-ward," or almost hopeless, cases seems to have occurred mainly because it achieved a "therapeutic atmosphere." An analysis of the Stockton procedure shows that this atmosphere was achieved in large part by destroying the status barrier and bringing professionals and attendants into close cooperation. *The physician was reaching the patient by doing therapy with the employees without attempting direct treatment.* See Galioni, E. F., et al., "Intensive Treatment of Back-ward Patients—a Controlled Pilot Study," *Am. J. Psychiat.*, vol. 109 (February, 1953), pp. 576–583. But to achieve the Stockton effect on a permanent basis, permanent changes are needed in Southern State Hospital. Dr. Robert W. Hyde has opened what may be the most promising line of attack on the problem of the mental hospital attendant. See his *Experiencing the Patient's Day: A Manual for Psychiatric Hospital Personnel* (New York: G. P. Putnam's Sons, 1955).

[8] The literature on state hospitals in the United States suggests to us that this is probably the central problem in these hospitals in the use of professional personnel. It is one which has been in effect for a very long time. There is an almost identical professional difficulty for the psychiatrist who works in the prison. See Powelson, Harvey, and Reinhard Bendix, "Psychiatry in Prison," in Rose, Arnold, editor, *Mental Health and Mental Disorder* (New York: W. W. Norton & Company, Inc., 1955), Chapter 31.

[9] This attitude is an important part of the motivation of the older attendants, particularly of the women. Many of these attendants are devout members of rural Protestant churches and tend regularly to frame their conceptions in terms of Christian religious duty. These attendants are largely responsible for most of the daily acts of kindliness and thoughtfulness we found in Southern State Hospital. They arranged birthday parties and bought presents for patients without families, and they often gave money to patients for small canteen purchases.

[10] There is considerable negative control by upper patient group members of this second group. Since the upper group monopo-

lizes most of the ward privileges, conformity by the second-group members is necessary if they want any of these privileges. Members of this second group who rise to the first actually seem to do so through the judgment of the upper group of patients rather than through the judgment of attendants or physicians.

CHAPTER TEN

[1] These terms, *admission* and *maximum-security*, are somewhat deceptive. Southern State Hospital does not have an actual admission service. The admission wards are simply those which are kept empty enough by transfers to receive newly admitted patients on a 24-hour basis. They are also used in showing many visitors the hospital. The maximum-security wards have been and to some extent still are substitutes in Southern State Hospital for a criminally insane hospital which the state does not have. Maximum-security wards are used both for the dangerous or potentially dangerous mentally ill and for prisoners convicted legally of being insane at the time of a crime or at the time of trial and whose mental condition has undergone no remission.

[2] The routine records include (1) a daily ward summary form showing ward capacity, number of beds, and number and physical condition of patients, for administrative report to the Superintendent's office; (2) an individual progress sheet, on which current information on the patient's condition is kept. When filled, these sheets go to the permanent file of the patient in the hospital's central file; (3) the record book, in which individual treatment records are maintained. In a thousand of the progress sheets we found only thirty-six containing anything except routine information.

[3] This practice, like the organization it is associated with, is at least 50 or 60 years old in Southern State Hospital. Old attendants told us of many other techniques employed to get rid of the "wrong sort" of attendants, ranging from mild to strong direct intimidation to sabotage of the attendant's work. These tech-

niques worked vastly better, we were told, in the old days when everybody lived at the hospital.

⁴ See Roethlisberger, F. J., "The Foreman: Master and Victim of Double Talk," in Hoslett, S. D., editor, *Human Factors in Management* (Parkville, Missouri: Park College Press, 1946).

⁵ The hospital has a psychiatric aide-training program, but it is designed not so much to train and familiarize the employee with the realities of his job as to "improve" him in background, in terms of rather vague professional specifications about his job. The aide-training program is regarded as "theoretical" and largely irrelevant by 80 per cent of the older attendants. Hyde has described the problem in Southern State Hospital and probably for hospitals in the rest of the United States when he comments as follows on aide training in Boston Psychopathic Hospital:

> It was with the thought of educating the attendant in psychiatric lore that I embarked some years ago upon classes for the attendants. They were unsuccessful. The basic principles of psychiatry and psychiatric nursing seemed to have little meaning or inspiration to the group, myself included. I found that for the most part I was peddling an old vocabulary, very poorly defined from the standpoint of the actual experiences in which attendants were immersed. I found, however, that whenever digressions occurred into the attendants' actual experiences with the patients, I began to learn a lot about an aspect of psychiatry that receives scant mention in the conventional textbooks. [From Hyde, Robert W., M.D., *Experiencing the Patient's Day: A Manual for Psychiatric Hospital Personnel* (New York: G. P. Putnam's Sons, 1955), Preface, p. iii.]

⁶ Our case material shows that this and similar instances are the rule in the hospital for new attendants. The new attendant is simply handed the ward keys, given no floor plan or door identification for the keys, warned carelessly about any particularly troublesome patients, and left on his own. In several cases new

attendants were given no instructions about patients locked into the lock-dormitories and had to ask other patients for instructions when the time came to wake up the ward. This lack of instruction characterizes even the assignment of attendants to the hospitals or infirmaries, where many gravely ill patients are kept. The attendants are given no emergency instructions and are often not briefed on how to record patients' conditions.

[7] An arrangement restraining the patient's arms without the painful and frightening restriction of the camisole or the tight sheet pack.

CHAPTER ELEVEN

[1] See *Proceedings of the Second Conference of Mental Hospital Administrators and Statisticians* (Washington, D.C.: Federal Security Agency, Public Health Service, 1953), pp. 2–6, for comparative figures on length of hospitalization in mental hospitals.

[2] In a majority of cases his legal status as a citizen, clouded by his commitment, may never be restored. Legal restoration proceedings for discharged mental patients from Southern State Hospital were initiated by the county courts in only 4 per cent of the cases we studied over a 20-year period. In a sample of 300 patients who had been discharged 5 years before, we found only 41 cases in which legal action had been undertaken to restore rights by patient, court, family, or friends.

[3] Our analysis of patient characteristics for this hospital shows a strong probability that the patient will have a less well-integrated family than the average.

[4] The so-called "geriatric centers" in South State are actually employed as residual centers for custodial cases. Our analysis of their composition shows that they are used for comparatively young patients as well as for old ones. The need governing assignment to these centers is the need to get rid of the accumulating sixth-level patients.

[5] National figures show that an active and well-trained social worker can produce a furlough success rate of 70 to 80 per cent

of all patients furloughed. See Mental Hospital Institute Proceedings, *Better Care in Mental Hospitals* (Washington, D.C.: American Psychiatric Association, 1949), remarks of Harriet Crutcher, pp. 153–156.

A program was attempted in Southern State Hospital during 1945 to 1948 which showed that even with an inadequate social work staff a tremendous improvement in furlough success occurred when social worker attention was concentrated on the placement of the patient outside the hospital. Returns of patients on leave not assisted by social worker placement activities averaged about 65 per cent. Returns of patients on leave who were assisted by social worker placement averaged 24 per cent.

[6] Two terms are used for the procedure of granting the patient a temporary leave of absence. The "leave of absence" is a temporary, usually brief, period, for which the patient is authorized to leave the hospital in the custody of a relative or other guardian. The "furlough" is a more extended visit to relatives or guardians. A leave of absence is any authorized absence that does not exceed 30 days, while anything in excess of 30 days—usually one year—is designated a furlough.

[7] The decision will be based thus either on his personal knowledge of his minority of selected cases on the wards or on the patient's status in the minds of the attendants and upper-level patients on the wards.

CHAPTER TWELVE

[1] "The Social Responsibility of Psychiatry: A Statement of Orientation," Report 13 (Topeka, Kansas: Group for the Advancement of Psychiatry, July, 1950). See also *Training and Research in State Mental Health Programs* (Chicago: The Council of State Governments, 1953), Chapter II. See also the definition of Malamud, in note 6, Chapter Two, above. Dr. Esther Brown and Dr. Milton Greenblatt have given a definite treatment of this problem in Greenblatt, Milton, Richard H. York, and Esther Brown, *From Custodial to Therapeutic Patient Care in*

Mental Hospitals (New York: Russell Sage Foundation, 1955), Chapter 21.

2 Jones, Maxwell, *Social Psychiatry* (London: Tavistock Publications, Ltd., 1952), and *Rehabilitation* (Geneva: World Health Organization, 1952). Grimes, Maurice, *When Minds Go Wrong* (Chicago: published by the author, 1951). See the remarks of Stanton and others in Williams, R. H., editor, *Panel Meeting on Rehabilitation Program Planning and Development* [Bethesda: National Institute of Mental Health, February, 1953 (restricted to staff circulation)]. See also Bateman, J. F., and Dunham, H. W., "The State Mental Hospital as a Specialized Community Experience," *Am. J. Psychiat.*, vol. 105 (December, 1948), pp. 445–448, and Weinberg, S. K., *Society and Personality Disorders* (New York: Prentice-Hall, Inc., 1952), Chapter XV. D. Ewen Cameron has made the general point of this statement in "Modern Methods of Treatment Require an Open Psychiatric Hospital," *The Modern Hospital*, vol. 74 (February, 1950), pp. 84, 86, 88; see also Ewalt, Jack R., "Mental Health Problems Affecting Social Relations," *Ann. Am. Acad. Polit. Soc. Sci.*, vol. 286 (March, 1953), pp. 74–80.

3 Lemkau, Paul, *Mental Hygiene in Public Health*, 2d ed. (New York: McGraw-Hill Book Company, Inc., 1955), Chapter III. Lemkau's view is that the hospital's general effect on research and development of an adequate mental health program is negative, since the massive appropriations for the hospital operations leave very little for the fundamental mental health programming and research.

4 See the discussion of these developments in *Training and Research in State Mental Health Programs*, Chapter Three, in particular Charts 4, 5, and 6, pp. 26, 27, 29.

5 For these figures see *Health Manpower Report*, Part I, Physicians (Washington, D.C.: Federal Security Agency, U.S. Public Health Service Publication No. 63, Preliminary, May, 1952). See also *Building America's Health*, Report of the President's Commission on the Health Needs of the Nation, five volumes

(Washington, D.C.: Government Printing Office, 1952), vol. II, section 5.

[6] *Building America's Health*, vol. II, section 5. The position of Southern State Hospital is far below these standards in all specialties.

[7] *Psychiatric Nursing Personnel* (Washington, D.C.: American Psychiatric Association, 1950), Plate II.

[8] *Building America's Health*, vol. II, section 5.

[9] *Statistics Pertinent to Psychiatry*, Report No. 7 (Topeka: Group for the Advancement of Psychiatry, 1949), p. 6.

[10] See the discussions in Chapters I, II, and III, and the works cited therein, particularly those of Deutsch, Jaffary, Weinberg, Bateman and Dunham, Lemert and Grimes, and the testimony of psychiatrists in *Better Care in Mental Hospitals*, Proceedings of the First Mental Hospital Institute (Washington, D.C.: American Psychiatric Association, 1949).

[11] See *Standards for Psychiatric Hospitals and Clinics*, Principle No. 10 (Washington, D.C.: Mental Hospital Service, American Psychiatric Association, 1951).

[12] See *Training and Research in State Mental Health Programs*, *loc. cit.*, and the Clinic Section, *Standards for Psychiatric Hospitals and Clinics*, *op. cit.* Some additions will have to be made to these schemes, particularly of qualified psychiatric nurses of liaison personnel in work with schools, churches, and city government, and in occupational rehabilitation. And the work must be organized to give actual team status to all members of the staff. Moreover, many problems of coordination with municipal and county welfare and medical services will have to be solved. This is one reason, in addition to the need to pin down local responsibility, for a local board of mental health.

[13] Maxwell Jones, *op. cit.*, reports on the success of an integrated occupation-therapy program conducted in terms of relationships approximating those recommended here with mental patients. On the broader aspects of local care, see Pollock, H. M., editor, *Family Care of Mental Patients*, particularly Chapter VII

by Edgar A. Dall, "The Gheel Belgium Plan" (Utica, N.Y.: State Hospitals Press, 1936).

[14] The recent study of Stanton, A. H., and Schwartz, Morris S., *The Mental Hospital* (New York: Basic Books, Inc., 1954) is a brilliant exposition of the fruits of the work of William Alanson White and Harry Stack Sullivan on this problem. See also Sullivan, Harry Stack, *Conceptions of Modern Psychiatry* (Washington, D.C.: W. A. White Psychiatric Foundation, 1947). Abraham Myerson and William Bryan were pioneers in the formulation of the advanced conception of the mental hospital as a total treatment agency. See Myerson, Abraham, "Theory and Principles of the 'Total Push' Method in the Treatment of Chronic Schizophrenia," *Am. J. Psychiat.*, vol. 95 (February, 1939), pp. 1197–1204, and Bryan, W. A., *Administrative Psychiatry* (New York: W. W. Norton & Company, Inc., 1936). William Menninger has given these ideas concrete and effective application. See his "Psychiatric Hospital Treatment Designed to Meet Unconscious Needs," *Am. J. Psychiat.*, vol. 93 (May, 1936), pp. 347–360, and his "Psychoanalytic Principles in Psychiatric Hospital Therapy," *Southern Med. J.*, vol. 32 (March, 1939), pp. 348–354.

[15] See Lemkau, Paul, *op. cit.*, p. 14, and Mustard, Harry S., *An Introduction to Public Health*, 2d ed. (New York: The Macmillan Company, 1938), Chapter I.

[16] Barnard, C. I., *The Functions of the Executive* (Boston: Harvard University Press, 1946), especially pp. 160–175.

The description of executive processes in the present study can be compared with the specification of organization and provision for organizational maintenance in MacEachern, Malcolm T., *Hospital Organization and Management* (Chicago: Physicians Record Company, 1935).

While there are of course many problems in general hospital organization which have not yet been solved, it is evident that this organizational form does provide all the essential auxiliary processes required by the physician to do his job. The contrast with the state mental hospital auxiliary processes shows the latter to be practically nonexistent for the physician.

Theory and Methods

FIELD METHODS AND THEORY

The case study of Southern State Hospital is an exploratory sociological analysis of the occupational roles of human beings in a specific social organization. The additional theoretical question considered in this analysis is whether these roles form part of a determinate system, and, if so, whether it is possible to indicate some of the consistent conditions of the system. The general theoretical foundation for this type of research and the scientific results to be expected from it are described by C. H. Cooley, Talcott Parsons, Florian Znaniecki, G. C. Homans, and R. K. Merton.[1] From a strictly scientific point of view, this study is to be classified as an initial attempt to outline a determinate social system and to state the conditions of the system in a way which will permit later more rigorous verification of the characteristics of the system and of its functional consequences.

A major focus of empirical interest in this study has been the social organization which emerges in the employment of specialist or professional services in a given organization. For modern society, with its increasing use of professional personnel, such as

[1] Cooley, C. H., "Case Study of Small Institutions as a Method of Research," in *Sociological Theory and Social Research* (New York: Henry Holt and Company, Inc., 1930); Parsons, Talcott, *The Social System* (Glencoe, Ill.: The Free Press, 1951); Znaniecki, Florian, *Social Actions* (New York: Rinehart & Company, Inc., 1936); Homans, G. C., "A Conceptual Scheme for the Study of Social Organization," *Am. Sociolog. Rev.*, vol. 12 (February, 1947), pp. 13–27; Merton, Robert K., *Social Theory and Social Structure* (Glencoe, Ill.: The Free Press, 1949), particularly Chapter I. Merton's specifications of the logic of procedure and his paradigm for functional analysis in the study of social organization were employed with much of our interview material.

engineers, research scientists, lawyers, and physicians, the effect of the social structure of the enterprise on the professional as a practitioner and as a person is becoming a critical issue. An equally important issue is that of the effect of the professional on the social organization of the enterprise.[2]

The analysis of the employment of medical professionals in a specific institutional setting is of particular value because of its bearing on this larger problem. The role of the physician and those of his auxiliary professionals, such as registered nurses, can be regarded without much question as among the most thoroughly organized of modern professional roles. The problems of these roles in concrete instances, such as the situations of private practice and the various kinds of institutional practice, will have by extension many implications for other professions: the engineering, teaching, and purely scientific disciplines, as they are employed in the universities and elsewhere.[3]

Field methods employed in this research consisted first of (1) a study from documentary sources of the history of the hospital selected; (2) a review of books and dissertations and other non-periodical literature on state hospitals in the United States and Europe, with a review of periodical literature in the psychological, medical, sociological, and anthropological journals; (3) a year spent in the hospital by a field staff made up of three paid interviewers, participant observers, and the author, interviewing

[2] Melville Dalton has outlined the general problem of professional use—considering the professional as a staff manager—in his "Conflicts between Staff and Line Managerial Officers," *Am. Sociolog. Rev.*, vol. 15 (June, 1950), pp. 342–351. See also Laski, Harold J., "The Limitations of the Expert," *Harper's Magazine*, vol. 162 (December, 1930), pp. 102–106, and Merton, Robert K., "The Machine, the Worker, and the Engineer," *Science*, vol. 105 (January, 1947), pp. 79–81. Robert Dubin has surveyed this problem in several administrative areas, with selected articles, in *Human Relations in Administration* (New York: Prentice-Hall, Inc., 1951), pp. 115–138.

[3] See "Social Structure and Dynamic Process: The Case of Modern Medical Practice," in Parsons, *op. cit.* For a general study of the complex social system required for the practice of medicine as a profession, see Hall, Oswald, "Sociological Research in the Field of Medicine: Progress and Prospects," *Am. Sociolog. Rev.*, vol. 16 (October, 1951), pp. 639–644; and Caudill, William, "Applied Anthropology in Medicine," in Kroeber, A. L., editor, *Anthropology Today* (Chicago: University of Chicago Press, 1953).

and observing in all levels of the organization. During the following year the author and seven volunteers among employees in the hospital, four former employees, and two former patients carried out 200 interviews of personnel employed and formerly employed in the hospital, using the following Master Research Schedule, the two semistructured schedules (I and II), and the check list (III) for each interview.

In the latter part of the third year of the study, the author helped to design and carry through a complete administrative study of Southern State Hospital and all other hospitals in the state system of South State, conducted by a professional research organization. This second study provided a source of independent data on job definitions, reporting practices, personnel practices, and medical administration of the hospital. It was possible to compare the original reports of our interviewers in Southern State Hospital with those of the other study at every important point. Where there was discrepancy between the reports we made further studies, and if the discrepancy could not be reconciled, the use of our own material was rejected. Only the material which passed this comparative test is employed in the present report.

In the synthesis of the reports of field interviews at the conclusion of the project, those who had conducted the interviews and the author functioned together as a panel in making judgments as to the way in which these reports fitted into a system. The imputation of structure or system to the isolated interviews and observations of a field study is still a difficult problem in the social sciences.[4] Our procedure amounted to the employment of a convergence of two or more interviewers and the author on the meaning of statements or behavior of those involved. This meaning was then checked against the related meaning of the compara-

---

[4] The method used in validation and interpretation of field material in the study of Southern State Hospital represented a form of panel or jury procedure, based on theoretical and methodological justification set forth in Firey, Walter, and Ivan Belknap, "The Problem of Standardizing Observation in Sociology," *Proc. Southwestern Soc. Sci. Assoc.*, vol. 1 (1951), pp. 60–67.

tive literature on the problem. By repeating this procedure through the steps of the Master Research Schedule, we were able to develop reasonable certainty that we understood the system of which these statements and behavior formed the parts. The basic test which must be made of the present report is that of comparative empirical adequacy and of the logical status of our deductions. Such a test can be provided only by independent studies of similar institutions which assume this test as part of their responsibility.

Schedules and the check list employed in the study are as follows:

MASTER RESEARCH SCHEDULE: SOCIAL ORGANIZATION

1. Review of literature on institution and similar institutions. Interpretation and establishment of purpose of study. Establishment of a role for the study personnel. Definition of study personnel to top-level personnel, supervisors, all employees.

2. Analysis of existing material on formal organization of the institution, including formal organization charts, job descriptions and evaluations, flow of work in central functions. Analysis of this material in relation to exterior organizations.

3. Selection for analysis of key systems, as indicated by Step 2.

4. Interpretation of the study to personnel in key systems and development of good informal relations by interviewers with personnel.

5. Role cycle analysis of the key system personnel, on interview and discussion basis (Schedule IA). Concurrently analyze formal job description (Schedule IB). Complete with formal role analysis from records (Schedule IB). Relate to system in which the position is operating (Schedule IC).

6. Concurrently with Step 5, accumulate interview data on how the person in the position relates himself to work flow and other persons. Types and patterns of on-job association; off-job association (Schedule II). Accumulate general social characteristics as needed (Schedule III).

7. Qualitative analysis and synthesis of the selected system, and relation of position in the system to the entire social system of the institution. Reinterviews will be necessary to answer questions raised by the qualitative analysis and synthesis.

8. Determination of the type of quantitative material significant in

further understanding of the selected system: turnover rates, pay-rate comparisons, production rates, medical treatment rates, accident rates, psychometric rates, comparison of social background variables, such as years of education, rural-urban background of personnel; time allocation to various functions in the job. These data should be secured and used to complete the final synthesis.

9. Decision in terms of the facts of Steps 1–8 as to use and dissemination of the analysis of the selected system. Comparison of the findings of the study with similar studies. Revaluation of Step 3 in the light of findings up to this point to see if other systems may be added to or subtracted from those selected.

10. Continue with study of the selected systems, beginning with Step 4.

Schedule I. Role Analysis

A. Interview Role Analysis and Observation. Interviewer observes utmost care in rendering *entire area of meaning* in words used by person in position. This description must be compared at least twice in the course of role analysis with *formal* description of Subject's position or job. All discrepancies are to be noted carefully.

B. Record Role Analysis and Supervisor Interviews as Necessary. Duties as assigned by the institution. Classification data: rates, evaluations. Psychometric and other criteria. History of positions. Problems, such as definition and rating. Development vertically and horizontally in relation to work flow and to vertical and horizontal positions.

C. Preliminary Estimates of Functional Position of Role:
    1. In immediate system
    2. In total system

These data must be wriitten up on the same day as gathered.

Schedule II. Social Relations

1. With whom does Subject associate while on the job and during breaks? Describe patterns of association and characterize as to emotional tone, frequency, duration, subjects of conversation (select typical ones), types of behavior, such as horseplay, kidding, and general role played.

2. Describe general ways in which others relate themselves to Subject on the job and during breaks; their attitude toward him, degrees of acceptance, their general definition of his role.

3. Preliminary description of functional relation of Subject's roles to those of others.

Schedule III. General Social Characteristics

Questions marked "R" can be taken from records. Those marked "I" are memorized and accumulated during role analysis.

Position _____

_____

1. (R) Age _____   2. (R) Sex _____

3. (R) Education, Level, Type _____

4. (I) Size of home town _____

5. (R) Marital status _____
(m, s, w, d)

6. (I) Number in present household and relationships _____

_____

_____

7. (I) Number of children and plans for their occupations _____

_____

_____

8. (R) (I) Religious affiliation _____

9. (I) Actual church attendance (weekly, *etc.*) _____

10. (I) Number close friends; at work and outside; visits and activities per week, month, or other unit _____

_____

_____

11. (I) Clubs, informal groups; activities; how often, degree of intensity _____

_____

12. (I) Patterns of occupational ambition, in school, at present, in

the future _____

_____

13. (I) Types of preferred leisure-time activities. Sports (participate; spectator); hobbies; reading; dancing; parties; movies; studies for advancement (Don't force questions here or try to cover

too much in one interview) _____

_____

_____

14. (I) Professional and occupational relationships (kind, amount,

role) _____

_____

_____

15. (I:R) Length of service since employment _____

16. (I:R) Previous employment _____

Index

L

Laski, Dr. Harold J., 260
Leadership structure in the hospital, 52
  conflict between formal and informal leadership, 52
Legal definition of problematic people, 32
Legal foundations, as agency of poor law, 33
  constitutional definition of, in mental hospitals, 33
  as custodial, 31
  hospital as residual to local welfare needs, 31, 32
  swamping of hospitals by nonpsychotic commitments, 31
Lemert, Dr. E. M., 9, 232, 257
Lemkau, Dr. Paul, 216, 256, 258
Levels of hospital organization, barriers between, 189
  communication between formal and informal, 76
  conflict between, 76
  contact as insulated from hospital treatment, 67
  movement between, 188
  ratio in staffing in, 210
Lipscomb, Governor, 20

M

MacEachern, Dr. Malcolm T., 258
Malzberg, Dr. Benjamin, 234
Massachusetts, Worcester State Hospital, conditions in 1833, 18
Master research schedule, social organization, 262
Maxwell, Dr. John, 256
Medical records, social worker role in, 58
Meltzer, Dr. Bernard N., 231
Menninger, Dr. William, 216, 258
Mental Hospital Survey Committee, survey of, 24
Mental hospitals, studies of, 230
  in social organization, 9
  in social system, 230
  in treatment effectiveness, 231

Mental illness, 229
  costs, 229
  hospital admissions in, 229
  individual probability of exposure to effects, 229
Merton, Dr. Robert K., 259, 260
Methods, job study procedure, 42
  and theories, study of, in occupational roles, 259
Millville, 19
  population and size, 37
  Southern Lunatic Asylum, 21, 239
  system of public relations, 208
Mineral Springs, establishment of psychopathic hospital, 22
Morale problem, 7, 8
Murray, Dr. Edwin, 92
Mustard, Dr. Harry S., 258
Myers, Dr. Jerome K., 248
Myerson, Dr. Abraham, 4, 216, 230, 258

N

National Committee for Mental Hygiene, recommendations of, 21
Newspapers, criticism by, of South State hospitals, 1
Nonpsychotic commitments to South State hospitals, 34
Nurse procurement, women, 156, 248
Nurses and attendants, criticism of, 2
Nursing service, 111
  as distinguished from attendants, 223–225
  intermediate line authority in, 100
  rejection of conditions in state mental hospitals, 207

O

Occupational roles, 259
  as study in, specialist or professional services, 259
  specific social organization, 259
Organization, of Southern State Hospital, authority distribution in, 147
  contradiction in functions, 204
  departure from formal chart, 46